INSTILLING TOUCHSTONES OF CHARACTER

Connecting What Matters With Common Core and 21st Century Skills

Gary Smit

"Instilling Touchstones of Character," by Gary Smit. ISBN 978-1-62137-476-3 (softcover); 978-1-62137-513-5 (ebook)..

Library of Congress Control Number: 2014911923

Manufactured in the United States of America.

Acknowledgements

There is a Chinese proverb that says, "A child's life is like a piece of paper and each passerby leaves a mark." When I began to delve into character education, I learned that the word character comes from the Greek word *kharakter*, which is a chisel or marking instrument for metal or stone. One's character, then, is a mark engraved into something permanent and enduring. Though I am far removed from being a child, I have come to the realization I've met many who have left a 'mark' or character on my life. I would be remiss if I didn't take time to express my heartfelt thanks and appreciation for the contributions and support of a few individuals who have helped chart my navigational course of a life of character.

I begin with a personal note to my wonderful wife Jayne who has been by my side through times of challenge and joy associated with being married to a school superintendent. So many of the beliefs that found their way into this book are from what you have shared with me. And, to our adult children and spouses, Erica and Scott, Alisa and James, Jason and Nikki, who have taught me the value of a life well–lived. Not only are we proud and grateful for all you have done but more importantly for whom you have become. By reflecting on 'marks' that can and will be left on a child, I can't help but think of our seven grandchildren: Tyce, Isaac, Ari, Mia, Lyla, Leo and Reese. My hope is that each of you will come into contact with committed and passionate teachers who will strive to help you to do your best work but also to be your best self.

Professionally, I have to acknowledge Cathy Fisher who sparked my interest and development in character by spearheading our CHARACTER COUNTS! initiative in Lombard schools. Without your level of interest, commitment and dedication to transforming lives through character, I might never have embarked on this most noble and rewarding path of school improvement.

Words alone cannot adequately express thanks to Joanne Ng for your encouragement, prodding and cajoling for me to write this book. I stand in awe of your steadfast commitment to promote, mold and shape the attitudes of teachers to directly impact students with effective and meaningful character instruction. Similarly, I express appreciation to Ken Fisher for your efforts with the Abraham Lincoln Center for Character Development as a way of kindling in me the continual desire to promote both excellence and ethics.

The knowledgeable and dedicated trainers for CHARACTER COUNTS! are to be acknowledged for having shared with me much of what I have learned about character. I have gained a greater understanding of the impact that character can and does have in schools and communities from all that I have captured when working with each of you. Especially, I have valued the work of Mark Britzman as you have motivated me to initiate character development experiences in ways that are meaningful and relevant. And to Randy Doerksen for inspiring me by sharing practical and effective school strategies for character development.

There would be no book if it were not for the contribution and assistance of Michael Josephson. I greatly appreciate your support and encouragement as we have trained together, wrote character content, created strategies and shared experiences associated with living one's life based on ethical values – trustworthiness, respect, responsibility, fairness, caring and citizenship. Thanks, Michael for all you have done. Acknowledging you and your efforts on this page of a book does not do justice to my personal growth and the cause of character development.

INSTILLING TOUCHSTONES OF CHARACTER:
Connecting What Matters With Common Core and 21st Century Skills

Table of Contents

Touchstones of Character

Character	Character counts all the time; all the time character counts.
Trustworthiness	Trust is essential to all my important relationships.
Respect	I will treat others the way I want to be treated.
Responsibility	It is an obligation that I do my best work and be my best self.
Fairness	People deserve to be treated fairly in all situations.
Caring	It is important to share care and concern for others.
Citizenship	I must contribute to my community and fulfill my responsibilities.
Collaboration	Working productively with others, as being part of a team or group, will allow me to accomplish more than I could alone.
Communication	It is my responsibility to communicate clearly with others and express my views effectively and respectfully.
Gratitude	I consistently identify, experience and express thankfulness for the good things in my life.
Perseverance	When something doesn't work right, try again and again.
Resilience	Even when life is tough, I know I can survive.
Growth Mindset	Intelligence and talent are not fixed; both can be improved with effort and practice.
Setting Goals	I will get better results if I set goals and plan out the steps to reach them.
Critical Thinking	It is important to understand and evaluate the information I am given.
Decision Making	I realize that my behavior and the choices I make affects others.

INTRODUCTION

A recent cold had me reaching for a bag of name brand cough drops. As I hurriedly popped one of the "triple soothing action" honey–lemon flavored drops in my mouth, I noticed that the company had redesigned their packaging. I was about to throw the wrapper away when I discovered a pleasant surprise: "A Pep Talk in Every Drop." Short phrases were written across the wrapper to inspire and encourage me to try to forget about my hacking cough.

The "pep talk" on each wrapper consisted of four different maxims, surrounded by the cough drop maker's logo emblazoned over a dozen times on the 2x3 inch piece of flimsy paper. By unwrapping the cough drops, I discovered uplifting and positive messages such as:

- Dust off and get up.
- Don't give up on yourself.
- Don't try harder. Do harder!
- Flex your "can do" muscle.
- Turn "can do" into "can did!"
- You've survived tougher.
- Take charge and mean it.
- Get back in the game.
- It's yours for the taking.
- Get through it.

Reading each cough drop wrapper made me realize that the sayings were not just there to make me feel better. Rather, many were motivational snippets specifically designed to help me make a change in my attitude or beliefs.

This started me thinking about other companies that embrace the moment when a consumer is holding their product in one hand and its packaging in another. I'm sure most chocolate lovers already know about the inspirational messages inside of a certain wrapped piece of candy. On each chocolate wrapper is a short quote or message. Some of my personal favorites include:

- Every cloud doesn't mean a storm.
- You are the star for which all evenings wait.
- Don't let anger rent a room in your head.
- Failure is...only the opportunity to begin again more intelligently.
- Never let others' opinions change the way you feel about yourself.
- To accomplish great things one must not only act, but also dream.
- Friendship is the gold thread that ties hearts together.
- Trust is the most valuable thing you'll ever earn.
- Do a little more each day than you think you possibly can.
- Footprints on the sands of time are not made by sitting down.

Again, it's the little things that can bring a smile to your face, or even recall a memory. Unlike the cough drops that are needed when we are feeling sick, eating chocolate is one of the pleasures we allow ourselves to enjoy when we are feeling well. One does not have to be sick in order to feel better. Life messages, even if they come from the wrappers of cough drops or chocolate morsels, can make a huge difference in how we approach life.

These life messages made me recall the funny, weird, often illogical, but sometimes inspirational sayings that mothers have told their children over generations. Although sometimes 'momisms' may seem like silly sayings, I've always been a true believer that a momism – no matter what it is – can stick with children and oftentimes shape their attitude and behavior into adulthood.

You have probably heard at least a few of these momisms or comparable sayings over the course of your life:

- Because I said so, that's why!
- What part of no don't you understand?
- I brought you into this world, and if necessary, I will take you out!
- Don't make me pull this car over!
- If all of your friends jumped off a bridge, would you?
- Shut the door – I can't pay to heat the whole neighborhood.
- There are starving people in India who would be happy to clean your plate for you.
- I'm not everyone else's mother – I'm *your* mother.
- Don't use that tone with me!
- As long as you live under my roof, you'll listen to my rules.

Why do sayings like these stick with us? I believe it is similar to the memories of our favorite books we have read, or memorable experiences we have had that we continue to reflect on throughout our lives.

C.S. Lewis reminds us that children love to have the same story repeated over and over, using the exact same words each time. Try to change the story, even just slightly, and the child will quickly interrupt to say, "That's not how it goes." There is the need and desire to have the same 'surprise' of discovering that Little Red Riding Hood's grandmother was actually the evil wolf in disguise. Likewise, it's easier for the child to appreciate the twists and turns in the story when they know what is coming. There is a measure of comfort because the child knows exactly what is going to happen and when. It is as if the memorization of the story has suspended all fear, freeing the child from being overwhelmed. Children can cope with the wolf that suddenly appears in the story because they know that everything will be okay in the end.

Lewis also points out that the 'unliterary man' reads a story only once, thinking that he is then done with it and can move on. However, Lewis claims that literary readers keep probing the same story in search of new insights. But they do this only because they already know how the story ends.[1]

I believe that this is also why some people return to a museum to gaze at the same painting or sculpture they've marveled at before, or why people buy copies of movies to watch more than once. They know these pieces of art so well, but they can never get enough. The collective insights of stories, regardless of whether they're read, overheard, or viewed, remain powerful lessons that we can use to teach children and young people about key beliefs we desire them to possess.

I have come to realize how important it is to solidify key beliefs and values regarding how we should live our lives. Whether these beliefs are instilled by a quote on a cough drop wrapper, a piece of art, or even a movie clip, they resonate with us like those words of wisdom espoused by mothers through the generations.

Hal Urban says this about words: "Lives can be changed through the power of words. They can hurt, they can heal. They can discourage, they can encourage. They can tear down, they can build up. They can express complaints, they can express thanks. They can make people cry, they can make people laugh."[2] Words can have a direct impact on how people feel or behave. A person's emotional or physical response to those words can help in forming their beliefs. It was Maya Angelou who said, "I've learned that people will forget what you said, people will forget what you did, but people will never forget how you made them feel."[3]

The Josephson Institute of Ethics has crafted "Model Standards for Academic, Social, Emotional, and Character Development." Critical educational outcomes have been written after synthesizing, summarizing, and augmenting the research findings, insights, and implementation strategies of the most influential school improvement programs.[4] Key beliefs have been prepared from these standards in the domains of academics, social and emotional learning, and character development, along with specific and practical instructional strategies to intentionally teach the beliefs.

The essence of those standards and the subsequent unpacking of the key beliefs have been simplified for inclusion in this book. The word 'touchstone' was chosen specifically for these key beliefs. There was a time when a touchstone referred to a black rock, such as basalt or jasper, which was used to test for the purity of gold and silver. Moneychangers would check the streaks on the touchstone to look for counterfeit coins. Although this usage of the word touchstone is archaic, the word still refers to a gauge, reference, benchmark, or standard. By definition, a touchstone can be a basic principle or standard employed to judge other things.

The word touchstone has come to have other meanings. Christine Brouillard, school counselor at Mill Pond School, a 2010 National School of Character has said, "Our touchstone will not be something that can be touched – it will be a touchstone of words. It will be like a pledge or promise that describes the high standard for speaking and acting that we will all try to achieve. We will try to live up to our 'Touchstone of Words!' It will also be something we can rely on to help us feel that we belong to our school community. It will make us feel safe and valued here!"[5]

Creating a meaningful and sustainable character education initiative can be accomplished with the aid of a schoolwide touchstone. This brief statement of purpose incorporates a shared set of commonly held values that will be held up to all staff and students as a message of what is important.. One could say that a touchstone incorporating shared values is critical for any successful organization, especially for a school. For some, this compilation of values can be found in a mission statement. A school's mission statement functions as its touchstone, guiding students and staff in how decisions are made. It can also serve as a framework for many aspects of school life, including parental involvement, after–school programs, and the hiring of staff.

By having a particular touchstone, or a statement of how things are done, can end up being the glue that holds effective schools together. One will find that the touchstone can keep schools focused on fulfilling their duties of preparing students to: succeed in school and in their future careers; live happy, worthy, and fulfilling personal lives; and become engaged, responsible, and productive citizens.

Furthermore, a creed or touchstone can be a powerful tool for building a sense of community in a class or school, as individuals tend to feel more connected to each other when joined by common values. The ideal is to have staff and students, in a deliberate and intentional manner, be in a constant and consistent relationship with the touchstone, while providing an environment that is conducive to learning. Ideally, the touchstone will then serve as a reference point for specific phases of ethical action related to conduct and behaviors of adults and students. When a decision needs to be made, the touchstone should assist in how one perceives and understands the situation, while creating the desire to take effective and ethical action that will produce the best possible result.

The school's mission formally articulates the core values, beliefs about learning, and the 21st century learning expectations that must serve to guide changes in all areas of the school. A school that uses these core values and beliefs about learning in this way is truly mission–driven and is delivering on its promise to its stakeholders. It is a school where students, teachers, parents, and administrators are very clear about the core values and beliefs about learning which serve as its foundation, ensuring that every student works to achieve 21st century learning expectations, while providing a challenging curriculum in support of schoolwide and course–specific learning goals.

In "Character Matters," Thomas Lickona speaks of creating a schoolwide touchstone: "The touchstone is a creed or way that expresses the shared values and aspirations of all members of the school community. Such a creed creates an intentional community, one in which members feel strong connection and a shared moral identity because they are joined by commonly held values."[6]

Allow me to share a few examples of schoolwide touchstones. These touchstones were created after soliciting input from staff, parents and students and clearly state the key beliefs directing the operation of the school:

Mann Middle School

'We are the Mustangs!
We believe that we ALL can achieve our goals.
As Mustangs, we hold ourselves and each other accountable and we are responsible for our own behavior and learning.
Mustangs have high expectations and work together to create a respectful and supportive environment.
As a Mustang, we encourage each other to do our best every day. Every day is a fresh start.
This is who we are. This is the Mustang Way!'

Lakes High School

"We show respect for ourselves and others through kind words and deeds'
We set high expectations for ourselves and accept responsibility for our own actions'
We support, encourage and challenge each other as we strive to be our best in school and life.
We celebrate our successes with enthusiasm.
We have courage to do the right thing.
We are the Lancers and this is the Lakes Way!"[7]

What you will find in the pages of this book is a collection of touchstone beliefs that capture the essence of what we, as educators, need to instill in the students who have been entrusted to our care. Sixteen "touchstones of character" or key beliefs will be shared, analyzed and studied, and are drawn from the academic domain, non–cognitive skills, and specific character traits that relate to moral right and wrong. I have found that, no matter what part of the world they are in, schools must give students the intellectual yet practical tools they can use within their classrooms, families, and communities. The beliefs being shared in this book provide many of these tools.

In determining the model standards from which these beliefs have been taken, Josephson concluded that historically, "formal standards directing and guiding the educational mission have focused on defining grade–appropriate academic objectives." However, we have now embarked on a journey where the "acknowledged objectives of education have been broadened as the result of a number of parallel reform movements vigorously urging educators to explicitly supplement content standards with outcome objectives concerning the development of critical and creative thinking, decision–making, and problem–solving abilities; social and emotional life skills, ethical character traits, and practical knowledge and competencies reflecting the demands of the modern workplace."[8]

Using these key beliefs as a resource allows for the teaching and organization of both classrooms and schools to assist students in achieving the set of skills they need in order to successfully manage life tasks. Evidence is present in creating an environment conducive to learning, forming relationships, communicating effectively, being sensitive to others' needs, and how students treat and get along with others. I am firmly convinced that when schools implement instruction that incorporates these beliefs effectively, academic achievement of students increases, incidence of problem behaviors decreases, the relationships that surround each child are improved, and the climate of classrooms and schools changes for the better.

This book is not meant to be an essay on the theoretical aspects of character; rather it is specifically designed to assist teachers in engaging students with practical and meaningful strategies to instill key beliefs. My vision for this book is that it not simply be read from beginning to end, front cover to back cover. Instead, you are encouraged to reflect on these words, and to intentionally outline how and when you will instill these "touchstones of character" based on your own understanding of what your students need, while aligning your actions with the operational values of your school.

From my own observations while working in schools, both as an administrator and a trainer, the values that are considered important to instill in students typically promote the development of skills in academic, social, and emotional learning, as well as help develop their character. Since I became involved in and committed to the framework of CHARACTER COUNTS!®, I have found there is an intentional and explicit desire to address these domains. For all students, the component of academic achievement is exemplified in the need to develop essential academic skills, while encouraging and assisting them to reach their highest intellectual potential.

Secondly, there is the stated and often mandated need to promote social and emotional growth, whereby schools strive to develop positive social and emotional life skills that will assist each student to lead a personally satisfying and socially responsible life.

Finally, there is the value and importance of the intentional integration of character development into the life of a school. For CHARACTER COUNTS!, this is portrayed by the desire to embed in each student the six core ethical values of trustworthiness, respect, responsibility, fairness, caring, and citizenship. When these domains form the fabric of a school, there is evidence of a nurturing, caring environment in which all students feel physically and emotionally safe.[9]

The "touchstones of character" included in this book are intended to be a practical and useful guide to successfully bring about this integration of the necessary knowledge, skills, and beliefs that will promote students' positive behavior and conduct. By no means is there a limit

---

[®] CHARACTER COUNTS! and "The Six Pillars of Character" are registered trademarks of Josephson Institute

being placed upon the beliefs associated with academic achievement, non–cognitive skills, or character traits that we should be striving to instill in students. Furthermore, there will be no distinction made in identifying the beliefs or activities related to a specific age range of students. Rather, the beliefs that have been identified provide a framework that teachers can use in helping students do their best work and be the best person they can possibly be.

"It is not the brains that matter most, but that which guides them – the character, the heart, generous qualities, progressive ideas." – Fyodor Dostoyevsky

CHAPTER 1: DEVELOPING GOOD CHARACTER AND PROMOTING KEY BELIEFS

It could not be more obvious that our school systems need to improve how they respond to our ever–changing world. Franklin D. Roosevelt once said, "We cannot always build the future for our youth, but we can build our youth for the future." We have an obligation as educators and parents to do whatever we can to help our students connect learning with real life, and to provide them with the necessary knowledge, skills, and attributes to prepare them for success.

Here's a riddle for you: You can hardly ever find this anymore – especially in politics or business. Numerous news stories have it as a common theme. Many schools cannot find time to teach it anymore, but we all want more of it in our children and in the adults who interact with them. It is what we want from the people for whom we work, as well as the colleagues we work with and the service people who work for us. Most of us believe we have plenty of it already.

What I'm talking about is character – or, more precisely, *good* character. So, what is character? Let's start with its root, which comes from the Greek word *kharakter*, which is a chisel or marking instrument for metal or stone. One's character, then, is a mark engraved into something enduring. Mannerisms can be molded, but we must chisel our character.

When working with students, one must be concerned with instilling positive, admirable, and ethical traits associated with good character. In one sense, character is what is inside of students, and behind how they respond to life. Their responses come from the habits and dispositions they have learned and developed. When we refer to a specific young person's character, we're concerned with the moral choices he makes and the virtues he may or may not practice.

In most situations, however, when we are talking about a person's character, we are referring to the sum total of his or her moral qualities: Is she a good or bad person? Is he or isn't he worthy of trust and admiration?

Therefore, when we say someone has good character, we are expressing the opinion that his or her nature is defined by worthy traits, such as honesty, integrity, respect, responsibility, perseverance, and compassion. People of good character are guided by ethical principles even when it is physically dangerous or detrimental to their careers, social standing, or economic well–being. They do the right thing even when it costs more than they want to pay.

Character is not inherited, nor is it forever determined by one's environment. We have to be taught character. Our true character is shown every day by our normal and consistent attitudes and behavior. It has often been said that character is what is inside of us and becomes evident in how we respond to life. When we are confronted with a situation, the response we give will come from the habits and dispositions we've learned and developed. No matter what we choose to do, there is no escaping the implications of character as it affects our attitude and behavior, along with every relationship we have.

Michael Josephson captures the essence of what character is in this definition: "A person's character refers to dispositions, values, and habits that determine the way that person normally responds to desires, fears, challenges, opportunities, failures, and successes."[1]

Character is first and foremost taught in the home. Even the best parents today need support, and many need instruction to better carry out their child–rearing duties. There is a growing need for those who care about children to assist families in instilling and reinforcing the ethical values and character traits children need to live socially constructive and personally meaningful lives. If children do not develop good character at home, and other institutions refuse to fill the gap, we not only abandon the child who has not been properly taught right from wrong, we also expose our own children to the actions and behavior of fellow students who may lack character.

Anne Frank, the 15–year–old victim of Nazi persecution, once wrote in her diary, "[T]he final forming of a person's character lies in their own hands." I have no doubt that she was right. Of course, efforts made by parents, teachers, and others to instill these values are still important. They can have a great deal of influence on the values one adopts, but we must never underestimate the roles that choice and accountability play in the formation of one's character.

Thus, character is both formed and revealed by how one deals with everyday situations as well as extraordinary pressures and temptations. Like a well–made tower, character is built stone by stone, decision by decision. The way we treat people we feel are inferior says more about our character than how we respond to people we think are important. How we behave when we think no one is watching or when we do not think we will get caught more accurately portrays our character than what we say or do in service of our reputations.

Of course, our assessment of another person's character is an opinion, and isn't always correct. Abraham Lincoln recognized an important difference between character and reputation. "Character," he said, "is like a tree and reputation like its shadow. The shadow is what we think of it; the tree is the real thing."

Because the angle of light and the observer's perspective both take part in determining the shape of a shadow, it is not a perfect image of the tree. In the same way, reputation is not always an accurate reflection of character. Some people derive more benefit from their reputation than they deserve; others are better than their reputations.

Still, reputation does matter. It determines how others think of and treat us and whether we are held in high or low esteem. Many people and organizations are so preoccupied with their image that they actually undermine their character by concealing or creating facts to make them look better. It is ironic that reputations are often the result of dishonesty or the lack of accountability.

Finding time for building character in schools and in students can be a challenge. However, school is the first social structure the child encounters, and it provides an excellent opportunity for character building.

School is not just about acquiring knowledge or the mastery of skills. It is also a place where a foundation can be built for students to become upstanding and productive adults. A teacher's role includes paying attention to a student's formation of habits and dispositions in critical areas of learning. This involves:

- Knowledge – what a student should know and understand, such as facts, concepts, theories, methods, techniques, and processes.
- Skills – what the student should be able to do, focusing on abilities and competencies.
- Beliefs (Values) – what the student should value and believe, including convictions, attitudes, mindsets, and point of view.
- Traits of Character – the characteristics and attributes of character the student should possess.

Hillary Wilce, a journalist and writer who specializes in all aspects of education, says, "A good life demands openness, courage, resilience, honesty, kindness and persistence. This is the true spine of success, without which we are all jellyfish. And since no one wants their child to be a jellyfish, our prime job as parents – and teachers – has to be to help our children build the backbone they need to make the most of their lives."[2]

Every school should strive to create a 'backbone' or framework that creates an environment where respect, honesty, responsibility, and genuine kindness for all students is advocated, promoted, and encouraged. Whether they like it or not, teachers are role models for students, and can provide examples of good character every day in the classroom. Students notice what teachers do, say, and tolerate, and how they handle challenges. I have often told both teachers and administrators that what you allow, you encourage; what you permit, you promote; what you condone, you own.

Character building can also be done proactively through planned actions and activities within the classroom. These activities will encourage students to develop and adopt quality ethical principles and behaviors that can last far beyond the classroom.

Developing good character takes work, and I do most readily admit that it is not easy. I have come to realize that character development is a slow, difficult, life–course project – even when it is done consistently and with the greatest of rigor. I believe that to be successful as a schoolwide endeavor, character education requires theoretical clarity, implementation consistency, unwavering confidence, and persistence over time. In an age where there is the demand for fast results and change, we must understand that character education is not a quick fix. It is not a project that can be reduced to posters on a wall, nor should be perceived as a passing educational fad.

Instilling Values In Students

"People do not automatically develop good moral character; therefore, conscientious efforts must be made to help young people develop the values and abilities necessary for moral decision making and conduct." – The Aspen Declaration on Character Education.[3]

Values are the building blocks of character and shape the nature and quality of our personal and social interactions. Beliefs are simply specific statements that people hold to be true. Depending on the importance we attach to them, beliefs can be described as convictions (usually, these are the most deeply held beliefs evoking passion), attitudes (often reflecting emotions and feelings), opinions, and preferences. A person's most important beliefs drive behaviors, but not always on a conscious level. One of the most effective ways to change a behavior is to change the beliefs behind that behavior.

Many of our values were formed and reside at a subconscious level, the result of generally held cultural norms, religious training, and the teachings and modeling of parents, teachers, and peers. Our values both shape and reflect emotional responses induced at a spontaneous or subconscious level, as well as responses formed as a result of conscious deliberative reasoning. Most people are unaware of all the beliefs that shape their attitudes and actions. Our values act as the compass that we use to direct our behavior, often unconsciously. It could be said that values are a core–defining element of our being; without them, we are just not ourselves.

When we conduct a character development seminar for CHARACTER COUNTS!, one of the activities we ask participants to do is to create an understanding and application of the concept of "Key and Lock Beliefs." Keys are positive values (beliefs and attitudes) that unlock potential and open doors to success, personal growth, and fulfillment. On the other hand, locks are the negative values that limit potential, impede achievement, and prevent personal growth and fulfillment.

One's beliefs exist on many levels, from global to personal, and serve as overarching frameworks for understanding and engaging with the world. They can be thought of as guiding principles that we hold to be true that serve as lenses through which new experiences can be understood. I would suggest that failing to examine one's own beliefs can have negative consequences, as these beliefs guide practice and priorities, determine what is ignored, influence decision making, and shape what types of interactions are valued.

We can conclude that values represent our aims, desires, and goals. They are usually abstract, and are further defined by criteria. Beliefs are judgments that connect our values and criteria to our experiences. They give our experiences meaning, and provide context for our values. Both values and beliefs shape the way we view ourselves and the world around us. They serve as filters for our perceptions, and actually create for us a map of reality. They literally *make* our reality, and in so doing, define who we are.

Barbara Lewis construes that instilling values is analogous to teaching a child how to ride a bike. "You do not learn how to ride a bicycle by looking at pictures of bicycles in a book and studying laws of physics. You learn how to ride a bicycle by getting on a bike and riding."[4] Similarly, you learn to be a good person by being a good person: by being honest, respectful, responsible, fair, caring, and a good citizen. You consistently put into practice the specific beliefs associated with reaching your desired goals through every choice that you make.

How are values learned? There are five ways for the classroom teacher to directly instill values in students, regardless of the students' ages. The first is through direct instruction. This could take the form of lecture or large group discussion. The teacher serves as the instructional leader for students, actively selecting and directing or leading the learning activities. Using common language to describe and teach character substantially increases the effectiveness of character–building programs by exposing young people and adults to consistent and pervasive messages.

The second method is to share quotations as a means to discuss what we can learn from others, while the third is to utilize experiential activities. Instead of simply telling students information, the teacher involves students at every turn, generating self–discovery and an emotional commitment to desired beliefs and behavior. The fourth way is to intentionally and explicitly integrate the key beliefs into academic content. Finally, a teacher can implement instructional practices by initiating vicarious experiences through oral storytelling, through books, videos, or movies. "Poignant narratives help listeners to transport themselves from the content of what is being spoken and into the experience itself. Because they create vivid images and provide concrete detail, stories are more understandable than terse lectures."[5]

What Is Character Education and Why Do We Need It?

Character education is not a 'quick fix.' It provides long–term solutions that address moral, ethical, and academic issues of growing concern to our society, and is key to the safety of our schools. Character education not only cultivates minds, it nurtures hearts. Character education gets to the heart of the matter – literally.

In "Educating for Character," Lickona states, "Moral education is not a new idea. It is, in fact, as old as education itself. Down through history, in countries all over the world, education has had two great goals: to help young people become smart and to help them become good."[6] Good character is not formed automatically, but developed over time through a sustained process of teaching, enforcing, advocating, and modeling. In schools, this occurs through direct efforts of character education. The intentional teaching of good character is particularly important in today's society, given that our students face many opportunities and challenges that previous generations did not encounter.

Character education interventions should be designed to support and complement the academic and social preparation of students, thus targeting the development of the whole child. CHARACTER COUNTS! has consistently based its efforts with schools in promoting a character initiative that is meaningful, measurable, and sustainable. We've found that character development is most effective when there is schoolwide implementation with instructional emphases in all classrooms. The teaching of character education is most effective when the instruction is integrated within daily lessons and taught as part of state–mandated standards–based curricula.

In order to create an effective school culture that promotes improved learning for all students, schools must first identify a set of core values and beliefs about learning that will function as their explicit foundational commitments to students and the community. Once identified, these core values and beliefs about learning will manifest themselves in a set of research–based, schoolwide, 21st century learning expectations, which the school must also identify through engagement in a dynamic, collaborative, and inclusive process informed by current, research–based best practices.

A school needs to take steps to ensure its core values, beliefs, and learning expectations are actively reflected in the culture of the school. These values and beliefs should be driving curriculum decisions, instructional strategies, and assessment practices in every classroom. Moreover, the school can use the core values, beliefs, and learning expectations to prescribe and direct the school's policies, procedures, decisions, and resource allocations. In time, the school can regularly review and revise its core values, beliefs, and 21st century learning expectations based on research and multiple data sources, as well as district and other school priorities.

Importance Of Non–Cognitive Skills

"The test score accountability movement has pushed aside many of these so–called 'non–cognitive' or 'soft' skills, and they belong back on the front burner."[7] With high–stakes testing, there is a tendency to advocate an education approach that tends to focus on intellectual aspects of success, such as content knowledge. However, I am convinced that for students to be successful, this is not sufficient. If our desire is for students to achieve their full potential, they must have opportunities to engage and develop a much richer set of skills. There is a growing movement to explore the potential of the "non–cognitive" factors – attributes, dispositions, social skills, attitudes, and intrapersonal resources, independent of intellectual ability – that high–achieving individuals draw upon to accomplish success.

The task of the teacher has to change from not only building students' content knowledge and academic skills, but also fostering a host of non–cognitive factors: sets of behaviors, skills, attitudes, and strategies that are crucial to students' academic performance. "The Common Core needs a vessel or a container to hold the knowledge and skill standards in order to move them forward. The best vessel is the school or school district that models ethical and performance character principles for students and adults, creating a culture of respect, responsibility and excellence in which all can thrive."[8]

Emphasizing the importance of integrating non–cognitive skills and character traits, Kristin Fink has concluded, "By embedding positive school culture and intentionally integrating pro–social education and character throughout instruction, the Common Core Standards will be strengthened and supported. Since the new standards will raise the level of cognitive rigor and require young people to develop more stamina, discipline and grit to handle more challenging work, [...] extra attention must be paid to building character. Common Core supported by comprehensive, high quality, social–emotional learning and character education is better than just Common Core."[9]

In the practical application of a classroom setting, if the target of change is contextual behavior (e.g., avoidance of cheating or fighting in school, being conscientious on assignments), we understand that external interventions such as rewards and sanctions can work. However, if the target is the development of the dispositions and habits that constitute character traits and non–cognitive skills (e.g., integrity, collaboration, conscientiousness), efforts must focus on beliefs and values.

Recent studies have demonstrated that non–cognitive skills might be as important as, or even more so than, cognitive skills in determining educational outcomes. Howard Gardner has gone even further by suggesting that in an increasingly interdependent globalized world, "our survival [...] may depend on the cultivation of this pentad of mental dispositions."[10]

In an article entitled "True Grit," Justin Minkel says, "Imagine academic skills as apps for an iPhone. Non–cognitive skills are the operating system for the iPhone itself. You might not need them to memorize state capitols or do twenty addition problems in one minute. But to do the kind of research built into the Common Core Standards, or to take on the engineering design challenges involved in STEM curricula, kids need to develop perseverance, collaboration, and other non–cognitive skills."[11]

Richard Roberts has presented research that paints a compelling portrait of the value of non–cognitive skills such as perseverance, communication, decision–making, collaboration, and goal–setting: "Devoting class time to these skills is a more effective way to increase academic achievement than spending all your time on the academic content itself."[12]

Filmmaker Woody Allen knew something about what we want from young people when he said, "Eighty percent of success is showing up." Thomas Edison concluded, "Genius is 1 percent inspiration, 99 percent perspiration." Americans read an Aesop's fable to their children about tortoises and hares, and a more modern story about the "little engine that could," both of which stress the values of character and perseverance. If we truly believe in what I have referred to as "touchstones of character," we will care not only about how well students perform academically, but also about the attributes and traits they possess and demonstrate in the choices made.

In my role as an administrator, I felt there was little disagreement regarding outcomes the public wanted besides literacy and numeracy from schools. While opinion surveys consistently include higher test scores as a school goal, the public does not believe that scores are the most crucial goal. In one recent survey, more than two–thirds of Americans felt that teaching values in public schools was more important than teaching academic subjects. Teachers, parents, and executives believe that higher–order, cross–disciplinary skills (such as writing, critical thinking, and problem solving) and self–motivation and team skills are more important than higher–level content in mathematics and science. This is particularly true when one considers the preparation necessary for students to handle the college experience or the workplace environment.[13]

For many schools, the Common Core Standards that have been adopted by almost every state provide a consistent, clear understanding of what students are expected to learn. The standards are designed to be robust, rigorous, and relevant to real world experiences, reflecting the knowledge and skills that our young people need for success in college and careers. These standards are research–based, internationally benchmarked, and more concise than previous educational standards. Advocates contend the Common Core is designed to lay out a vision of what it means to be a literate person in the 21st century. From state educational agencies that have adopted Common Core, there is agreement that the established standards raise the level of cognitive rigor and require students to develop the stamina and skills that are necessary to explore and complete challenging work.

The Common Core, however, makes it clear that it does not attempt to identify all that should or could be taught, or specify the supports that schools must continue to put in place to help all young people be successful. We have to remember that these are standards – they do not identify the curriculum or teaching and learning strategies that teachers will use. What we have come to understand is that teaching through the Common Core requires aligning instructional practices to move teachers away from an emphasis on preparing students for low–level, multiple–choice tests to more real–world, performance–based assessments. The level of rigor has been increased, with daily reading and writing across the curriculum in a wide range of texts, including literary and informational.

While the standards lay out what students need to know and be able to do in a 21st century global society, they fall short on identifying what students need to 'be like,' or the dispositions and qualities of character they will need to develop to be well–prepared for what it means to be educated in today's world. Clearly, character and non–cognitive skills are implicitly built into the new standards, although not directly named or identified as key to successful implementation of the standards. I would contend it is these skills that form the important structural foundation and common denominator that will help students effectively cope with all of these greater demands.

For schools, Common Core can be implemented with a comprehensive, integrated, values–based initiative that focuses on the sixteen values and "touchstones of character" that are identified and elaborated on in this book. This could be accomplished by utilizing a school improvement committee with an established objective to connect the key beliefs with the Standards. This schoolwide initiative would encourage teachers and administrators to emphasize:

- Explicit and intentional planning for the values and beliefs that students will need to acquire to be ready for college, careers, and the real world, while grappling with the greater performance demands of the Common Core.
- The importance of providing a curriculum grounded in values and key beliefs so that students have a clear vision of the kinds of people they might become.
- Intentional and deliberate planning designed to work towards a pervasive sense of community for every student, and the caring relationships that foster optimal human development across all domains – academic, social/emotional, and ethical.
- Teaching practices to encourage students to learn the skills of collaboration, critical thinking, communication, problem solving, questioning, analysis, decision–making, planning, researching, building arguments, and reading/writing.
- A greater demand for students to develop the cognitive rigor and stamina to do more and better work.
- Developing an ethical learning community based on clearly determined and identified norms as espoused in the key beliefs valued by the school.
- Weaving values through every aspect of school life, including the academic curriculum, co–curricular activities, staff modeling, and all human relationships.
- Collaboration to create a school and classroom culture rooted in the values and beliefs that allow for a positive learning environment.

This will require a real paradigm shift for educators as they move towards analysis and evaluation skills, while providing them with a lens on creating more cognitively engaging and challenging tasks. Instruction will need to shift from quantity of content to quality of learning and reasoning. An explicit focus on character, with instruction on values and non–cognitive skills through direct teaching and experiential activity, is the value–added piece that the Common Core Standards must have in order to develop high–performing schools and ethical human beings. A comprehensive and engaged emphasis on these skills will be in alignment with the goals of Common Core. When teachers initiate both character and Common Core, students will be put on a positive life path that will help them develop all of their talents and gifts in a manner that allows them to be used to enhance the lives of others.

This judgment only restates what Thomas Jefferson called upon public schools to accomplish – to not only raise students' academic proficiency, but also to ensure they will "understand duties to neighbors and country, and [...] observe with intelligence and faithfulness all social relations [...] ."[14]

"It is primarily the teacher's responsibility to engage the students, as opposed to the teacher expecting students to come to class naturally and automatically engaged." – Richard Jones

CHAPTER 2:
CRAFTING CHARACTER LESSONS TO ENGAGE STUDENTS IN PUTTING KEY BELIEFS INTO PRACTICE

The chapters that follow identify sixteen key beliefs, categorized as "touchstones of character," that teachers should intentionally strive to instill in students. There are key beliefs written to address academic skills, non–cognitive behaviors, and character traits. The key beliefs follow a standard format for teachers to utilize in planning a lesson or incorporating directly into the academic content they teach. The lessons could also be used as part of an enrichment class, student activity club, after school program, or summer leadership experience.

A teacher may use these belief statements in a variety of ways. One idea is for a belief statement to be posted, read, and discussed at the beginning of each week. It could then be read daily with the students. The teacher could incorporate intentional and direct instructional practices into everything related to academic content. A culminating experience would be for the teacher to ask students at the end of the week about what they learned or how the key belief applied to their lives or activities during the week. Depending on the age of the students, they could give written or oral examples, or draw pictures to illustrate their ideas.

Another way to use these belief statements is to choose one of the beliefs to focus on for the week. As the teacher, you can refer to the belief when discussing a lesson, while reviewing a story that the students have read, or while viewing a video clip. You can then have students identify the choices one must make to ensure the beliefs become a behavior.

A third way would be to initiate what I will call "Take Five for Character." Each day, a teacher could promote one of the "touchstones of character" with direct instruction, telling a story, sharing a video clip, having a discussion, or conducting an activity.

Another technique would be to have the key beliefs become a component of clearly established expectations for the attitudes, conduct, and behavior of students. The key beliefs would help the class identify what is valued. Moreover, the beliefs demonstrate to students the expectations for which they will be held accountable.

Teach, Enforce, Advocate and Model

No matter how a teacher utilizes the resources, the process can be reinforced using a simple structure that CHARACTER COUNTS! promotes called T.E.A.M. The acronym stands for four things a teacher can do to intentionally instill the key beliefs: Teach, Enforce, Advocate, and Model.

Teach
- Make it clear that you expect students to live up to the school's values.
- Make sure they understand what the values mean in terms of their own conduct.
- Point out positive and negative examples from relevant experiences students observe.
- Intentionally and explicitly initiate instructional strategies to promote the key beliefs.
- Use the language of the important beliefs consistently and continuously.

Enforce

- Demonstrate the importance of your school values by consistently conferring appropriate positive and negative consequences. Positive: praise, awards, responsibilities, or special privileges. Negative: disciplinary consequences, informing parents, denying privileges, etc.
- Emphasize with students that upholding the values are outcomes of expected behaviors.

Advocate

- Communicate clearly and continuously the importance you and your program attach to character and the traits you want to instill.
- Constant encouragement while making sure you are not neutral about the importance of good character.

Model

- Be self–conscious about setting a good example in what you do and say, as your conduct sends a message to your students about what you value by the choices you make.
- You must be conscious of the message you are sending to assure it affirms the school's values.

Practical Strategies to Instill Values and Character Traits

The resources provided in this book will assist the teacher in utilizing the process of T.E.A.M. to instill values within the academic curriculum. Under each touchstone, there will be supporting beliefs that correlate with the identified value. For each of the sixteen identified values, you will find five specific and practical methods that a teacher could use to instill the values as touchstones in students. We have learned from the Common Core and 21st century skills that a teacher needs to initiate a variety of instructional practices to promote an opportunity for producing desired attitudes and behaviors in students.

1. **Explain it – Teach what students need to know.** This could also be categorized as direct teaching. Here you will find a few salient points of reference related to the belief that a teacher could use to design a lecture or craft a large group presentation and discussion. Primarily, this section is designed to put the belief into context, show how it relates to students, and explain the importance of building the belief as a "touchstone of character." The assumption made is that one can explicitly teach students the knowledge associated with a specific belief.

2. **Explore it – What we can learn from others.** One would consider this to be the adult modeling of the identified belief. As teachers, we need to realize that our students may not listen to much of what we say, but they notice when we put our own words into action. We demonstrate the beliefs we wish to instill in our students not just in words but also in action. In addition to your own modeling of the specific belief, quotations are provided for use in the classroom, as a tool to encourage students to learn others' words spoken about the belief. Using the quotations provides the opportunity for students to:

- Reflect on the meaning of the quotations and apply their thoughts to better understand the world around them and their own lives.
- Express in their own words the underlying wisdom of the quotations.
- Be encouraged to live more meaningful and effective lives by incorporating new insights into their daily experiences.

Teachers could use the quotations as prompts for journal writing. They can also be used as a tool for discussion in small groups or with the entire class, using specific questions such as:

- What circumstances do you think prompted the speaker to say this?
- Why do you suppose this quotation is famous, or at least notable?
- Is there something you can learn from this quote in regards to how you should live your life?
- How would the school be different if everyone lived by this quotation?
- How would the school be different if no one lived by this quotation?
- Is this quote realistic or idealistic?

3. **Engage it – How beliefs and content can be taught at the same time.** I'll admit, changing one's values seems to be a daunting task. So daunting, in fact, that teachers sometimes use this as an argument when they choose not to integrate character and values within the context of their classroom or the content of their curriculum. Values seem to be ingrained, especially in older students, and the very thought of trying to directly and intentionally change another's values seems overwhelming, if not impossible. Regardless of what we teach, our instructional task is to help students understand how to make good choices. When a decision is made and students put into action the choice they have chosen, they are promoting and advocating a change in beliefs. If the belief becomes a habit or disposition, we can then say a value has been altered, changed, or modified. From my perspective, this process can be directly integrated into the academic content a teacher is required to teach.

Promoting effective instruction requires preparing a lesson plan that not only begins with standards–based curriculum, but also includes integrated or infused character formation experiences. The expression "integrated character education lesson" is used as the reference for this method of instruction. Classroom teachers can incorporate learning experiences that address aspects of character formation along with their instruction of the standards–based curriculum. This approach, involving the design of integrated curriculum, can occur within any subject area and across all grade levels.

The list of instructional strategies under each of the key beliefs outlined in this book is not by any means exclusive; however, each is an effective way to actively engage students and to make each student more responsible for their own education. While the specific examples might not be ones that you would use in your own academic discipline, they are useful templates for designing your own assignments and activities.

Lickona has concluded that teachers need to move from incidental to intentional methods of teaching character and values. If teaching sound character is left to incidental or opportunistic instruction, then we can be confident that students' application of sound character will be similarly sporadic and occasional.[1] This means a teacher is to "mine the academic curriculum" for its character–building potential. A teacher needs to look at the subject matter and ask: "What are the natural intersections between the curriculum I need to cover and the values I wish to foster?"[2] The intersection between content and values creates character connections. This should encourage teachers to use the ethically rich content of academic subjects as the vehicle for teaching character, by intentionally incorporating values into teaching objectives.

4. **Enhance it – Learning from stories read, told or viewed.** Effective instruction in the key beliefs can come from having students vicariously experience an event that is derived by

watching, hearing, or reading what someone else may have done, rather than doing it themselves.

Stories can be a powerful and effective tool for communicating, because they enter our hearts by engaging our imaginations. They are how we have endowed history and values, wisdom of the mind, and wisdom of the heart for thousands of years. Sharing stories speaks to the human heart and often generates an emotional connection, which may enrich our own experience. We all have stories to tell, whether they are from our own personal experiences or if they are gathered from what we have read or heard from others. When we tell our stories or read those of others who have made choices and put values into action, we are engaging students to discover and create meaning in the key beliefs we are intentionally desiring to instill.

These experiences can extend the learning that occurs in the classroom beyond the textbook or lecture. In this section, stories and links will be provided for a particular movie or video clip, allowing the teacher to develop and craft a discussion that supports the desired belief. The stories and video clips are shared as a way to inform, stimulate, inspire, and touch students. Michael Josephson, founder and president of Josephson Institute and its CHARACTER COUNTS! project, has written a number of the stories. Others are taken from parables or anecdotes. Though sources are provided when they are known, some stories' origins cannot be determined.

Utilizing movies or video clips can be a great tool for teachers. Instead of being just a time filler, a movie or video clip can reach students in ways that a class lecture cannot. With so many movies available to the public, a teacher can find a film to fit any subject or curriculum. If followed by an interactive group discussion, students will gain valuable insight in seeing character traits in action, while learning how effective decisions are made. I have found that the stories viewed can be used to help teachers and students discuss character issues in a meaningful way, particularly when the discussion includes reflection about how actions affect the outcome.

One of the best sources for short clips comes from The Foundation for a Better Life. This organization creates public service campaigns to communicate the values that make a difference in schools and communities. These uplifting messages model the benefits of a life lived by positive values.

Another excellent source comes from Film Clips for Character Education. This company has produced DVDs that incorporate short segments from over 90 different movies. The clips allow students to discuss character issues in a meaningful way and reflect on how actions affect the outcomes.

Motivational Media is a source that has selected prime examples of great messages on character from recent movies. Character in the Movies™ includes easy–to–use lesson plans with guides that will generate discussion and motivate students to think or feel deeper about their actions.

Teach With Movies is a useful site that provides movies or clips, along with lesson plans, that teachers can consider when teaching specific beliefs.

Finally, Wing Clips has made showing movie clips convenient for teachers to use when working with students. They also have edited clips to better illustrate specific points associated with numerous beliefs.[3]

There can be numerous video clips found on the web by typing a value or character trait into a search engine. I have found this to be an excellent source for clips that can be used to unpack a value or character trait.

5. **Experience it – Using experiential activities to promote learning by self–discovery.**
Putting into practice experiential activities with students generates self–discovery and an

emotional commitment to desired beliefs and behavior. This book will include numerous activities that can be used when working with students or even adults. As a teacher, you do not need to present yourself to students as a paragon of virtue or as the one who has character all figured out. I like you, am on a journey of practicing the beliefs that are shared in this book to live a productive and successful life.

These various approaches address the essentials for developing critical values, skills, and traits. Through these five distinct and practical elements, effective teachers can accomplish the intentional teaching of the identified beliefs, in any classroom.

For teachers to instill the "touchstones of character" in their students, attention must be placed on making sure that the lessons are:

- Purposeful – intentional and focused on a significant outcome/objective.
- Relevant – must be evidently pertinent to the life of students.
- Clear – message must be easily understood.
- Memorable – message or strategies must be practical, applicable, and lasting.
- Emotional – must evoke an emotional commitment to change attitude, behavior, or conduct.

By placing such an emphasis on the need to instill touchstones, it is not meant to imply that most students are not caring or moral. I'm convinced that the majority of them are. My belief in students, in regards to their attitudes and behaviors, grows each time I watch them gently comforting others, when I read about students unselfishly volunteering, or I hear stories of youths putting their own needs aside to help others less fortunate. Our students just don't hear as much as they should about the compassionate, humane gestures people do for others. Instead, they are too often exposed to the visual images or written descriptions of disrespect for others, hate, harassment, cruelty, violence, and vulgarity.

So, can we overcome the forces perpetuating hateful, fearful, and uncaring images and still raise students with caring hearts, responsible actions, respectful attitudes, and decent souls? This is the question I am often asked in my workshops by hundreds of parents and teachers each year, and I'm sure it has crossed your mind. And the answer I always give is a resounding yes. Parents and teachers can make a difference in a child or young person's moral life, and it can be significant enough to have long–term effects.[4]

Why am I so certain? Because years of research have confirmed that non–cognitive skills and the traits of strong character are all learned. This means we can teach them to our students, and in doing so we can nurture the qualities that enhance their moral growth and development.

We can no longer just sit back and hope our children and young people will grow up to become caring, respectful, responsible, and decent human beings. We must deliberately and passionately teach and model key beliefs so that our students really can become the best they can be.

This book is intended for use by parents, teachers, school counselors, activity program leaders, and administrators. The quotes, activities, and ideas contained in this book can help educators deliberately plan a variety of character education activities. These activities capitalize on the daily teachable moments we encounter, as well as utilize teachers' creative resources to integrate the information into daily lessons and various classroom experiences. It is my hope educators will use the material to enhance the moral ethos and climate of the schools. Anyone who has spent time working as a teacher has come to know that "character education creates the climate for learning and caring in schools."[5]

"Education is the kindling of a flame, not the filling of a vessel." – Socrates

CHAPTER 3:
FACILITATING EFFECTIVE CHARACTER DEVELOPMENT EXPERIENCES

There is an ancient Chinese proverb that says, "Tell me, I'll forget. Show me, I'll remember. Involve me, I'll understand." From the writings of Benjamin Franklin we read, "Teach me and I remember; involve me and I learn."

As old as these two quotes are, it seems that we often fail to grasp the importance and value of involving students in the learning process. Kindergarten and primary school grades seem to be the exception to this, when teachers engage students in learning key concepts and skills. Unfortunately, as we progress through the grades, educators tend to rely on more traditional teaching styles. We have come to the realization that that these styles are becoming less effective at reaching today's students.

Teachers can tell you that student boredom is a deterrent to learning, and there are many who are critical of the educational process for not sufficiently challenging students. Research confirms that students learn most effectively from active engagement with information and ideas.[1] Common Core and 21st century skills are promoting that students learn better when they apply concepts to practice. Solving problems, making decisions, and reflecting on what they have learned has applicability and relevance to their own lives.

Learning is not a spectator sport. Students do not learn much just by sitting in class listening to a teacher, memorizing prepackaged assignments, and then spitting out the answers on a test, only to immediately move on to the next component of the mandated syllabi. To master a skill, students must discuss what they are learning, write about it, relate it to experiences, and then apply the knowledge gained to their daily lives. Students learn more when they are actively involved in the learning task, rather than just being passive recipients of instruction.[2]

All genuine learning is active, not passive. Purely verbal presentations – lecturing at large groups of passive students who are expected to absorb concepts – can be of limited value.[3] Even while working with adults in a character education presentation, I have found there is a need to limit the amount of time spent in large group direct instruction, and instead commit to utilizing experiential learning activities and discussion as educational tools.

We all learn by doing. Schools should provide experiences to reach and actively involve students. Gallup surveyed 600,000 students in grades five through 12 on "their feelings of hope, engagement, and well-being. Forty-five percent of students felt 'not engaged' or 'actively disengaged' from school, with rates of disengagement increasing by grade level. Teachers have the biggest influence on student-engagement levels. Students who have "at least one teacher who makes me excited about my future" and feel their school is "committed to building the strengths of each student" were 30 times more likely to be engaged at school."[4]

Experiential learning is the intentional combination of experience with engaged learning so that each enhances the other. By involving students in the learning process, the traditional classroom experience is enhanced through interactive application of theory and practice. Students are engaged in critical thinking skills, problem solving, and decision-making strategies in contexts that are personally relevant to them. This approach to learning also involves providing opportunities for debriefing and consolidation of ideas and skills through feedback, reflection, and the application of the ideas and skills to new situations.

Experiential learning is also known as the following terms: learning–by–doing, active learning, and hands–on activities. Tom Jackson sees experiential learning as students "participating in their own learning process by [being involved] in some type of activity where they physically become a part of the lesson. Simply put, it's learning by doing."[5] The learn–by–doing approach allows students to experience something with very little adult guidance. Instead of being told 'the answers,' they are presented with a problem, situation, or activity, which they must figure out for themselves.

Specific examples of this instructional strategy include: role–playing, simulations, debates, activities, demonstrations, decision–making initiatives, skits, discussions, and games. This book will use the term experiential learning, providing specific examples of practical and applicable tools that a teacher could use to instill key beliefs in students.

John Dewey originally wrote about the benefits of experiential education, explaining, "there is an intimate and necessary relation between the processes of actual experience and education."[6] He contends that in order for education to be progressive there had to be an experiential component to the lesson. Dewey would argue that by focusing only on the academic content of the lesson, a teacher eliminates the opportunity for students to develop and enhance their own opinions of concepts that would be based on interaction with the information. For Dewey, a classroom that focuses on experiential or active learning would tend to mimic society, where all people have different views of topics, thinking and information.

You may be wondering if we are able to identify the benefits of experiential learning. Does teaching beyond the lecture or direct instruction prove to have value? Research has concluded that actively involving students leads to a greater impact on learning and retention. We know that when we have students participating it affects the emotions, feelings, and attitudes more than just direct teaching would. When activities are initiated in the classroom, learning is more fun for students, and teaching is more enjoyable for teachers. In his book "Teaching Tips for College and University Instructors, A Practical Guide," David Royse presents 50 years of research regarding the way teachers teach and learners learn.[7] Instructional practices that involve students in the learning process through experiential activities increase the opportunity for the mastery of skills or concepts. Moreover, utilizing these experiences serves as the vehicle to promote and support the skills identified in Common Core.

Initiating experiential learning practices does not completely eliminate the need for direct teaching. The desired balance is to have students participating in the learning process that will help to embed concepts presented through direct teaching. The importance of creating an active learning environment is well recognized if the objective is one of deep (rather than surface) learning. It can encourage students to empathize with the position and feelings of others. Finally, life skills can be learned, instead of only academic content. It was John Dewey who said, "All genuine learning comes through experience."[8]

Furthermore, Edgar Dale's Cone of Learning posited that after just two weeks, we tend to remember:

- 10% of what we read
- 20% of what we hear
- 30% of what we see
- 50% of what we hear and see
- 70% of what we say
- 90% of what we say and do

He concluded that receiving and participating while actively engaged produces the greatest degree of retention.[9]

When we review 21st century learning skills, we come to understand that the students of the future need to have the ability to:

- Solve problems
- Think creatively – invent and produce/generate new ideas and knowledge
- Communicate and collaborate
- Think critically – challenge, debate, discuss
- Take the initiative and self–direct
- Make decisions – compare, analyze, select, justify
- Analyze and evaluate information and ideas
- Set goals[10]

Surveys conducted by business groups, governmental agencies, and various education policy groups have consistently shown that employers complain far more about job applicants' communication skills, punctuality, responsibility, attitude, teamwork ability, and conflict resolution skills than about their verbal and mathematical levels.[11] Employers report that students need to demonstrate the following skills for future employment:

- Communication skills
- Collaboration and team work
- Effective decision–making
- Positive attitude
- Ethical behavior
- Resilience
- Planning and organizing
- Life–long learning
- Use of technology

Even though we are cognizant of the need for developing these skills, engaging students through experiential learning can be a challenge for some teachers. Implementing activities into the curriculum might require more preparation on the part of the teacher. It will also require patience and guidance, as a decentralized approach can seem less orderly and may initially be uncomfortable for an authoritarian–style teacher.

In addition, some teachers claim they may not be able to cover as much course content in class within the time available. Admittedly, the use of in–class active learning strategies reduces the amount of available lecture time that can be devoted to instructor–provided content coverage. Though many view lecturing as a useful means of transmitting information, direct teaching does not necessarily give rise to student learning. Evidence of this can be clearly seen in the disparity between what a teacher thinks he or she has taught effectively and the actual assessment of course content successfully demonstrated by students on an exam.

A second set of potentially more difficult obstacles to overcome involves increasing one's willingness to face two types of risks. First, there are risks that students will not (a) participate actively, (b) learn sufficient course content, (c) use higher–order thinking skills, and (d) enjoy the experience. And second, there are risks that a teacher will not (a) feel in control of the class, (b) feel self–confident, (c) initially possess the skills needed to use active learning instructional strategies effectively, and (d) be viewed by others as teaching in an established and accepted fashion.[12]

If these challenges can be overcome, teachers will find that using experiential learning as a teaching tool is a powerful way to make connections between the concepts you want to emphasize (cognitive), the feelings you want students to experience that help link the concept (affective), and their actions (behavior).

As a way to provide a teacher with guidance on how to initiate experiential learning strategies in a classroom setting, one must effectively address:

- Setting up the activity
- Monitoring what is transpiring with students
- Processing/debriefing the activity upon completion

Setting up the Activity

In leading an activity, it is important to remember these key points:

1. Lead from the content that came before – what was just taught, what students experienced, and what were they feeling about what they were learning.
2. Plan for the transition – think about how to introduce the activity in a way that helps students see a practical connection to your overall purpose, goals, or content.
3. Grouping – plan ahead for how you will group the students so that having them work as a pair or team doesn't interrupt the flow of their thoughts and overall experience. Later in this chapter, I will share numerous ways to group or pair students.
4. Never let slip what you want them to learn. For example, don't tell them that you are going to do an activity to demonstrate why they shouldn't be disrespectful. You want them to emotionally experience it, and then they should be able to tell you what it is they learned.
5. Be sure you give clear instructions before the activity begins. It is often helpful to include specific instructions on a PowerPoint slide.
6. With the initial instructions, inform students how they will know when to stop the activity. For example, when you raise your hand or ring a bell, they are to stop, be quiet, and look to you for the next instruction.
7. Provide direction and guidance by letting students know in advance the time allotment you have given to complete the activity.

Monitoring the Activity

While your students are completing the activity, it is important that you are equally engaged in monitoring what is happening. For example:

1. Watch the time, making sure that the activity is progressing and that you allow for processing and debriefing.
2. Watch the dynamics of groups for any confusion about what they are supposed to be doing.
3. Know when to stop the activity by being aware of when students' interest begins to wane.

Processing/Debriefing the Activity

At the heart of all learning is the way we process what has been experienced. Teachers recognize that significant learning occurs as a result of critically reflecting upon the experience – in and out of the classroom, between teacher and student, and among students themselves. It is necessary for reflection to be part of the debriefing process.

Debriefing is the name given to what teachers do in class to help students process the information and make generalizations from their experience. This is an important phase of experiential learning because it helps students to learn what they have done, consolidate concepts, and deduce generalizations about the topic being studied. It also helps them to be able to determine what knowledge could be applied to new situations.

Students are responsible for linking the meaning of the activity with their experience and then applying what they have learned from the experience to relevant situations in their own lives. True facilitation and processing relies on the knowledge, feelings, and actions of the students to focus on the content. The teacher's job is to ask the right questions.

The experiential learning activities in this book for each of the identified key beliefs include a three–part sequence that can be used for processing:

1. **An Event – What?** – Questions are asked about what the students did and what happened while they were doing the activity.
2. **A Feeling – So What?** – Specific questions are asked that provide the stimulus for students to connect what they felt within the activity as it relates to content or objectives for the lesson.
3. **Taking Action – Now What?** – Questions are crafted to lead students to establish connections to concrete and relevant situations in their own lives, especially when those connections will lead to a change in attitude or behavior.[13]

A teacher should conclude the activity by summarizing, making any observations that will highlight the intended purpose for doing the activity.

Crafting Processing Questions

"A good teacher makes you think, even when you don't want to."[14] It is important within the above sequence of processing/debriefing an activity to prepare open–ended questions that will be asked of the students. Open–ended questions allow for the students to elaborate and share in their own words what was experienced in the activity. A teacher should try to avoid using closed–ended questions to which the students can provide just one–worded answers. Effective teaching is more about asking the right questions than getting the right answers.

A State of Illinois survey of 6th–12th grade students revealed the importance of asking the correct questions that will allow for students to make connections to relevant situations. The students were asked simple but revealing questions on a statewide survey: "Does your teacher ask difficult and challenging questions in class?" Their answers were an eye–opener, with nearly 50% disclosing that they were either never or very seldomly asked hard questions in their main academic classes.[15]

To make the debriefing process effective, teachers need to ask students at least three higher – order thinking questions per experiential activity being conducted in the classroom. This is verification that you are presenting your students with challenging questions and meeting the needs of your advanced learners.

On the following pages are examples of what could be considered as open–ended processing questions for teachers to use when debriefing an activity:

Analyzing Question Starters:
- How could you break down…?
- What components…?
- What qualities/characteristics…?

Applying Question Starters:
- What practical application…?

- What are examples…?
- How could you use…?
- In your life, how would you apply…?

Assessing Question Starters:
- By what criteria would you assess…?
- What is different because of…?
- Can you think of way that you could improve…?

Categorizing Question Starters:
- How might you classify…?
- Are you able to think of a way to categorize…?
- How can you explain…?
- What ideas might you add to…?

Comparing/Contrasting:
- How would you compare…?
- What similarities do you find between…?
- What are the differences that exist…?
- If ___ happened, what might the ending have been?
- How is ___ similar to…?
- Can you distinguish between…?

Connecting Question Starters:
- Can you tell me what you already know about…?
- What are all of the connections you can make between…?
- Why did… changes occur?

Decision–Making Question Starters:
- Do you think… is a good or bad thing?
- Do you believe…?
- What are the consequences…?
- Why did the character choose…?
- What is the cause of…?
- How does ___ effect ___ ?

Defining:
- How would you define…?
- What principle could you apply…?
- What can you say about…?
- In your own words, what is…?

Drawing Conclusions/Inferring Consequences:
- What conclusions can you draw from…?
- If you changed ___, what might happen…?
- Can you see a possible solution to…?

- How would you describe/summarize…?
- Do you agree with the actions/outcomes?
- What do you imagine would have been the outcome if ___ had made a different choice?
- If you could, what would be a new ending?

Evaluating:
- Do you prefer…?
- What are the positive and negative aspects of…?
- What are the advantages and disadvantages…?
- On a scale of 1 to 10, how would you rate…?
- What is the most important…?

Interpreting:
- What is the significance of…?
- What role…?
- What criteria would you use to assess….
- How would you determine…? How could you verify….? What information would you use…?
- What is the moral of…?

Observing:
- What observations did you make about…?
- How does change happen?
- What patterns can you find…?

Strategies For Choosing Partners and Dividing Into Groups

Often when a teacher does an activity that involves participation, there must be an organizational strategy to pair up students or create a group to accomplish an identified task. Having students choose their own partners is one way to determine whom they will work with for the activity. However, this can create a problem if there are an odd number of students in the class. Regardless of the number of students in class, there is also the risk of dealing with cliques that always want to work together. Moreover, feeling left out when trying to find a partner or group is not a positive experience for a student under any circumstances. Here are a number of methods for dividing students into partners, groups, or teams:

Appointment Clock – Students can draw a clock with four hands showing – 12, 3, 6, and 9.

Have the students find a partner to share an appointment for one of the times. Both will put down on the line next to the time the other student's name. They will continue until they have four appointments.

Weekly Appointment Chart – A similar strategy as the clock is to have students find partners for appointment times.

Appointment Chart	
Appointment 1:	
Appointment 2:	
Appointment 3:	
Appointment 4:	
Appointment 5:	

Incorporations – Here are some group configurations to consider:

- Elbow partners
- Groups of three
- Groups of three plus one
- Groups of three or more formed by students wearing the same color shirt
- Groups in which all members share the last digit of a phone number
- Groups of eight in which members have to arrange themselves so as to form the letter H with their bodies
- Groups in which everyone shares a birth month

Forming Groups or Teams

- A simple strategy is to count off by however many students you want in a group.
- Make up a sentence that contains the number of words equal to the size of the group you need. For example, if you would like groups of five, you could use, "Character Counts all the time," as your sentence. Go around the room and have each student say one word of the sentence. The sentence would be repeated as many times as necessary to allow everyone to say one of the words. When finished, students who have said all of the same words would group together.
- Have the class count off from one to however many students there are in the class. Then, have the odd numbers form one team and the even numbers form the other team. If you need four teams rather than two, then repeat this process one more time with each of the two original teams numbering off separately, and then once again split them into odds and evens.
- Have everyone circle up in birthday order (date only, not birth year). The goal is to form a circle starting with January birthdays, going month by month until ending with December birthdays, with all students in the correct order. The challenge is that this must all be done silently. Writing is not permitted, either – not on paper, not on the ground, not in the air. Students may communicate using only fingers and a nod or shake of the head. After the circle is formed, break into smaller groups of 3, 4, 5, or 6 based upon where students are standing.
- Write a character trait on an index card and then write elements of that word on the next two, three, or four cards. For example, you could have a character trait card of trustworthiness and three other cards consisting of honesty, integrity and promise–keeping. Do the same with additional sets of cards using different sets of character traits/elements for however many number of groups you want. Ask each student to pick a word, any word. Once everyone has a card, explain that they will be working in value groups. Students then form themselves into

groups based on the matching elements of a core value. This approach could also be used for homonyms, antonyms, figures of speech, or pretty much anything else that can be categorized.[16]

- Write numbers on Popsicle sticks. These numbers should correlate to the number of groups that you would like and the number of people in each group. For example, if you want six groups of four students each, then you would have four 1s, four 2s, and so on. All of these numbered sticks then go in a cup or can labeled '6 of 4.' Have the students draw sticks to determine their grouping.

- Allow students to group themselves according to a shared preference. For example, they can put themselves in groups of favorite authors, reading genres, historical periods, or countries they've studied in social studies. This grouping system is good to use when student success is not dependent on choice, or when you want students to take the lead.

- Use a five or six piece puzzle. Give each student a puzzle piece. When it is time to form a group, have them find the other students holding the same puzzle's pieces to put the puzzle back together.

- Give each student an index card or Post-it note with different farm animal names written on them (e.g., Cow, Pig, Horse, Sheep). To find the rest of their group, students must make the sound of the animal from their card, and then assemble into groups based on their animal.

- With 3" x 5" index cards, create a card for each student in your class. Student names or pictures can be placed in the middle of cards. Various grouping criteria will appear in the card's four corners. Determine how many students you want in the first group and how you want them to be grouped. This will be your largest grouping; if you have 24 students and want three groups of eight, then you will use numbers 1–3. Place the appropriate number (1–3) in the top left corner of each student's card.

Pairing Strategies

- From a roll of double raffle tickets, give each student a ticket that includes a number. Have students pair up based upon the number on their ticket.

- Randomly assign students a playing card. Pairs can then be created by:
  - Having students find someone with the same number card but in a different suit.
  - Finding the opposite color suit card (i.e., if a student is holding a black suit card, that student can simply find someone holding a red suit card).
  - A student holding an even-numbered card finding someone with an odd-numbered card.
  - Card runs.

- Have everyone form two circles with equal numbers in each, one inside the other. While music is played, have the two circles walk in opposite directions. When the music stops, the two students standing across from each other are partners.

- On a piece of paper, write the names of half of your class and assign each name a number. List these numbers on the board. The other half of the class takes turns picking a number from the list on the board. Write their name next to the number they chose. When everyone is finished, reveal to whom the numbers on the board belong.

- Write the names of everyone in your class on index cards. Put the cards in a hat or box and pull them out two at a time.

- Use greeting cards you have received. Cut the front picture, image, or graphic in half. Have students draw card halves and find the person who has the correct matching half to form partners.

- Write two identical quotations on separate index cards. Divide your class in half to determine the number of quotations needed. Pass out the quotations and then have students find their match. Begin the activity by having the pair discuss what the quotation means and what it says as to how one should live their life.
- Divide a character quotation into two segments, writing each phrase on an index card. Mix the index cards up and pass them out so each student has a card. Half of the class will have the start of the quotation while the other half has the ending. The objective is to have students form a pair based upon the successful completion of the quotation.

CHAPTER 4:
CHARACTER BELIEFS
Action Steps to Instill the Key Beliefs

Touchstone Belief	
Character	Character counts all the time; all the time character counts.
Trustworthiness	Trust is essential to all my important relationships.
Respect	I will treat others the way I want to be treated.
Responsibility	It is an obligation that I do my best work and be my best self.
Fairness	People deserve to be treated fairly in all situations.
Caring	It is important to share care and concern for others.
Citizenship	I must contribute to my community and fulfill my responsibilities.

CHARACTER

Touchstone Belief: Character counts all the time; all the time character counts.

Supporting beliefs that will bring positive results and opportunity for student success:
- I am responsible for making the right choices and being a person of character.
- It is important to be an ethical person.
- The formation of my character lies in my own hands and affects all parts of my life.
- My values shape my choices, which shape my behaviors.
- I believe that I can change behaviors and choices, and ultimately values.

Explain it – Teach what students need to know

Students need to understand the personal and social importance of character and ethics. As a teacher, you need to seek out the opportunities in your academic content to share the basic terminology and concepts of character and ethics. In doing so, you can assist students in acquiring the knowledge and developing the skills, traits, and conduct patterns of a person of good character.

Good character consists of attributes reflecting positive moral values, traits, dispositions, habits, and attitudes. Students will learn that character will define them, shape their reputation, and determine how they are likely to act. For example, will they be generous or indifferent to a person in need, kind or cruel to a person who made a mistake, honest or devious in dealing with others?

It is critical to teach that good character is more important to success, meaningful relationships, self–respect, and the esteem of others than other commonly valued attributes, including beauty, talent, money, and status. Character not only defines who students are, but it also determines their future.

When working with students, strive to reach an understanding that values are the building blocks of character, shaping the nature and quality of all personal and social interactions.

Teach students that character is a product of one's values and choices. As a result, students need to accept and demonstrate personal responsibility to create and improve their character by conscientious efforts to strengthen their commitment and adherence to ethical values and principles.

Finally, a teacher should share that the concepts of character and ethics refer to principles establishing standards of right and wrong. It is these standards that define morality and prescribe how a good person should behave. Importance is placed on students comprehending, understanding, and applying:

1. There is a difference between universal ethical values and personal ethical values. The universal ethical values are beliefs about virtue and morality consistent across time and cultures. Personal ethical values are the beliefs about right and wrong, often based on political or religious convictions that are not universal because people of character disagree on whether they establish ethical duties for everyone.
2. Ethical duties and moral obligations are different from, and sometimes more demanding and important than, legal duties. For example, civil disobedience, the deliberate and open violation of unjust laws, is an expression of an ethical duty.
3. Ethics and values are not interchangeable terms. Ethics concern what is right and wrong, whereas values are simply what is important to an individual and what drives one to take action.

Explore it – What we can learn from others

1. Of all the properties which belong to honorable men, not one is so highly prized as that of character. – Henry Clay
2. Character is what you are in the dark. – Author unknown
3. Character, in the long run, is the decisive factor in the life of an individual and of nations alike. – Theodore Roosevelt
4. Our lives teach us who we are. – Salman Rushdie
5. Character is like a tree and reputation like its shadow. The shadow is what we think of it; the tree is the real thing. – Abraham Lincoln
6. The function of education is to teach one to think intensively and to think critically... Intelligence plus character – that is the goal of true education. – Martin Luther King Jr.
7. Character is an essential tendency. It can be covered up, it can be messed with, it can be screwed around with, but it can't be ultimately changed. It's the structure of our bones, the blood that runs through our veins. – Sam Shepard
8. Character is much easier kept than recovered. – Thomas Paine
9. You can easily judge the character of a man by how he treats those who can do nothing for him. – Johann Wolfgang von Goethe
10. Happiness is not the end of life: character is. – Henry Ward Beecher
11. Character is power. – Booker T. Washington
12. You cannot dream yourself into a character; you must hammer and forge yourself one. – James A. Froude
13. Hard work spotlights the character of people: some turn up their sleeves, some turn up their noses, and some don't turn up at all. – Sam Ewing
14. The content of your character is your choice. Day by day, what you choose, what you think and what you do is who you become. Your integrity is your destiny; it is the light that guides your way. – Heraclitus
15. People of character do the right thing even if no one else does, not because they think it will change the world but because they refuse to be changed by the world. – Michael Josephson

Engage it – How beliefs and content can be taught at the same time

- Incorporate character building into everyday lessons and activities, by the questions asked or the discussion that takes place.
- Develop a class motto that evokes key beliefs you desire to instill in students, and find the existing connection to the motto in the context of your curriculum.
- Discuss responsible and authentic social media interactions.
- Explain and illustrate character traits in connection with a lesson.
- Ensure as a teacher that you model and illustrate the importance of ethics and values in schoolwork and beyond.
- During one of your lessons, make time to illustrate the positive examples of ethical values in action. Or, highlight when a poor choice has been made and then identify what would have been a decision that could have produced the best possible result.
- Have students write in their journals about character, the specific traits they are studying, and when they may see these attributes in action.
- Institute a "Character Honor Roll" for your class.
- Discuss how living a life of character promotes being a good student.
- Have students assist in creating classroom rules based on your school values.
- Designate a section in the school library that contains books with stories depicting character traits and other moral lessons.
- Share an everyday hero, mentor, or source of character of yours and tell the students why and how this person has impacted you.
- Use announcements, school/classroom bulletin boards, and/or the school newsletter to highlight various accomplishments – particularly character–oriented ones – of students and faculty members.
- Read and discuss biographies of accomplished individuals. Encourage students to be discerning, to see that an individual may have flaws but still be capable of much admirable action.
- Publicly recognize the work of a school's 'unsung heroes' – custodians, secretaries, cafeteria workers, bus drivers, and volunteers – and connect what they do to the school's values.
- Have athletes and coaches collaborate to develop a code of conduct for athletics.
- Communicate with parents appropriate ways they can help their children in promoting character and specific values while at home. This can be done by sending out monthly newsletters to parents that include references to ongoing character development in the classroom.

Enhance it – Learning from stories read, told or viewed
Stories Told

Story 1 – The Seven C's of Character by Michael Josephson[1]

As you consider your goals for the New Year, I hope you'll think about working on your character. No, you're not too old and I don't mean to imply you're a bad person. As I've said often, "you don't have to be sick to get better." In fact, it's a lot easier to make a good person better than a bad person good.

The struggle to be better takes place during our daily choices. People of exceptional character stand out from the crowd because they develop the wisdom and strength to know and do the right thing in the face of pressures and temptations to do otherwise.

There are seven core qualities I call the Seven Cs of character: conscience, compassion, consideration, confidence, control, courage, and competence.

1. CONSCIENCE. Your conscience is your moral compass. Take care of it. Use it. Trust it.
2. COMPASSION. Nurture, express and demonstrate compassion by caring about, giving to and helping whomever you can, whenever you can in all ways that you can.
3. CONSIDERATION. Be considerate. Always be aware of how your words and actions affect others so you can do more good and less harm.
4. CONFIDENCE. Approach every opportunity and challenge with confidence that you are worthy enough and able enough to succeed. Never doubt your inner strength to overcome temptations, difficulties and misfortunes with honor and dignity.
5. COURAGE. Protect who you are and what you believe with courage. Master your fears and preserve your integrity by doing what you know is right even if costs more than you want to pay.
6. CONTROL. Control the emotions, urges and appetites that demean you, damage your name or diminish your future.
7. COMPETENCE. Continually build your competence, the knowledge, skill and ability to ethically and effectively solve problems.

Story 2 – Obedience Respected

More than a century ago the nobility of England, in their colorful finery, were on a foxhunt. They came to an area with a closed gate where a ragged youngster sat nearby.

"Open the gate, Lad," said the leader of the hunt.

"No, this property belongs to my father, and he desires it left shut," answered the boy.

"Open the gate, lad. Do you know who I am?"

"No, sir."

"I am the Duke of Wellington."

"The Duke of Wellington, this nations hero, would not ask me to disobey my father."

The riders of the hunt silently rode on.

Story 3 – Weakness or Strength?

Sometimes your biggest weakness can become your biggest strength. Take, for example, the story of one 10–year–old boy who decided to study judo despite the fact that he had lost his left arm in a devastating car accident. The boy began lessons with an old Japanese judo master. The boy was doing well, so he couldn't understand why, after three months of training the master had taught him only one move. "Sensei," the boy finally asked, "Shouldn't I be learning more moves?" "This is the only move I know, but this is the only move you'll ever need to know," the sensei replied.

Not quite understanding, but believing in his teacher, the boy kept training. Several months later, the sensei took the boy to his first tournament. Surprising himself, the boy easily won his first two matches. The third match proved to be more difficult, but after some time, his opponent became impatient and charged; the boy deftly used his one move to win the match. Still amazed by his success, the boy was now in the finals. This time, his opponent was bigger, stronger, and more experienced. For a while, the boy appeared to be overmatched. Concerned that the boy might get hurt, the referee called a time–out. He was about to stop the match when the sensei intervened. "No," the sensei insisted, "Let him continue."

Soon after the match resumed, his opponent made a critical mistake: he dropped his guard. Instantly, the boy used his move to pin him. The boy had won the match and the tournament. He was the champion. On the way home, the boy and sensei reviewed every move in each and every match. Then the boy summoned the courage to ask what was really on his mind. "Sensei, how did I win the tournament with only one move?" "You won for two reasons," the sensei answered. "First, you've almost mastered one of the most difficult throws in all of judo. And second, the only known defense for that move is for your opponent to grab your left arm." The boy's biggest weakness had become his biggest strength.

Stories Viewed

From Foundations For a Better Life

- The Greatest – A change of perspective shines a bright light of realization that you just might be succeeding in other ways.
- Concert – Based on a true story, this poignant moment in a concert hall reminds us how even the most embarrassing situations can be turned around with a little patience and encouragement.

From Film Clips on Line

- The Sandlot – Against the wishes of his teammates, a young man insists a new kid without much talent be given a chance to join the team.

From Wing Clips

- Amistad – Put to the task of defending African slaves who lead a mutiny on board a slave ship, Tappan suggests that winning the case is not as important as giving the men their dignity.

Experience it – Using experiential activities to promote learning by self–discovery
CHARACTER

#1   What Do You Think?

Learning Objective: To provide opportunity for students to express where they see character
Three – Step Interview
Each table group gets a different character question. Examples of character questions include:

- What does it mean to be a responsible person?
- How do you make a decision when confronted with an ethical dilemma?
- How can you explain the poor and ineffective choices some students make when faced with a challenging situation?
- What would our school be like if everyone was honest in how they dealt with others?
- What role does character play in the workplace?
- What are examples of how students at our school put into action various traits of good character?
- Why is it important to be honest?
- What does integrity mean to you?
- How do you feel when someone treats you disrespectfully?
- Can values be taught to students today?

After a question is read to a table group, students pair up.
1. One person interviews the other about the question.
2. Switch roles with the interviewer becoming the interviewee.
3. Pairs come together and each individual presents to the others at the table what their partner shared.

Think – Pair – Square
One person reads a question out loud to the others at their table. Partners on the same side of the table then pair up to discuss the questions and their answers. Then, all four students at the table come together for an open discussion on the question.

Process and Reflection:
What?
- What were the various activities you had to do?

So What?
- Discuss responses to the questions.

Now What?
- How do the questions and responses relate to what it is we do here at our school?

#2   Moral Courage Treasure Hunt

Learning Objective: To realize that character is reflected in what it is we do
Materials: Moral Courage Treasure Hunt
Instructions:
Give each student a copy of the Moral Courage Treasure Hunt. Instruct them that they are to:
- Find one of the statements they can respond to that explains what it is they do or have done.
- Students need to move around with their Treasure Hunt and interact with other members of the class.
- They have to ask other students to initial or sign a box that they can honestly say they do. Each person may only sign one box.
- The goal is to have as many of the boxes signed or initialed within the allotted time.

MORAL COURAGE TREASURE HUNT

Never got a detention	Always completes my homework on time	Have not sworn at another student when angry	Been an assigned buddy for another student in school	Never use profanity while at school or with my friends
I am proud of the grades I achieve this year	Show respect for others even when they did not deserve it	Have apologized to someone for something I said or did	Would admit to a mistake even if there would be consequences	Think about potential consequences when making a decision
Have never bullied someone	Always do my share without whining or complaining	Have never cheated on a test	Can complete this sentence: "Character is ..."	Accepts responsibility for my decisions and behavior
Said something when I saw someone being bullied	Returns money when given too much change	Showed someone else that I cared	I would be considered a good listener	I am worthy of others trusting me
Would refuse a great deal on stolen merchandise	Understand values are those things that motivate me to action	Can recite The Golden Rule	Follows through with my commitments to others	Has done a service project or volunteered in past 3 months

Process and Reflection:
What?

- What were you asked to do?

So What?

- Were any boxes hard to find someone to sign? Which words made the exercise difficult?
- Would the responses be different if you completed this activity anonymously as part of a student survey? Why or why not?
- How did it feel to be looking for squares to sign if your 'favorite' ones were already taken?

Now What?

- What does this activity have to say about your own character?
- Why do you think it is highly unlikely to have all of the squares signed by someone else?
- What would be other statements that could be included in the Moral Courage Treasure Hunt that would relate to the students in our school?
- "I'm not so bad; other students are worse than me." Give your reaction to this statement and describe what it has to say about character.

#3   When You Look at My Values

Learning Objective: To explore how others perceive and react to values
Materials: Value cards
Instructions:

- Cut the sheet of identified values into individual cards and place them down on a table. Have each student take a card. That tag will represent what he or she values during the activity.
- Introduce the activity by informing the students that certain values are not received equally well by others. Some may like your values; others will not. Remember, your values are those things that shape your behavior and motivate your actions.
- Have the students hold the card so others can see it.
- Tell them to walk around the room and look at each other's values and respond nonverbally.
- Have them respond to a value they dislike by frowning at it, showing a thumb down, or shaking their head. They can respond to values they like with a thumb up, smiling or nodding. They can smile mockingly at values that seem silly or extreme.
- After five minutes of circulating have the students sit down.

Process and Reflection:
What?

- What was the purpose of having others reflect upon the values you were showing them?

So What?

- How did most people react to your value – positively or negatively?
- Why do you suppose they reacted this way?
- How did you feel when you observed their reactions?

Now What?

- Based on their reactions, what do you think of that particular value? Why do you think that way?
- What values are important to you that motivate you to take action?

- If you had to compare the values that are important to you to those you see by others at our school, what conclusion could you make?
- Are all values equally acceptable? Defend your position.
- Defend or attack the position that some values are more effective than others when it comes to establishing positive relationships and/or helping society generally.
- Is there a difference between ethical values and those that are ethically neutral?

Value Cards		
1. Honesty	2. Wealth	3. Caring
4. Power	5. Possessions	6. Fame
7. Status	8. Wisdom	9. Honor
10. Integrity	11. Helping Others	12. Competition
13. Hard Work	14. Courage	15. Respect
16. Responsibility	17. Approval	18. Fairness
19. Hobbies	20. Love	21. Trustworthiness
22. Perseverance	23. Athletics	24. Resiliency
25. Getting Even	26. Callousness	27. Ruthlessness

#4   Say It and Do It[2]

Learning Objective: To understand the importance of modeling
Instructions:
- Have the entire group stand up and face you. Explain that you're going to point your arms in one direction and they're to copy you by pointing their arms in the same direction, calling out the direction they're pointing.
- You can only do four directions. You can point your arms up, down, left, or right. Demonstrate this and have the students copy you, calling out each direction. Be sure they understand that the directions they move and call out are how they see them, not how you see them. That means while you're pointing your arms left, they'll be pointing right.
- Move your arms to one of the four positions and wait for them to move and call out the direction. Repeat this several times.
- Stop and explain that you're now changing the assignment. This time you want them to move their arms the same direction as you but to call out the opposite direction. For example, as you move your arms down, they must move their arms down but call out 'Up.'
- For the third round, they're to call out the direction your arms move, but they're to move their arms in the opposite direction. For example as you put your arms up, they should say 'Up' but move their arms down.
- Finally, start from the beginning again, but this time if they make a mistake, they have to sit down. See how may remain after each round. The additional pressure of having a consequence for making a mistake closely relates to the pressure of how our character affects our choices.

Process and Reflection:
What?
- What did the leader do?

So What?

- How did the change make you feel when the rule was added about being out if you made a mistake? Did you feel any added pressure?
- How hard was it to move your arms and call out the same direction I was pointing?
- How hard was it to say the correct direction and move your arms in the opposite direction?
- How hard was it to say the opposite direction and move your arms in the correct direction?
- How hard is it for you to say one thing but think another?
- How hard is to act one way when you feel another?

Now What?

- Can we act differently from what we believe? Explain.
- What does this have to do with one's character?
- How does this activity apply to making decisions?
- How does having conflicting thoughts or messages affect our ability to make good decisions?

#5   Values Commercial

Learning Objective: To create a commercial that 'sells' a character trait

Materials: Anything that is available in the room can be used for the commercial

Instructions:

Divide the class up into table groups of six or fewer students. The job is to create a commercial that will 'sell' their assigned value. The rules are:

1. Review the components of your assigned value – choose what your group thinks are the most important parts to include.
2. Your group may create a jingle, a skit, song or role–play that will get others to buy into why the value is important.
3. Think commercial – TV or radio – not documentary
4. It cannot be longer than two minutes.
5. All members of the group must participate.

Allow 20 minutes for each group to prepare their commercial. Then have each of the groups present their commercial to the entire class.

Process and Reflection:

What?

- What was the purpose of doing a commercial?

So What?

- How did you determine what was to be included in your commercial?
- How did you prioritize the elements of the value you were assigned in preparing a script for the commercial?
- Compare the benefit of presenting a commercial with just providing knowledge as to the elements of the value.

Now What?

- What was the message that your group wanted to send that could be applicable to our school and the students who are here?
- What is the relationship between the value you were asked to present and real life experiences?
- What did you learn about the value that personally relates to your life as a student?

#6   Paper Folding

Learning Objective: To demonstrate the importance of being intentional and explicit in our teaching of character and values – not leaving it up to chance

Material: Everyone needs a blank sheet of paper

Instructions:

After the paper is distributed, explain the following rules of the activity:

- Eyes must be closed, there is to be no talking and the students cannot ask any questions
- With an understanding of these rules, the following directions are given: (pause after each)
  1. Fold the paper in half
  2. Tear off the upper right corner of the paper
  3. Fold the paper in half again
  4. Tear off the lower left corner of the paper
  5. Fold the paper in half again
  6. Tear off the lower right corner of the paper
- Have the students unfold the paper. They may now open up their eyes. Have students hold the paper above their head and compare. If the teacher has done the activity as well, he/she should hold up their paper.

Process and Reflection:

What?

- What were you asked to do?

So What?

- Why are not the papers all the same? Did we not all hear the same instructions?
- What are the differences you observed in the final product of others in the room in comparison to yours and the teacher?

Now What?

- What could have been done differently?
- How does this apply to what many teachers do related to teaching specific character traits to students?
- How can a teacher intentionally teach values?
- If teaching of character is to be effective, what a teacher does has to be relevant and engaging. Describe what this statement means.

#7   Quotations to Teach Character[3]

Learning Objective: Quotations can be a powerful and vital tool for teachers to use in the intentional teaching of character or specific values

Materials: Quotation sheet either as a PowerPoint or handout

Instructions:

- Have each student choose one of the quotations.
- If using a quotation handout, students can mark the box of the quotation they chose. If using a PowerPoint slide, have students write the selected quote on an index card.
- Have students be prepared to discuss the following questions:
  1. What do you think this quotation means?
  2. What are the most important ideas and values embedded in the quote?
  3. Give a 'real life' example of what this quote is about.
  4. Is there something you can learn from this quote about how you should live your life?

- Pair students or use a grouping strategy to select partners.
- Have the students share their quotation and responses to the questions.

Process and Reflection:
What?

- What impact can quotations have on how one lives his or her life?

So What?

- What circumstances do you think prompted the speaker to say this?
- Why do you suppose this quotation is famous or at least notable?
- If this quote doesn't apply to you directly, what kind of person or situation would it apply to?

Now What?

- Have students find five quotes about one topic, such as honesty, collaboration or respect.
- Have students research and write a biography of the person who said their favorite quote.
- Have students rewrite five quotes using language a 10–year–old could understand.
- Have students find and explain one quote that uses a simile and one that uses a metaphor.
- Give students the first part of a quote and have them think of different endings. For example, "Most folks are about as happy as... _____." (The original quote, from Abraham Lincoln, ends with "they make up their minds to be").
- List 10 quotes for students and have them rank the quotes in order of how meaningful they would be to a child, a teenager, a parent, or a senior citizen.
- Select a quotation and write it on the board. Have students copy it, write what it means in their own words, and give an example from their own lives.
- Assign a group of three or four students a particular maxim and have them prepare a one to two–minute skit to illustrate the essential message of the quotation.

#8   Character Questions

Learning Objective: Having students write their own questions about character is an effective method for reviewing key concepts. When students know how to ask their own questions, they take greater ownership of their learning, deepen comprehension, and make new connections and discoveries on their own.

Instructions:

- With a partner, use the question starters below to create complete questions. You could modify or add specific sentence starters related to the values you are striving to instill.
- Exchange your questions with another team to answer.

Question Starters:
1. How would you describe...
2. What role does character play...
3. Does character...
4. How honest...
5. How do you decide...
6. What would you do if...
7. How would you feel if...
8. What is the importance of...
9. Do your actions...
10. Who deserves...

As a table group, choose one of the ten questions to share with the class. Be prepared with a response. Others in the class can also respond differently to the question.

Process and Reflection:
What?
- What were you asked to do?

So What?
- On a scale of 1–10, how effective was this activity in making you think about character?
- Why do you think this activity involved you as students in writing questions rather than having you answer questions written by the teacher?
- What did you learn from writing the questions?
- What did you learn when answering questions written by others?

Now What?
- If you were asked to rewrite the question based upon the feedback received, what would you do differently?
- How could the answers to the questions be used to create an agreement related to expectations for our class?

#9   What Just Happened?[4]

Learning Objective: To provide a summary of key points made in a lesson or presentation
Materials: Chart paper for each group; markers
Instructions:
- In setting up the activity, try and have no more than four students assigned to a table.
- Assign the tables to either an A or B group

Group A Poster Instructions: Your job is to design a poster that presents the key points of this lesson.
- Your poster must only use words. You may not use any graphics, pictures, or diagrams.
- All members should contribute to the creation of the poster.
- The final version of the poster should be ready in 10 minutes.

Group B Poster Instructions: Your job is to design a poster that presents the key points from the lesson.
- Your poster must only use pictures (including graphics, symbols, and diagrams without words.)
- You should not use any letters, words, or numbers.
- All team members should contribute to the creation of the poster.
- The final version of the poster should be ready in 10 minutes.

Each group shares their poster. You can also combine elements from each to create a single poster.

Process and Reflection:
What?
- What did we learn?

So What?

- What were the common themes you saw between groups A and B?
- Which group had an easier task? Why?
- What steps did you take as a group to decide what would go on the poster?

Now What?

- How can our class use what we have learned? Our school?
- How did the contributions of everyone in the group lead to a more detailed and effective poster?

#10   Gotcha

Learning Objective: To help students get to know each other and to reinforce specific character traits or concepts previously taught

Instructions:

- Students stand in a circle with their arms out to the side. The left hand palm should be up and the right index finger pointing down and touching the neighbor's outstretched palm.
- I am going to say a number of words. "When I say the word "CHARACTER" do two things.... grab the finger in your left hand, and prevent your right finger from being grabbed. Let's practice. I'll count 1–2–3 and then I will say the word "CHARACTER."
- 1–2–Th.... (make it sound like you are saying three) then say, "Think about this." Three! – CHARACTER (how many moved on three?)
- "Okay this time I won't count to three, instead I will say different words but you have to listen – don't go until I say character. Okay, ready? – CHARACTER!"
- Let's do it again: Ready? Ethics, Honesty, Respect, CHARACTER!"
- "Okay you have to listen carefully. Ready: Responsibility, Citizenship, Respect, Caring CHARACTER!"
- "One last time but now wait until you hear the word KINDNESS. Ready: Honesty, Fairness, Caring Character, KINDNESS."

You can stop at any point and ask who has been successful in grabbing the finger of their partner. A character question could be asked of that student. Or, all those who had their finger grabbed must answer a character question from their partner.

Process and Reflection:
What?

- What were the directions?

So What?

- What was important about the activity?
- What were the challenges associated with this activity?

Now What?

- Why is it that we are so often jumping to conclusions without facts or information?
- Tips and comments: For this activity there are some different variations that can be done to enhance the level of the activity and change it up a bit. One would be to have the students switch between which hand they grab with and which hand they pull with. The other would be to have them do it palms up with the finger pointing down on top of the palm.

#11　Pipe Cleaner Partner

Learning Objective: To provide students with an opportunity to express which character trait best describes them

Materials: Pipe cleaner (one for each student)

Instructions:
- Students pair up to introduce themselves to each other.
- Tell students they need to include in the introduction the value that best describes them.
- Students can then form a pipe cleaner into a shape that represents what the other person has told them about the value.
- Each student introduces his or her partner and pipe cleaner to the class.

Extension:
Each member of the group gets one pipe cleaner. Students form a shape that represents a value that they can use to describe themselves. The shape can be literal or abstract. As students introduce themselves to the group, they share their symbol.

Process and Reflection:
What?
- What are the core values for our school?

So What?
- What were the values that best describe the students in our class?
- Why did you think the value you chose best describes you?
- Identify the ways you are able to put your value into action.

Now What?
- What choices do you face as a student?
- How do students put values into action at our school?
- What makes it difficult to always uphold character traits or values?
- Identify specific strategies you use to overcome obstacles.

#12　Dodgeball[5]

Learning Objective: To review character and values while generating and answering questions

Materials: Five blank index cards per student

Instructions:
- Divide the students into two teams.
- Write review questions on a specific value you have been studying. Give five blank cards to each team member. Have team members write a review question (and the answer) on each card. Ask each team to collect the review cards from its members and remove duplicates.
- The goal of this activity is to eliminate opposing players by getting them 'out' by asking a question that stumps them or by correctly answering a question presented by an opposing player.
- Ask all students to stand and provide an explanation as to how the game is played.
  1. A member of Team A will call on a member of Team B and read a question.
  2. Team B member must answer the question within 20 seconds. If the answer is correct, Team B member remains standing and Team A member (who asked the question) sits down and is 'out.' If the answer is incorrect, Team B member sits down and is 'out' and Team A member (who asked the question) remains standing.

3. Whichever team did not get 'out' will ask the next question.
4. The first team to eliminate all members of the opposing team wins the game.

Variations:

- Play the game for exactly 10 minutes. The team with the most players standing when time is called is the winner.
- Don't want to penalize players for writing easy questions? Change the rules so that you can only get 'out' by answering a question incorrectly.

Process and Reflection:
What?

- What were you asked to do?

So What?

- What were the various components of this activity?
- What did you learn from writing the questions that were asked as part of the game?

Now What?

- Can there be an application of this activity to what happens in our school? Explain.
- Does this activity speak of competition or collaboration? Provide examples of a collaborative activity for students.
- In what ways does working together with others prove to be a critical lesson for one to learn?

#13   Mirror Image[6]

Learning Objective: To understand our actions speak louder than words
Instructions:

- Invite a volunteer to stand facing you about two feet apart. The teacher initiates action with the other person following in 'mirror image.'
- Make your movements interesting and slow enough for the other person to mime as if they were being viewed in a full–length mirror.
- Also include zany stretches/contortions, especially facial gymnastics. Include action sequences for tasks like brushing your teeth, combing your hair or drinking from a glass.
- In pairs, one person does the movement, the other follows. Then, after some time, have the students swap positions.

Variation:
Reverse–mirror image. Try following partner's movements in reverse–mirror image (i.e., swap left <– > right).

Process and Reflection:
What?

- What was the purpose behind this activity?

So What?

- What made it difficult to follow the other person's motions?
- What did you have to do to make the exact motions of the other person?

Now What?

- What does this activity have to say about modeling?
- Who do you look up to as a model? What reasons do you have to consider someone else a model?
- Describe how it would make you feel if someone named you as a model for his or her life.
- How does having a role model make a difference for you in how you live your life?
- "I am because of who you are." Explain what is meant by this African proverb.

#14   Character Reflections

Learning Objective: To collect and share concepts, opinions, and examples related to character
Materials: A set of questions cards (one card for each student)
Preparations: Prepare five question cards. Each card must contain a number and a different open-ended question related to character and values. You may come up with your own questions or select from this list that has been created using "The Six Pillars" of CHARACTER COUNTS!

Trustworthiness

- What does it mean to trust others?
- How can I be honest when talking with others?
- Why is it important to have trustworthy relationships?
- What is integrity?
- When trust is broken or absent, what are the results?
- Can trust be repaired?

Respect

- What are respect and self–respect?
- What can I do to treat others the way I'd like to be treated?
- How can I live by the Golden Rule?
- How can I gain respect?
- What are the actions of respectful people?
- What does it mean to be tolerant of those who are different?

Responsibility

- Why do I have to do things and what would happen if I didn't do them?
- How can I manage my responsibilities?
- How can we share responsibilities and be effective?
- How can I develop my self–control?
- How can I prioritize my responsibilities?
- What does it mean to have self–control over my behavior?

Fairness

- What makes some things fair? Unfair?
- How can I learn to make fair decisions?
- What moral obligations are involved in fairness and unfairness?
- How can I accept fairness when it means I don't get what I want?
- What course of action should I take when I see something unfair?
- What and who will be affected by my being unfair?

Caring

- What does caring mean?
- What happens when I hurt someone? How do I feel when I am hurt?
- How can I learn forgiveness?
- How can I show conviction for and commitment to being a caring person?
- What should I do when someone hurts me?
- What can I learn from people who've forgiven me for mistakes I've made?

Citizenship

- What does it mean to be a good citizen?
- What are rules and why do we have them?
- Why should I do my share?
- What are my civic duties?
- What communities do I belong to?
- When is civil disobedience appropriate?

Instructions:

- Make copies of the five cards so you have equal numbers of each card.
- Distribute the question cards making sure that approximately equal numbers of different cards are distributed.
- Have each student read the question on the card and independently come up with one or more responses. Encourage the students to jot down the key points in their responses.
- Ask the students to interview as many others as possible within five minutes and get their response to the question on the card. Tell the students to jot down the key points.
- At the end of five minutes, ask the students with the same number to form a team.
- Have the members of each team share the responses they collected during their interviews. Ask them to discuss these responses and identify the frequent responses and unique ones. Tell the teams to prepare a poster on a sheet of chart paper and advise them to select a spokesperson to make a one–minute presentation.

Process and Reflection:
What?

- What did you notice about this activity?

So What?

- What did you learn from your interviews?
- What did you find out when you got together as a team?
- Were there specific responses to the question that made the most sense?
- As a team, did you find that compiling the responses to the question created the best possible answer? If so, why do you think this happened?

Now What?

- How could we use this activity when discussing values?
- What kind of questions would you write if you were designing the activity?
- In what way did the answers you heard differ from how you might have responded?
- Compare and contrast your chosen responses to what you think other students in our school might have said. How about students who are on the Honor Roll? What about those who are often in trouble because of poor choices? Your best friend?

TRUSTWORTHINESS

Touchstone Belief: Trust is essential to all my important relationships.

Supporting beliefs that will bring positive results and opportunity for student success:

- Honesty is the best policy.
- It is not worth to lie or cheat because it hurts your character.
- It is better to try and fail and learn from the process than to take shortcuts by cheating.
- It is important to keep promises and commitments.

Explain it – Teach what students need to know

In working with students, it is important to instill appreciation for the fact that trust is essential to:

- Meaningful personal relationships
- Enduring and rewarding friendships
- Successful associations in school, activities, and the workplace.

Trust is merely a state of mind. In cynical times, it is difficult to create and easy to destroy. Students need to be reminded that towers of trust can be toppled by even small lies and deceptions. They are built stone by stone, yet no tower is so tall or so strong that it can stand when lies and deceptions undermine the stones at its base. We find these elements of trustworthiness when we look more closely at how a tower of trust is built:

1. Honest Communications. Students recognize the central role honesty plays in generating trust, and they demonstrate honesty in their communications in three ways:
   - Truthfulness. Students are truthful; everything they say is true to the best of their knowledge.
   - Sincerity. Students are sincere. This means they always convey the truth as best they can, avoiding all forms of accidental or intentional deception, distortion, or trickery (e.g., it is dishonest to tell only part of the truth or to omit important facts in an effort to create a false impression).
   - Candor. Students know that certain relationships (e.g., parent–child, teacher–student, best friends) create a very high expectation of trust. In these relationships, honesty requires them to be candid and forthright by volunteering information to assure that they are conveying the whole truth, and nothing but the truth.
2. Honest Actions. Students demonstrate honesty by honoring the property rights of others (they do not steal) and playing by the rules in sports and other activities (they do not cheat).

To be a trustworthy person, one must uphold the following attributes:

1. Honesty – As teachers, we should strive to teach students that being honest will help them succeed in school and life and strengthen any relationship they will have. In so doing, they will learn to reject common rationalizations for lying and cheating as false and short–sighted, examples of this being that one has to lie or cheat in order to succeed, everyone cheats, or it's only cheating if you get caught.
2. Integrity – This is the direct connection between what you say you believe and what your actions prove you believe. It is a moral wholeness demonstrated by a consistency of: thoughts, words, and deeds. Although living up to personal values and "walking the talk" are critical aspects of integrity, they aren't enough. A person of integrity must also recognize and live up to universal moral

obligations. Aspects of integrity include self–reflection, a commitment to ethical principles, having moral courage, resoluteness, and fortitude.

3. Promise–keeping – Keeping promises represents a vital moral aspect of reliability, as the promises we make create duties beyond legal obligations. People have a right to rely on us to perform what we commit to do whether or not there is an enforceable obligation. Promise–keeping directly applies to good work habits. There is an ethical dimension to good work habits – the work ethic – when others depend on us to show up on time, be prepared and ready to do our work, and be dedicated to stick with the job until it's done well.

4. Loyalty – This aspect of trustworthiness implies a steadfast and devoted attachment that is not easily turned aside. It is defined as constancy, devotion, fidelity, faithfulness, and allegiance. Loyalty is an important discussion issue with students as they struggle with the desire to fit in and to belong in situations where they feel required to move away from their own values in order to do so. In these discussions, it is important to underscore the need to stand by, stick up for, and protect their family, friends, school, community, and country. It is important to keep secrets and not betray a trust. However, students must realize that protecting someone or being loyal does not include allowing anyone to hurt themselves or others.

Instilling the value of trustworthiness requires more than creating a list of desired behaviors, or even the direct instruction as to the various elements that define the value. We need teachers to instill in students the ability to put the value into action. Character is formed and shaped by the choices a student makes.

Explore it – What we can learn from others

1. We must not promise what we ought not, lest we be called on to perform what we cannot. – Abraham Lincoln
2. The pursuit of truth will set you free – even if you never catch up with it. – Clarence Darrow
3. A lie has speed, but truth has endurance. – Edgar J. Mohn
4. What you don't see with your eyes, don't witness with your mouth. – Jewish proverb
5. Truth is like the sun. You can shut it out for a time, but it ain't goin' away. – Elvis Presley,
6. The great enemy of the truth is very often not the lie – deliberate, contrived, and dishonest – but the myth – persistent, persuasive and realistic. – John F. Kennedy
7. The liars punishment is not in the least that he is not believed, but that he cannot believe anyone else. – George Bernard Shaw
8. How many times do you get to lie before you are a liar? – Michael Josephson
9. If you tell the truth, you don't have to remember anything. – Mark Twain
10. Truth is such a rare thing, it is delightful to tell it. – Emily Dickinson
11. The highest compact we can make with our fellow is – Let there be truth between us two for evermore. – Ralph Waldo Emerson
12. Who lies for you will lie against you. – Bosnian proverb
13. The truth needs so little rehearsal. – Barbara Kingsolver
14. The reputation of a thousand years may be determined by the conduct of one hour. – Japanese proverb
15. Avoid suspicion: when you're walking through your neighbor's melon patch, don't tie your shoe. – Chinese proverb

Engage it – How beliefs and content can be taught at the same time

- Provide examples of key character in a classroom story or historical figure that demonstrated the importance of trustworthiness.

- Explore and examine people and situations within the context of the curriculum as to how issues of honesty or integrity were addressed, and the consequences of their actions.
- Have students role–play scenarios in which telling the truth could hurt, and then other scenarios in which telling the truth could help.
- Develop an honor code for homework, tests, and projects, with real consequences agreed upon by all.
- Examine situations (historical, literary, or current) in which promises were broken, and what the results were of the actions taken within the context of the story.
- Study historical figures and characters in literature that have exemplified loyalty through good times and bad.
- Many people complain that political leaders cannot be trusted. Develop a checklist for evaluating the trustworthiness of political leaders. Test out your checklist by listening to a politician speaking on TV or by what is written in a newspaper or magazine article.
- Divide the class into small groups. Have each group develop a list of do's and don'ts for being a trustworthy person. Have them give oral reports to the class addressing the following questions: What happens when people live in accordance with these guidelines? What happens when they don't? How does trustworthy/untrustworthy behavior affect our community and society? In what ways can/do young people demonstrate trustworthiness?
- Have the students watch a movie, TV drama, or sitcom, paying particular attention to the behavior of the main characters in regards to trustworthiness. How much trustworthy behavior did they find? How much untrustworthy behavior? Have a class discussion about these issues.
- Have students write an essay describing what our society might be like if nobody were trustworthy; if suspicion, dishonesty, and betrayal were the norm; if nobody could be counted on to keep commitments.
- Students can write about someone they trust. Why do they trust that person? How important is that trust to them? How do they reciprocate?
- Students can keep a journal for a month that focuses on their relationships with their friends and family in the area of trustworthiness. If there are things they don't like, they can develop some ideas for improving the situation.
- Within the context of the curriculum, determine a time when trust was lost. Was this trust ever regained? How?

Enhance it – Learning from stories read, told or viewed
Stories Told

Story 1 – Opportunity of a Lifetime or a Wise Choice?

Imagine you're a parent of twin 11–year–old boys attending a community hockey game. The game is a fundraiser for a hockey association in which your sons participate. Before the game, you agree to buy raffle tickets for your sons. The winner will be drawn at halftime, and that person will get the chance to take a nearly impossible shot – from center–ice to a tiny opening barely bigger than the puck itself, 89 feet away. If the raffle winner makes it, he'll take home $50,000.

Halftime comes, and one of your sons' names is drawn! Unfortunately, he's outside the stadium with some friends. You decide to send your other son out in his place. "No harm in that," you figure, since the shot is basically impossible anyway. "Just let the kid have some fun." Then, the impossible happens. He makes the shot! Your family has won $50,000. The only problem was that Nate hadn't won the raffle. The name on the winning ticket belonged to his identical twin brother, Nick.

You are truly troubled about what has transpired. You know it's up to you either to accept the money or teach your kids a lesson in ethics. What do you do?

The parent decides to make a very difficult phone call to the organizer of the event and come clean. The game organizers thank the parent for being honest, and said they'd have to report the situation to the insurance company responsible for paying winners. After investigating the situation, the insurance company decides they would not award the prize money because they didn't want to set a precedent that would come back to haunt them legally. But, they would donate $20,000 to the hockey program in the town where the boys live.

"Being honest and truthful, it turns out good in the end," said the boys' mother. "That's all you can hope is that my sons have seen that we really do need to tell the truth."

What do you think? Was this lesson on the meaning of trustworthiness worth $50,000?

Story 2 – The Make–Up Test

Chad and his three friends were college seniors and doing well in their classes. Even though the final physics exam was on Monday, Chad persuaded his buddies to take a weekend trip several hundred miles away. He told his worried friends they could study in the car and when they got back Sunday night. Instead, the boys partied all weekend. By Sunday night, they weren't ready for the exam.

Chad, an A student, told them to relax. He had a plan. He called the professor at home Monday morning and told him they were on the road and ready to take the final, but they'd had a flat tire. They didn't have a spare and couldn't get help. Chad persuaded the professor to let them take a make–up exam the following day.

When they showed up, the professor placed them in separate rooms and handed each a test booklet. They were relieved that the first problem, worth 5 points, was simple. They were less pleased when they read the second problem, worth 95 points: "Which tire was flat, and what time did the repair truck come?"

Chad's exam had an additional note: "Chad, I just received a reference request for you from Harvard. How you do on this exam will determine how I fill it out." Then he added a P.S.: "You took two exams today. One was on physics. The other was on integrity. It would have been much better if you only flunked physics."

All choices have consequences. Chad and his friends took a risk by not studying, but they took a greater one when they made up a phony excuse.

Story 3 – Trust, Promises, and Good Friends by Michael Josephson[7]

Sarah was 16 and when her mom saw that her grades were slipping she said, "No parties until you get your grades up." This led to a nasty fight with Sarah calling her mom unfair and her mom calling Sarah irresponsible. Later Sara tried a different approach.

"You're right," she said. "School is important and I will do better, but Emily's having her Sweet 16 party Saturday, and I promised Jessica I'd go with her. If I promise to do better at school, can I go, please?"

Sarah's mom reluctantly said, "Okay, but only if there is no drinking at the party." Sarah replied, "I don't know if others will be drinking but I promise if Jessica or I see anyone drinking, I'll call you to pick us up."

"Okay," her mom said, "but if you let me down, you can forget about getting that used car we discussed."

At the party, two boys who were clearly high, offered pot to lots of the girls, including Sarah and Jessica. Some said yes, but Sarah and Jessica said no. Then Jessica said, "We better call your mom."

Sarah: "No way! It's totally unfair that we can't stay just because someone else is smoking pot, besides my mom only talked about drinking, and no one is drinking."

Jessica: "Come on. You know your mom won't buy that. It isn't worth getting her super upset and losing the right to get your car."

Sarah: "Maybe, but she'll never know."

Jessica: "If you don't call your mom I will."

Sarah: "If you do, you'll never be my friend again."

Jessica got mad: "I'm just trying to look out for you!"

Sarah: "I've already got a mom. I need you to be my friend."

Jessica: "I'm trying to be your friend but you are making me your accomplice. Your mom trusts me and you're asking me to lie or cover–up for you. That's not fair."

Sarah: "You don't have to lie unless you are asked and she'll never ask you."

Jessica: "And if she does? I don't think you are being a very good friend."

Jessica called her parents to pick her up saying she didn't feel well. She told Sarah she wouldn't say anything about the pot. Sarah stayed at the party.

The next morning Sarah's mom asked, "Was there any drinking or drugs at the party?" Sarah hesitated for a moment because she asked about the drugs but she trusted Jessica not to say anything so she said: "Of course not. I would have called you if there was."

"Really? Emily's mom called to tell me that quite a few kids were smoking marijuana, but she wanted me to know you were offered some and you refused. Is that true?"

- What do you think Sarah should say now?
- What should Sarah's mom do?
- Do you think Sarah should be rewarded for not accepting the marijuana or punished for breaking her promise? Or both?
- What about Sarah's lie when her mom did ask about marijuana?
- Did Sarah actually break her promise? Did she break the spirit of the promise?
- How does the technicality that her mom didn't mention drugs in the first conversation affect trust?
- Was Jessica being a good friend or bad friend? What would you have done if you were Jessica?

Stories Viewed

From Foundations for a Better Life

- Peer Pressure – Peer Pressure can be used as a positive force, as seen in this scenario. Watch as a group of teens influence their friend to 'do the right thing' while hanging out at a music store.
- Purse – Watch the drama unfold and wonder if the young man is stealing or returning the purse – until the last triumphant moment.
- Honesty – Cheating in class is a widespread problem. It affects the cheater and all who feel pressured to participate. One person making a decision to be honest can make a big difference.

From Film Clips on Line

- Liar, Liar – A lawyer cannot lie for 24 hours due to his son's birthday wish. He argues that everyone has to lie, but his son won't buy it.
- Shrek – An ogre, in order to regain his swamp, travels along with an annoying donkey in order to bring a princess to a scheming lord, wishing himself King. Princess Fiona tells Donkey a secret then, despite Donkey's protests, demands that he tell no one.
- The Legend of Bagger Vance – A tournament golfer counts an extra stroke on himself when he accidentally moves the ball even though the judges didn't see it.
- Cool Runnings – An Olympic bobsled coach explains to a member of his current team why he cheated in the past.

From Wing Clips

- Courageous – When he refuses to fudge numbers to benefit his boss, Javier learns that his boss' request was just a test of his integrity and he got the promotion.

50

- The Pursuit Of Happyness – After spending the night in jail for unpaid parking tickets, Chris is forced to run straight to his prestigious interview in dirty plain clothes.

From Teach With Movies
- The Adventures of Milo and Otis – This is a story of the friendship of Milo, a farm kitten and Otis, a farmyard puppy. They portray their adventures, and how they grow up and return to the farm with their own families.

From Motivational Media – Character in the Movies
- Despicable Me 2 – Students will see the importance of honesty and honest communication in our dealings with others as Gru, the ex–supervillain, is about to be approached by Lucy, an Anti–Villain League agent. He wants to avoid talking with her.
- 42 – Branch Rickey makes history in professional sport by opening an opportunity for Jackie Robinson, a black player, to enter baseball. He challenges Robinson to be a dependable person of character.

Experience it – Using experiential activities to promote learning by self–discovery
TRUSTWORTHINESS

#15   Tossing Balloons

Learning Objective: To build consciousness and commitment to the truth, emphasizing the energy it takes to keep a lie going and the vulnerability of lies
Materials: One balloon for each student (make sure you ask if anyone is allergic to latex)
Instructions:

- Give students a balloon and instruct them to blow up and tie off the balloon.
- Have students take their balloon, which represents a lie, and stand in a circle.
- Tell them that when you say, 'go' they are going to toss their balloons in the air toward the center of the room and try to keep theirs in the air. If their balloon touches the ground, their lie has been discovered and they are 'out.'
- You may end the activity here and go to the processing questions or have those that were left still keeping their balloons in the air add two or three more balloons each to their effort to keep them all going and not touch the floor. You can also do the activity again but this time the students not only try and keep their lie afloat but are given license to try and knock down (and discover the lie) the balloon of others.

Process and Reflection:
What?

- What did we have to do to try and keep the lie going?

So What?

- What was it like trying to keep your lie going?
- What strategies did you use to keep your lie going? Did any of you have someone get in the way of you keeping your lie aloft? How did that feel? Did it result in your lie hitting the floor or did you try to keep away from them?
- Did anyone purposefully try to get your lie to hit the floor?

Now What?

- Share three things you have learned about trustworthiness from this activity.
- Describe how this activity relates to your life at home, school, and work or with your friends.

- When an untruth is discovered, how will it influence the perception of others about your worthiness of trust?
- Is an omission or misdirection considered dishonest? Explain.

#16   Oh What a Tangled Web We Weave

Learning Objective: To learn the importance of telling the truth
Materials: Ball of yarn
Instructions:
- Arrange ahead of time to have a student help you with this demonstration. Secretly ask the student to give false answers to each question that you ask. This will begin after he or she has taken a seat in a chair at the front of the class.
- Ask your seated student a simple question such as, "Why didn't you get your homework done for today?" As she answers with a lie, such as the dog ate my homework, wrap a long string of yarn around her once.
- Then ask a follow–up question based on her reply, such as, "How did the dog get your homework?" As she makes up another answer, wrap the yarn around her again.
- Continue to ask follow–up questions until she is entangled in a web of yarn.

Process and Reflection:
What?
- What did you observe?

So What?
- What does telling lies do to someone?
- What result will be achieved by the person who always tells the truth?

Now What?
- How did you feel and react when you were caught in a lie and had to tell another lie in order to cover it up?
- Why is it important for us to always tell the truth?
- When you find out someone has lied to you, what else do you wonder about?

#17   The Honest Mouth

Learning Objective: To understand not being truthful can leave a stain on one's reputation
Materials: Black licorice
Instructions:
- Ask the students if anyone knows what happens when you eat black licorice? (A mouth that has eaten black licorice turns black).
- Not only does your tongue look horrible, but soon your teeth and even your lips get black. It takes a long time before your mouth returns to its normal color. Like licorice that leaves our mouths black for a long time, we can see the results of telling lies long after we've told them. Others will lose their trust in us, privileges will be taken away and friendships will be lost. It's always best to be honest and truthful; don't let the stain of dishonesty leave its mark on you.

Process and Reflection:
What?
- What does our mouth look like after eating the black licorice?

So What?

- Finish the sentence, "It will take a long time before…"
- What does this activity say about being dishonest?
- What do others think of us when a lie is discovered?

Now What?

- What can be the effect on our relationships with other students when one lies? With our parents? Teachers? Our reputation?
- How is it possible to have trust restored when one is caught in a lie?
- Why do you think it is hard to restore trust?

#18 The Tower of Flour

Learning Objective: To come to the realization when we are not honest, the trust others have in us is damaged or destroyed

Materials: Flour; dime; hard plastic cup; newspaper; butter knife; paper plate

Instructions:

- Begin by spreading newspaper on a table.
- Place a dime in the center of the bottom of a plastic cup.
- Scoop flour into the glass. Pile it to the brim and press down firmly to make it compact.
- Place the paper plate on top of the glass and turn them over together on the newspaper.
- Tap the glass gently and carefully lift it off. The flour will remain standing in the shape of the glass with the dime on top.

Explanation:

- Explain that the dime represents the trait of honesty.
- Next, take the knife and carefully slice off the edge of the 'flour tower' being careful not to cut too deeply. This represents what happens when we tell lies. Our reputation is weakened. Others will not trust or respect us and eventually the tower of trust falls.
- Notice how each time more flour is removed the dime's position becomes more precarious.
- Continue until the dime drops in.

Process and Reflection:

What?

- Why is this activity called the Tower of Flour?

So What?

- Finish the sentence, "It will take a long time before…"
- What does this say about being dishonest?
- What do others think of us when we are not honest?

Now What?

- Why do students sometimes lie to others? Are there any benefits that can be gained from not being truthful?
- What are the potential consequences of a choice to be dishonest?
- How many times can someone lie to you before you consider them a liar? Explain.
- Why do you think it is hard to restore trust?

#19   The Cover Up

Learning Objective: Telling one lie often leads to another making it hard for others to trust us

Materials: Bucket; one quarter; a penny for each student

Instructions:

- Fill the bucket with six to eight inches of water and put the quarter at the bottom in the center.
- Begin by saying, "Telling a lie may seem like a simple way out of a problem. However, usually when we tell a lie we end up telling even more lies in order to cover up the first lie."
- Explain to the students that their challenge is to cover up the quarter by using a penny. Have students come up one at a time and try to drop their penny (from at least two inches above the water) into the bucket and try to cover up the quarter. If you have space, this could also be done at individual tables.

Process and Reflection:

What?

- What are we trying to cover up?

So What?

- How well did the penny cover the quarter? How many actually landed on the quarter?
- How does this activity compare to trying to cover up a lie that we told?
- Does someone have to tell more lies to cover up the first lie?

Now What?

- What happens when you are caught lying?
- How easy is it for others to trust you again?
- Why is telling the truth easier than lying even if the truth may get you in trouble?

#20   Two Truths and a Lie

Learning Objective: To have students realize the fragility of trustworthiness

Instructions:

- Ask each student to think of two true statements about him or her and one that is false.
- When ready, they turn to a partner and say the three statements in any order.
- The partner's job is to guess the false statement.
- Then they switch places and the partner does the same.

Process and Reflection:

What?

- What were you asked to do?

So What?

- Was it easy to guess the lie? Why or why not?
- Was it easy to say a lie?
- Telling even a 'white lie' is wrong. What do you say to defend your response?
- How do we know it's wrong to not be honest with someone else?

Now What?

- Were the things we lied about important?

- What do we call those kinds of lies? (white lies or fibs)
- When you find out that someone lied to you, what do you think? (what else did this person lie to me about)
- What if I told you one thing today and something different tomorrow? Even if it is an unimportant thing, would it break our trust and make you wonder if anything else I had said was true?

#21   Trustworthiness Skit[8]

Learning Objective: To understand the elements of trustworthiness: honesty, integrity, promise–keeping and loyalty

Materials: Copies of the Trustworthiness Skit

Instructions:

- Say: "Trust… our world operates on trust. Countries sign treaties based on trust. Banks loan money based on trust that the loan will be repaid. Businesses accept checks, trusting that there's enough money in the checking account to cover the check. Restaurants serve us food, trusting us to pay after the food is eaten. Families operate on trust also."
- Distribute copies of the Trustworthiness Skit.
- Call on six volunteers to read the skit in front of the class.

Process and Reflection:

What?

- What was the skit about?

So What?

- How can we believe someone with a history of lies?
- How can you have faith in someone whose 'walk' doesn't match his or her 'talk'?
- Can you think of ways that we count on someone who doesn't keep promises?
- How can we entrust our well–being or interests to someone who has been disloyal?

Now What?

- How would you rewrite the skit to reflect issues that students face in our school?
- Even though it only takes a few seconds to destroy trust, it takes a long time to build trust, and even longer to rebuild it once it has been destroyed. What does this mean as it relates to decisions you make every day?

Extension:

Take the activity further by having students help Erin figure out how to rebuild trust. Say: "You'll work in groups to list things Erin can do to earn trust at home, with friends, at school and on her job." Create groups of four. Your assignment is as follows:

- You have 10 minutes to create a thorough, detailed list of specific ways to earn trust through honesty (group #1's task), integrity (#2), promise–keeping (#3) and loyalty (#4).
- Be very specific with things Erin needs to do at home, at school, with friends and at work.
- When each group is finished, have them report out what Erin would do.

Trustworthiness Skit

Mom: "No, Erin! You may not take the car to a cabin party this weekend!"
Erin: "Mom, why don't you trust me?"
Mom: "You're right, Erin. I don't trust you. Why? Just think about it, Erin, just think about it." (Mom walks away, shaking her head.)

Erin: (Talking to herself) "What does she mean? I'm 17! I'm her daughter! She should trust me!" (She puts her head in her hands, or on the table in her arms.)

Conscience Voice #1: "Hey, Erin, this is your conscience. Remember last summer when you told your mom you were going to the library? Everything was fine until she ran into you at the mall with Bryan… and Jason… and Ryan… and Marcus! And remember the time last spring when you told her you were going to McDonald's? You just forgot to tell her it was the McDonald's in Atlantic City. Then there was the time you told her you loved the birthday necklace… just before you sold it for a new set of Rollerblades! Where was your honesty?"

Conscience Voice #2: "Yo, Erin! This is your conscience. While you're remembering, think about the time you let Megan talk you into buying the $304, 52–volume CD set of the Beach Boys greatest hits. And you don't even own a CD player! And remember the time you pretended to be homeless… just so you could meet the cute volunteer at the shelter? And remember the time you let your little sister take the rap for the broken lamp? Where was your integrity?"

Conscience Voice #3: "Erin, Erin! This is your conscience. Think about your promise–keeping record. Count the times you promised to clean your room and you just stuffed everything under the bed. It was O.K., until your mom found a family of small rodents nesting there. Count the times you promised to be home by curfew and missed it by two time zones!"

Conscience Voice #4: "Whoa, Erin! This is your conscience. Where was your loyalty when you went to a swim party and left your mom to single–handedly control the Anderson triplets you had agreed to babysit? She could've managed if she hadn't been in that body cast at the time. Bicycle tracks on a body cast…. not a pretty sight!"

Erin: (Sitting up) "OK., OK., enough is enough! Maybe I haven't always shown honesty, integrity, promise–keeping and loyalty. Nobody's perfect. I'll start now being worthy of Mom's trust."

#22   Is It Trust or Distrust?[9]

Leaning Objective: To identify and apply factors that increase and decrease people's trustworthiness

Materials: Sheets of chart paper; felt–tipped pens; masking tape

Instructions:

Part 1

- Tell the students to think of three people they trust very much: One of them should be a public figure, one should be a friend or a family member, and one should be a person from school. They do not have to reveal the identity of these people to anyone else.

- Ask the students to identify what makes them trust these three people very much. Have them make a list of the trust factors on a piece of paper. These trust factors could be common to all three or they could be specific to one or two of the selected people.

- Ask the students to select three other people they distrust the most. One of these should be a public figure they do not trust at all, another should be a friend or a family member, and the third one should be a person from school.

- Have the students identify what makes them distrust one or more of the selected people. Have them to make a list of these factors on a piece of paper.

- Use a strategy to pair students. Ask the students to share the trust factors they had identified in the first thought experiment. Ask them also to discuss the distrust factors.

Part 2

- Form a team of three to five students
- Distribute a sheet of chart paper and a felt–tipped pen to each team. Instruct the team members to share their ideas and to prepare a two–column poster with a list of do's and don'ts for increasing trust level.

Part 3

- Have the teams attach their posters to the wall and invite students to review the posters from the other teams to discover common items and unique ones.

Process and Reflection:
What?

- What is so important about trust?

So What?

- Which trust factor appeared in most of the posters?
- Which trust factor is unique to a single poster?
- Was there a difference between what was said about a public figure, friend or someone from our school?
- What are the benefits of being trustworthy?
- What is negative about someone who cannot be trusted?
- Were there common themes when discussing the don'ts of trustworthiness?

Now What?

- Which trust factor is most frequently neglected in our school?
- Which factor can produce the most increase in the trust level for students?
- What would you like to see more of related to trust from other students? From teachers?
- What would you like to see less of?

RESPECT

Touchstone Belief: I will treat others the way I want to be treated.

Supporting beliefs that will bring positive results and opportunity for student success:

- It is important to treat everyone with respect, even if I feel they don't deserve it.
- I need to treat everyone the same by accepting their differences, whether they are my friends, or people I don't know very well.
- I must respect the personal space of others and keep my hands to myself.
- It is important for people to be included.

Explain it – Teach what students need to know

Respect is the act of valuing others. When we respect others, we take their preferences and ideas seriously. We thoughtfully weigh our own insights and experiences against theirs. However, cultivating respect does not mean insisting that all ideas, beliefs, or actions are respectworthy. What it does mean is that we recognize the basic human dignity of others, even when their ideas or values are different from our own.

We need to teach students to believe that the well–being and dignity of all people is important. This means that they need to treat all individuals with respect, judging them on their character and ability without regard to race, religion, sexual orientation, political ideology, gender, age, or other physical or personal characteristics. Respect is the foundational basis for relationships that we have with others.

Often, admiration is equated with respect. Admiration implies that you agree with the actions of another, and in so doing you hold them in high esteem. Respect, on the other hand, is to treat someone else with civility just because he or she is a fellow human being. This is hard for all of us to accept when someone does something we find undesirable or even dishonorable. Regardless of what they did, we still have an ethical obligation to treat them with respect. We do not have to like that person or befriend them, but we must treat them with basic civility.

Students need to be reminded the value of respect is not about 'someone else.' Rather, it is about us as individuals. It isn't about whether someone treats you with respect – it is about whether or not you are showing respect to others. The essence of respect is to show solemn regard for the worth of people, including oneself.

Students often believe respect is something given after it has been received, or that respect from others has to be earned. A level of consciousness must be built about the subtle but powerful ways that we as individuals are disrespectful – often without an awareness of how it is affecting others.

Students demonstrate respect by:

1. Being civil, courteous, and polite (i.e., they use good manners).
2. Refraining from offensive and disrespectful profanity, insults, and gestures.
3. Listening respectfully to others even if they think what's being said is wrong or foolish.
4. Paying attention to the well–being of others and striving to make them feel comfortable and welcome.
5. Learning about and treating with respect the customs and traditions of people who come from different cultures. This can also apply to ensuring that students understand the universal Golden Rule ("Do unto others as you would have them do unto you") and how it applies as a standard of respect. There is a tenet like the Golden Rule in every major religion and philosophy of the world.

- *Confucius.* What you do not want done to yourself, do not do unto others.
- *Aristotle.* We should behave to others as we wish others to behave to us.
- *Judaism.* What you dislike for yourself, do not do to anyone.
- *Hinduism.* Do nothing to thy neighbor which thou wouldst not have him do to thee thereafter.
- *Islam.* No one of you is a believer unless he loves for his brother what he loves for himself.
- *Buddhism.* Hurt not others with that which pains thyself.
- *Christianity.* Do unto others as you would have them do unto you.

Teachers are compelled to instill in students the understanding that respect is demonstrated when we seek to create and support a kind, caring, respectful, and emotionally and physically safe school climate. For students, this means refraining from and discouraging others from engaging in violence, threats, intimidation, and other conduct intended or likely to cause physical injury, emotional pain, humiliation, embarrassment, or a feeling of being left out or excluded. This includes, but is not limited to:

- Unwelcome physical touching (i.e., they must keep their hands to themselves).
- Cruel, unkind, or deliberately hurtful or embarrassing gossip.
- Physical intimidation, cyberbullying, harassment, and mean–spirited teasing or taunting.

Finally, acknowledging and honoring each other's rights to privacy and personal space demonstrates respect. Examples of being disrespectful in this regard include reading someone else's diary, looking through someone else's backpack, hacking someone's Facebook page, or eavesdropping on conversations.

Explore it – What we can learn from others

1. You can easily judge the character of a man by how he treats those who can do nothing for him. – Johann Wolfgang von Goethe
2. There is a secret pride in every human heart that revolts at tyranny. You may order and drive an individual, but you cannot make him respect you. – William Hazlitt
3. The true measure of an individual is how he treats a person who can do him absolutely no good. – Ann Landers
4. Prejudice is the child of ignorance. – William Hazlitt
5. I shall allow no man to belittle my soul by making me hate him. – Booker T. Washington
6. When you go to a donkey's house, don't talk about ears. – Jamaican proverb
7. Respect yourself and others will respect you. – Confucius
8. I'm not concerned with your liking or disliking me... All I ask is that you respect me as a human being. – Jackie Robinson
9. We must learn to live together as brothers or perish together as fools. – Martin Luther King Jr.
10. One of the basic causes for all the trouble in the world today is that people talk too much and think too little. They act impulsively without thinking. I always try to think before I talk. – Margaret Chase Smith
11. Men are respectable only as they respect. – Ralph Waldo Emerson
12. Respect your efforts, respect yourself. Self–respect leads to self–discipline. When you have both firmly under your belt, that's real power. – Clint Eastwood
13. It is not sufficient to be worthy of respect in order to be respected. – Alfred Nobel
14. Respect a man, and he will do all the more. – John Wooden
15. Be beautiful if you can, Wise if you want to... But be respected – that is essential. – Anna Gould

Engage it – How beliefs and content can be taught at the same time

- Explain and illustrate how it is possible to treat everyone with respect, specifically when you are reading a story or having a discussion related to academic content.
- Establish an environment of civility and politeness in the classroom, especially when conducting a class discussion or an experiential activity.
- Practice courteous communication for email, phone, and in–person interactions.
- Trace the influence of music throughout cultural traditions both here and throughout the world.
- Have students role–play some typical situations in which disrespectful behavior leads to hostility and maybe even violence. Then, change one of the disrespectful actions into one of respect to demonstrate how the outcome is altered.
- Use examples from current events or literature to demonstrate the effects of bullying and discuss what can be done to strive for creating a culture of kindness and respect.
- Brainstorm ways to make your school environment more respectful. Create a list of recommendations and place them in your school newspaper or on a poster.
- Conduct a lesson on social media privacy options. Make sure everyone knows how to use them and have students consider why they should respect them being used both online and in the real world.
- Divide the class into small groups. Have each group develop a list of do's and don'ts for being a respectful person. What happens when people live in accordance with these guidelines? What happens when they don't? In what ways do respectful and disrespectful behavior affect our school and community?
- Bring in articles from newspapers and magazines describing situations in which respect or disrespect are issues. Talk about who is acting respectfully in these situations, and then discuss who is acting disrespectfully. Using the articles as evidence, teach the class about the consequences of disrespectful and respectful behaviors.
- How does government "of, by, and for the people" depend on respect? Have students connect the concepts of democracy and respect. What is it about the concept of democracy that relies upon mutual respect among people? How is the very concept of democracy related to respect for the individual?
- Bullies often try to make people 'respect' them. Is this really respect, or is it fear? What is the difference? How is bullying and violent behavior an act of disrespect?
- Have students identify three things they could do to be a more respectful person. Consideration should be given as to how respectful behavior would affect a student's relationship with others.

Enhance it – Learning from stories read, told or viewed
Stories Told

Story 1 – R–E–S–P–E–C–T by Michael Josephson[10]

R – E – S – P – E – C – T. Aretha Franklin reminded us how it's spelled, but a lot of us need coaching on how to show it. In both personal and political relationships the failure to treat each other with respect is generating incivility, contempt and violence.

There's an important distinction between respecting a person in the sense that we admire and hold that person in especially high esteem and treating others with respect. While respecting others is desirable, respectfulness is morally mandatory. Thus, people of character treat everyone with respect, even those who are not personally respect worthy.

The way we behave toward others is an expression of our values and character. Thus, we should treat others with respect, not because they have a right, but because we have a moral duty to do unto others the way we want them to do unto us. Again, it's not because they deserve it, but because doing less would diminish our own character.

That's the message in an old story about a politician who found himself being drawn into mudslinging and name-calling. Once he realized he was lowering himself to his opponent's level, he stopped and said, "Sir, I will treat you as a gentleman, not because you are one, but because I am one."

It can take a lot of self-control to be respectful to people who are nasty, dishonorable, or disrespectful to us. Still, our inner sense of integrity should help us resist temptations to "fight fire with fire." As Lily Tomlin said, "The problem with the rat race is that, even if you win, you're still a rat."

Story 2 – Most Important Lesson

During my second month of nursing school, our professor gave us a pop quiz. I was a conscientious student and had breezed through the questions, until I read the last one: "What is the first name of the woman who cleans the school?"

Surely this was some kind of joke. I had seen the cleaning woman several times. She was tall, dark haired and in her 50's, but how would I know her name?

I handed in my paper, leaving the last question blank. Just before class ended, one student asked if the last question would count towards our quiz grade. "Absolutely," said the professor. "In your careers, you will meet many people. All are significant. They deserve your attention and care, even if all you do is smile and say 'hello'."

I've never forgotten that lesson. I also learned her name was Dorothy.

Story 3 – Jesse Owens and Luz Long by Michael Josephson[11]

In 1936 the Olympic Games were hosted by Germany, governed by Adolf Hitler's Nazi regime. Hitler's well-known hatred of Jews and his disdain for non-white races was part of the atmosphere of the Games and, to America's most famous and accomplished African American athlete Jesse Owens, competing in a stadium filled with swastikas and "Heil Hitler' straight-arm salutes to the German dictator was distressing, to say the least.

Owens, who held the world record in the long jump, foot-faulted on his first two qualifying jumps. If he fouled again, he'd be eliminated. According to Owens, Luz Long, the only man who had a chance to beat Owens, introduced himself and suggested that Owens play it safe by making a mark a foot before the takeoff board to assure he could qualify. It worked, and Owens advanced to the finals to compete against Long.

This decision to help a competitor is still viewed as one of the great acts of sportsmanship but the fact that Long was Germany's premier long-jumper and made the act even more extraordinary.

In Long's first jump he set a new Olympic record, but Owens beat that jump, setting a new World Record. In the end, Owens won the gold medal and Long took the silver.

Though he knew it would not please Hitler, Long was the first to congratulate Owens. That's sportsmanship. But Long went further. He embraced Owens and walked around the stadium with him arm-in-arm before the astonished German crowd. Later they posed together for pictures. That's character.

Describing the event, Owens said, "You can melt down all the medals and cups I have and they wouldn't be a plating on the 24-karat friendship I felt for Luz Long at that moment." Though they never saw each other again, they kept in touch and as a soldier fighting for Germany in 1942, Long wrote this letter to Owens:

My heart is telling me that this is perhaps the last letter of my life. If that is so, I beg one thing from you. When the war is over, please go to Germany, find my son and tell him about his father. Tell him about the times when war did not separate us and tell him that things can be different between men in this world. Your brother, Luz.

Luz Long died from battle wounds a year later at age 30. In 1951, Jesse Owens kept his promise and found Long's son in war-torn German. He later said that what he valued the most from Olympic experience had been his friendship with Luz Long.

Stories Viewed

From Film Clips on Line

- Ant Bully – When bullies bigger than he is torment Lucas, he takes out his anger on ants.
- Boundin' – A wise Jackalope helps a recently sheered sheep learn how to dance and regain his self-respect.
- Remember the Titans– The coach of football team divided by racial cliques insists that members of these cliques get to know each other or else.
- Forest Gump: A young man with a disability is shunned by everyone on the school bus except for a girl who isn't afraid of doing the right thing
- Mean Girls – A new girl gets the run-down on the do's and don'ts of the school's most popular clique.

From Foundations for a Better Life

- Homecoming Queen – Shellie Eyre school years were a wonderful time of learning a gaining many friends. This culminated in her senior year when she was selected as Homecoming Queen. Shellie's inspirational life is an example of what true beauty can be and where love, acceptance, and inclusion can triumph over any disabilities.
- Cafeteria – A story that shows simply being new is reason enough were verbal aggressiveness to hurt and what one does to stand out and make a difference.
- Crosswalk – This message playfully portrays the classic scene of helping an elderly lady across the street. In a plot twist that both teaches "Good Manners" to our young hero, we see that values are sometimes best communicated with humor.
- Locker – This clip models a positive example of reaching out to someone else in need. It also positions the athlete in the spot as part of the solution – not part of the problem.

From Wing Clips

- Not Easily Broken – After a racial fight breaks out, Dave teaches his little league team that they all a part if the same race: the human race.
- 17 Again – Watch a scene in which Mike confronts the bully in the cafeteria, humiliating him, and providing an introduction to the psychology of bullies.

From Motivational Media – Character in the Movies

- Saving Mr. Banks – Students will see the consequences from people being inconsiderate or cruel, tearing apart relationships. Pamela Travers, the author of the Mary Poppins book series, has arrived in California to meet with the movie studio wanting to gain the rights. It turns out to be the Disney studios and she is less than enthusiastic.

Queen Creek High School – Shy Johnson: http://www.youtube.com/watch?v=8jE6j5oCay4

Experience it – Using experiential activities to promote learning by self-discovery
RESPECT

#23   Playing Card Hierarchy

Learning Objective: To raise consciousness of respect and how student's feelings are impacted by the interactions with others

Materials: Deck of playing cards; make four signs to represent the four hierarchy groups. Label each sign as follows:

A, K, Q, J	10, 9, 8
7, 6, 5	4, 3, 2

Instructions:

- Place the signs in separate corners of the room. Remove cards from the deck equal to the number of students with roughly the same number of cards for each of the four groups.
- Pass out the cards face down, one to each student, not looking at the card that has been given. Be sure not to allocate a low card (2,3,4) to anyone who is perceived by others or themselves as being a low card in real life.
- Say: "Don't look at your card. Even when I signal the end of the activity, don't look at your card until I say so. When I say 'Go,' place your card on your forehead so others can see it. The higher your card is, the more 'popular' you are. Everyone must treat and react to others based on their cards. For example, if someone is a King, show that you want to hang out with him or her. That person must in turn respond to you based on your card."
- "When I say 'Go,' mingle and ask people if they want to have lunch or do something with you this weekend. Respond verbally and non–verbally based on the person's card only. When you find people you want to be with and who want to be with you, stay with them."
- When students think they know what range their card falls into, ask them to move to the designated sign that you have placed in the corners of the room.
- When everyone's reorganized, say, "Look at your card. Was it what you thought it was?"

Process and Reflection:
What?

- What were the various components of this activity?

So What?

- How many questions did it take before you knew which group you were in?
- What verbal responses did you get? What non–verbal responses did you get?
- Ask each of the four groups: "How does it feel to be in your group?"
- How does this activity relate to respect?

Now What?

- How is this activity similar to what happens in a school or community?
- Why do such groups form? Where do these judgments come from? Is that a good thing? Why or why not?
- How do such judgments show disrespect and prevent people from getting to know others?
- If you don't like someone or don't want to spend time with him or her, is there a way to get that across respectfully?

#24   Accepting Differences[12]

Learning Objective: To understand that despite differences, we still should respect others – not just those who can help or hurt us

Instructions:

- Choose five – eight categories with four options for students to consider.
- Ask students to complete this sentence: *I am a(n)* _____.
- After they have done this, ask them to complete the same sentence four different ways.
- Have each student place his or her list (written side down) on the table and pick up someone else's list.
- Debrief by calling out various categories and asking for examples from different lists.

Here are some suggested categories:

Activity level

Ethnicity

Outside of school activity

Physical characteristic

Age

Family type

Personal characteristic

Birth order

Interests

Personality type

Variation:

This can also be done as a stand–up activity by having students move to different corners of the room based on four options you have made up for the category.

Process and Reflection:

What?

- What was the process used to group the members of our class?

So What?

- Did you notice as you changed from one group to another as various categories were presented that there were different people in each group? What conclusion can you reach?
- How often do we categorize others either by race, national origin, background or academics and them create assumptions as to what they are like?

Now What?

- What does this say about how we should treat others, particularly those we do not know well, or pre–judge?
- In our school, how would you apply the principles around the value of respect?
- How should we respond to those who are different than us?

#25 $1 or 100 Pennies

Learning Objective: To realize respect is desirable and represents the way we want students to treat each other

Materials: A dollar bill and 100 pennies or depending upon your local currency, a bill with an equal value of coins

Instructions:

- Show a dollar bill and 100 pennies. Divide a sheet of chart paper in half, using the heading of 'Differences' on one side and 'Similarities' on the other. Ask the class to brainstorm ways in which the $1 and 100 pennies are different first and then ways they are the same.
- Ask table groups to decide what this activity has to say about respect and how we would like students to treat each other.
- Conclude that the $1 and 100 pennies are equal in value. Make the comparison to students. Even though we are different in many ways, we are all of equal value or worth.

Process and Reflection:

What?

- What did the currency represent?

So What?

- Are there more differences or similarities in the people we meet?
- Even though they are different in many ways, what is true of the dollar bill and the 100 pennies?

- What does this activity say as to how we should treat others we associate with or come in contact with on a daily basis?

Now What?
- Why is it hard to treat everyone as if they have the same worth?
- What are practical applications of this activity to what we would like to see at our school?
- Can you think of what would be different at our school if everyone clearly understood that in spite of differences, all students have the same worth?

#26   Rule Cards

Learning Objective: To learn the importance of respecting others and themselves
Materials: Three different colored sticks or pencils (one set of three for each group); three different color index cards (two sets for each group); rule cards
Instructions:
- Divide the class into groups of four. Ask all of the ones to gather together in an area, all of the twos in another, and so on.
- Before distributing the rules, explain that each number has a different rule. They are not allowed to share their rule with anyone from any other group, but they may talk about it to people of the same number if needed. The activity depends on the rules being kept secret.
- Distribute the rules to each of the number groups. Allow some time for students to familiarize themselves with their rule. When they all understand their rule, create teams with one student from each of the numbers.
- Remind everyone that they must follow their individual rule at all times.
- After ten minutes have the groups count the items. Ask the second highest group to explain what happened. Next have the lower end group (but not the last one) explain how their team worked. Finally, have the winning team explain what they did to collect their items.

Process and Reflection:
What?
- What do you think was the objective of this activity?

So What?
- How did the team collect the items needed and show respect for the members who had different rules?
- What was difficult about it?
- What conclusions can you draw from this activity related to respect? Responsibility?
- What other values were evident in this activity?

Now What?
- How could the game be done differently?
- What does this game tell us about how we work with others who have different opinions and backgrounds?
- How can we solve problems when working with others and still be respectful of what others say and do?

RULE CARDS

Rule Card One	Rule Card Two
1. Your group has to collect one green stick, one red stick and one yellow stick 2. Your group has to collect two cards of each of the following colors: blue, red, green 3. You cannot touch any stick, but you can touch cards 4. You can only say yes or no.	1. Your group has to collect one green stick, one red stick and one yellow stick 2. Your group has to collect two cards of each of the following colors: blue, red, green 3. You cannot touch any cards, but you can touch sticks. 4. You can ask questions to people with Rule Card One, but you cannot answer questions.
Rule Card Three	**Rule Card Four**
1. Your group has to collect one green stick, one red stick and one yellow stick 2. Your group has to collect two cards of each of the following colors: blue, red, green 3. You can touch sticks and cards 4. You cannot speak at all.	1. Your group has to collect one green stick, one red stick and one yellow stick 2. Your group has to collect two cards of each of the following colors: blue, red, green 3. You cannot touch any sticks or cards 4. You can ask questions to anyone in your group and you can answer questions.

#27   Bully Busting

Learning Objective: To have students reflect on the issue of respect in journal writing exercises and discussions

Materials: One small notebook for each student

Instructions:

- Either as a take–home or in–class assignment, have the students write short entries in a "Respect Journal."
- First, discuss what it means to be respectful.
- Write down the following points on the board and tell them to list these on the first page of their journals as a reminder of what respect means: Upholding the Golden Rule (treating others as you would like to be treated), resolving conflicts nonviolently, showing courtesy and consideration to everyone.

This activity should be done with regularity (every day, every other day, or once a week) and followed by a discussion about what the student wrote. Have them make journal entries about respect beginning with the following sentence stems

1. When talking with other people, I show respect by…
2. I can be a better listener by…
3. When people make fun of me, I feel…
4. People show their respect for me when…
5. Insulting others is…
6. My parents know I respect them when…
7. My parents respect me by…

Make the connection to the "touchstone of character" and supporting beliefs that you believe to be critically important for putting the value of respect into action.

Process and Reflection:
What?

- What were you asked to do?

So What?

- What was the hardest part of the activity?
- If you remember back to the start of keeping the journal, what did respect mean to you? In what ways has your views changed or been strengthened?
- What did you find were the benefits of reflecting and then writing down your response rather than just participating in a discussion of the sentence stems?

Now What?

- By writing what you did, how will you change your attitude or behavior by making different choices related to respect?
- What is the process you use to make a decision?
- What happens in a class or school when students make better choices?

#28   Courtesy Charades

Learning Objective: To understand rudeness and discourteous behavior has consequences
Materials: Samples of rude and discourteous behaviors written individually on sheets of paper
Instructions:

- Write down examples of rudeness and discourtesy on sheets of paper. You can have students create these by working in groups. Let them think of behaviors they have seen in class, the playground, hallways, bus, or lunchroom.
- In pairs, students choose a sheet and then act out that example. Situations could include: interrupting one another, cutting in line, not saying please or thank you, talking back.
- Have the other students guess what discourteous example is being acted out by the pair.
- Discuss ways to show proper courtesy and manners in similar situations that students may face at school.

Process and Reflection:
What?

- What was the objective of this activity?

So What?

- How hard was it to come up with rude and discourteous behaviors that you have seen at our school?
- How often do these behaviors occur? Are these behaviors increasing, decreasing or staying about the same?
- Why do you think students act this way?
- What are examples of similar behavior you may have seen in adults?

Now What?

- How does this apply to what we do in our class or how we ought to act when there is no adult around?
- What do want to be remembered for by others?
- How would our class be if everyone acted rude and discourteous toward others?
- How would our class be if everyone acted kindly and was respectful toward each other?

#29   Get Off That Gossip Train

Learning Objective: To understand that gossip or rumors can be a destructive force in a classroom and is hurtful in establishing positive relationships

Materials: A tube of toothpaste; a paper plate; document camera or overhead projector (optional)

Instructions:

- Take a tube of toothpaste and have each student squeeze out just a bit of it onto a plate. Tell them you are conducting an experiment to see how much toothpaste the whole class will be able to squeeze out.
- After everyone has had a turn, begin the second part of the experiment by asking a student to get the toothpaste back into the tube. Pass it around and let a few of them actually try to force the toothpaste back into the tube.
- Talk about how gossip is a bit like the squeezed-out toothpaste. Once it is said or passed along, it is very difficult to reverse. You may want to talk to your students about the power of words and the value of a person's reputation, as well.

Process and Reflection:
What?

- What does gossip mean to you?

So What?

- Why do people gossip or spread rumors about others?
- "Sticks and stones will break your bones but words will never hurt you." Do you think this is true? Explain your answer.

Now What?

- What are the kinds of things others say about students at our school?
- How do you think our students could change what others say about each other?
- Can you think of a difference that this would make at our school if there was no gossiping or rumors being spread about others?
- Do you think this is possible? Why or why not?

#30   Classification Game

Learning Objective: To understand the negative impact that can occur when classifying or stereotyping someone

Instructions:

- Explain the concept of 'pigeon-holing someone,' which means classifying someone as something or stereotyping someone. It should be made clear that this type of classification is subjective and unhelpfully judgmental.
- Divide the group and have the students quickly discuss some of their likes, dislikes, etc.
- Share with the teams that it will be their job to discover how they can classify themselves as a team into two or three subgroups. They may not use criteria that contain negative, prejudicial, or discriminatory judgments. Examples of subgroups can include athletes, technology wizards, morning people, artists, travelers, fast food lovers, etc.

Process and Reflection:
What?

- What can be negative about 'pigeon-holing' people?

So What?

- Why are we so quick at times to classify others?
- What can be an impact if we rely only upon first impressions when meeting someone else?
- Was it a challenge for your team to choose specific ways to classify yourselves? Explain.
- What did it take to arrive at different ways to classify your team?

Now What?

- Do students in our school pre–judge others without getting to know them? If so, provide examples of what you see or hear.
- Why do you think students 'pigeon–hole' others at our school?
- What steps could be taken as students to make sure we do not stereotype others?
- If we were able to change what others say about fellow students, what could happen at our school?

RESPONSIBILITY

Touchstone Belief: It is an obligation that I do my best work and be my best self.

Supporting beliefs that will bring positive results and opportunity for student success:

- By my choices, I determine what kind of person I am and how others will view me.
- I am responsible for my actions and their consequences.
- It's up to me to have a positive attitude, which is more likely to have positive results.
- I should do what I have to do without whining or giving excuses.

Explain it – Teach what students need to know

There are critical elements of responsibility that need to be taught to students. First, students need to demonstrate the trait of responsibility by taking ownership of their lives and acknowledging their power to choose what they think (including their attitudes and mindsets), say, and do. At the same time, they are accountable for the consequences of their choices. Similarly, students should accept responsibility for the consequences of what they say, recognizing that their words can have serious and lasting impact on others. For example, insults can harm another's self–image, and revealing secrets can destroy relationships. As a result, students need to accept responsibility for the consequences of their actions/inactions and recognize their obligations to:

1. Foresee and avoid harmful outcomes, including unintended but predictable consequences.
2. Help others in need, through gifts of time or resources.
3. Protect others from harm or abuse.

It is a student's responsibility to do what they are required to do by their parents, teachers, coaches, and other adults who have legitimate authority. Students need to accept their responsibility and review their actions to allow them to learn from all experiences. Holding themselves accountable like this helps them determine what they could have done differently to get a better result, helping them decide what they should do in similar situations in the future.

Students acknowledge their responsibility to strengthen their chances of success in school, in life, in the quality of their relationships, and in their own well–being and happiness by consciously choosing positive attitudes and mindsets (including optimism, enthusiasm, gratitude, and cheerfulness) and rejecting self–defeating attitudes (e.g., pessimism, cynicism, defeatism, and hopelessness).

Finally, students demonstrate responsibility by making healthy choices to protect their well–being by eating well, getting sufficient sleep and exercise, and by refraining from the use of illegal drugs and other intoxicating or mind–altering substances. They also demonstrate responsibility by not abusing prescription drugs, using alcohol or tobacco, or engaging in self–abusive practices.

Explore it – What we can learn from others

1. Every right implies a responsibility, every opportunity an obligation, every possession a duty. – John D. Rockefeller, Jr.
2. You can't escape the responsibility of tomorrow by evading it today. – Abraham Lincoln
3. Provision for others is the fundamental responsibility of human life. – Woodrow Wilson
4. I am only one, but still, I am one. I cannot do everything but I can do something. And, because I cannot do everything, I will not refuse to do what I can. – Edward Everett Hale

5. It is better to light a candle than to curse the darkness. – Chinese proverb
6. The value of life is not in the length of days, but in the use we make of them; a man may live long yet very little. – Michel de Montaigne
7. Any man's life will be filled with constant and unexpected encouragement if he makes up his mind to do his level best each day. – Booker T. Washington
8. I long to accomplish some great and noble task, but it is my chief duty to accomplish small tasks as if they were great and noble. – Helen Keller
9. A man can do only what he can do. But if he does that each day he can sleep at night and do it again the next day. – Albert Schweitzer
10. We become just by the practice of just actions, self–controlled by exercising self–control, and courageous by performing acts of courage. – Aristotle
11. When you're thirsty, it's too late to think about digging a well. – Japanese proverb
12. If a link is broken, the whole chain breaks. – Yiddish proverb
13. A civilization flourishes when people plant trees under which they will never sit. – Greek proverb
14. We are made wise not by the recollection of our past, but by the responsibility for our future. – George Bernard Shaw
15. In the long run, we shape our lives and we shape ourselves. The process never ends until we die. And the choices we make are ultimately our responsibility. – Eleanor Roosevelt

Engage it – How beliefs and content can be taught at the same time

- Create a list together of ways in which students can help others.
- Use historical examples, literary characters, or current figures to model how each individual is responsible for his/her own character.
- Examine the meaning and power behind words.
- Have students keep records of their own successes and missteps.
- Examine the consequences of not being accountable for actions in literature, history, or current events.
- Have students role–play situations in which the action (or lack of action) has a great impact on a character.
- Explain and illustrate how, despite the fact that we can't control our situations, we can choose our attitudes.
- Remind students that others look up to them, even though they may not know it. List some examples of who might think of them as role models.
- Have students write a letter to their five–year–old selves giving advice on how to be successful.
- Provide realistic information about the consequences of unhealthy choices.
- Examine statistics, physiological effects, or celebrity examples of making unhealthy vs. healthy choices.
- Divide the class into small groups. Have each group develop a list of do's and don'ts for being a responsible person. What happens when people live in accordance with these guidelines? What happens when they don't? In what ways does irresponsible behavior affect our community and society? In what ways can/do young people demonstrate personal responsibility?
- Have students search for the word responsibility on the Internet. Make a list of resources. Then create a Responsibility Web Page with links to these resources. E–mail this list to several of the websites, recommending that they in turn link to these resources.
- Ask this question of students: What responsibilities do you believe you personally have for: 1) yourself, 2) your family, 3) your community, 4) the world?

- Have students write an essay about the relationship between their age and level of responsibility. How do responsibilities differ for people their age and for older adults? How has their sense of responsibility changed as they have gotten older? At what age should we become totally responsible and accountable for our actions?
- Instruct students to write at least five things they could say to themselves when they are tempted to act irresponsibly. Explain the meaning and significance of each.
- Describe what this society might be like if nobody was accountable for his or her actions, or if nobody kept their commitments.

Enhance it – Learning from stories read, told or viewed
Stories Told

Story 1 – Not My Job by Bernard L. Brown, Jr.[13]

Brown once worked in a hospital where a patient knocked over a cup of water, which spilled on the floor beside the patient's bed. The patient was afraid he might slip on the water if he got out of the bed, so he asked a nurse's aide to mop it up. The patient didn't know it, but the hospital policy said that small spills were the responsibility of the nurse's aides while large spills were to be mopped up by the hospital's housekeeping group.

The nurse's aide decided the spill was a large one and she called the housekeeping department. A housekeeper arrived and declared the spill a small one. An argument followed.

"It's not my responsibility," said the nurse's aide, "because it's a large puddle." The housekeeper did not agree. "Well, it's not mine," she said, "the puddle is too small."

The exasperated patient listened for a time, then took a pitcher of water from his night table and poured the whole thing on the floor. "Is that a big enough puddle now for you two to decide?" he asked. It was, and that was the end of the argument.

Story 2 – Just Wait

We stood in front of a black sign with white letters that read, "Please Wait to Be Seated." I was hungry and impatient, and not in any mood to wait. Two couples that arrived ahead of my weary four–woman group waited too, even though at least half of the tables in the restaurant were empty. I took that as a sign that the restaurant's staff was slow and incompetent. That made me even more impatient.

When we were finally seated and our food arrived, I lost it. "You call this a fresh fruit salad?" I scolded Lindsay, the nineteen–year–old waitress who delivered a bowl of faded honeydew and overripe cantaloupe that the kitchen had, for some reason, thought I would eat.

I expected Lindsay to tell me it wasn't her fault because she didn't make the salad. But she stunned me. "No," she agreed, "it doesn't look fresh at all. The kitchen is just about out of fresh fruit. I'm sorry." I didn't know what to say. I knew it wasn't her fault, yet she apologized. Lindsay directed my attention to the plump, red strawberries that garnished the sandwich platters my friends had ordered. "How about a big bowl of those?" she offered.

She returned in a hurry, eager to salvage my supper. But steps away from our table, she stumbled over a kink in the carpet and released the bowl, sending strawberries flying all over my dinner companions and me.

"Did everybody get some?" Lindsay asked, and she started to giggle. It infected all four of us. We laughed. This teenage ray of sunshine helped us pick berries out of our hair and sped back to the kitchen to slice up some more.

We left her a huge tip, this young woman who spilled food all over us. As we left, I pulled her aside. "You didn't get upset because I didn't like my salad or even when you tripped. You didn't blame the kitchen or the carpet or us for arriving so late. You just handled it. How do you do that?"

Her response was mature beyond her nineteen years. "I'm responsible for making sure you come back," Lindsay explained. "You'll base your decisions on my actions." She was responsible for every mess she made. She was responsible for serving me the wilted cantaloupe. She was responsible for tossing strawberries all over my friends and me.

I asked Lindsay one more question before I turned to leave: "Why were so many people waiting to be seated when we arrived, even though so many tables were empty?"

She replied, "They wanted to sit in my section, so they had to wait for tables to open up."

Story 3 – Lessons From the Monkey Pot by Michael Josephson[14]

Many years ago a man came to a village in India to catch monkeys so he could sell them to zoos. The monkeys, however, were very clever and every sort of trap he set failed. A young boy watched the man's pathetic efforts and laughed.

The man said, "If you can catch me a monkey I'll give you $2." (That was a huge amount of money then.)

The boy went to his home and took a clay pot with a narrow neck. He placed a few nuts around the pot and put lots of nuts inside. He then tied the pot to a tree and he told the man, "We should have a monkey in a few hours. Let's wait in the village. The monkey will call us when he is ready."

Sure enough, a band of monkeys soon discovered the nuts and the pot. One slipped his hand in the pot and grabbed a handful of nuts, but he couldn't pull his hand out of the narrow opening of the pot because his fist was clenched. The monkey panicked and started making loud noises. Some of the other monkeys tried unsuccessfully to pull the pot off his hand.

The boy and the man heard the ruckus and the boy got a sack. As they approached the monkeys they all ran away except the one with its hand in the pot. The boy grabbed the monkey and the pot. The man was amazed and asked the boy the secret of his monkey trap. "Why was it so easy for the monkey to get his hand in but so hard to get it out?"

The boy laughed and said, "The monkey could have easily got his hand back out and escaped, but he would have had to let go of the nuts in the pot, and he just wasn't willing to let go. They never are."

What lessons can be learned from this story? Do people sometimes trap themselves by holding onto things that they should let go? Do you?

This story is often used to illustrate the power of greed. The trappings of success, trap people by wealth, and by a limitless desire to acquire and hold onto material things – even when the things they hold do not give them what they want or need. But there are other dimensions to the story as well. Many people trap themselves by holding onto negative feelings – resentment, anger, and jealousy – that both lessen and limit their lives. Like the monkey who derives no pleasure or nourishment from the nuts he holds in his hand, we can derive nothing of value from these negative emotions. Many of us could improve our lives instantly by the simple act of letting go.

It's so simple, yet so hard.

Stories Viewed

From Foundations for a Better Life

- Change the World Making a Difference – At first it seems so daunting. It implies that you must have some sort of influence, special talents and time. In fact, it takes only the desire to make just one thing a little better.

From Film Clips on Line

- Christmas Story – A boy is double–dog–dared to stick his tongue to the flagpole.
- Pay It Forward – A social studies teacher challenges his students to come up with an idea that can change the world.

From Wing Clips
- Imagine That – In the middle of an intensely critical time in his professional career, Evan must take sole care of his daughter.
- Groundhog Day – Knowing he's living the same day over and over, Phil decides to eat, drink, and smoke to his heart's content.
- Braveheart – After a tremendous victory against the English, Scottish nobles would rather bicker over titles instead of preserving their freedom.

From Teach With Movies
- The Lion King – Tells the story of Simba, his birth, the murder of his father by his Uncle Scar, Simba's exile, and his return.
- Thelma and Louise – Students will learn how to use, analyze and interpret foreshadowing and characterization through showing rather than telling.

From Motivational Media– Character in the Movies
- After Earth – This clip will help students understand the importance of growing in responsibility and leadership. General Cypher Raige and his son, Kitai, have crash–landed on the now–quarantined planet Earth. Due to his father's critical injuries, Kitai must now save them both by retrieving a special beacon.

Lateefah Simon – http://www.youtube.com/watch?v=BDmOZZ3mork

Experience it – Using experiential activities to promote learning by self–discovery
RESPONSIBILITY

#31   Filling the Jar

Learning Objective: To be reminded of the need to prioritize responsibilities before fun
Materials: A clean empty jar; golf balls or ping pong balls to fill the jar to the top; a container with enough uncooked rice to fill the jar once the balls are inside
Instructions:
- Before you begin this activity, fill a jar to the top with plastic golf balls or ping–pong balls. Pour rice over the balls, filling in all the gaps to the top. Empty the jar and separate the rice and balls into two containers.
- Begin by stating that the jar represents the amount of time you have available in a day. The balls represent responsibilities or duties and the rice represents the fun things one wants to do.
- If one chooses to do the things he or she wants to do, all the rice is dumped in the jar. Then one realizes the day is mostly over and tries to add the balls or responsibilities. It isn't long before the day is full and responsibilities have not been done. Then dump everything back out and suggest an alternative scenario.
- Choose to take care of responsibilities first, and then do the things one wants to do. As the balls are put in first and then the rice is added, everything fits.

Process and Reflection:
What?
- What value is being presented in this activity?

So What?

- Do you relate more to the first experience with this activity or the second?
- What do you think are the benefits of conducting your life based on the second way of filling the jar in comparison to the first?
- How does it work if we do some of our responsibilities, and then have some fun, followed by fulfilling additional responsibilities?

Now What?

- To make things concrete for younger students, have them suggest what responsibilities some of the balls represent. (e.g. doing homework, walking the dog, practicing the piano) and what some of the rice could represent (e.g. playing a video game, talking on the phone, going to the movies).
- What do you think the majority of students do at this school? Explain your answer.
- Why is responsibility important for students? How about as an employee in the workplace?
- In your own words, what does it mean to be a responsible student?

#32   Leadership Advice From Your Role Model[15]

Learning Objective: To explore different pieces of advice on leadership styles, characteristics, attitudes, behaviors, and skills

Materials: Index cards

Instructions:

- Ask students to individually select a role model who has inspired them. This role model could be a family member, a teacher, a friend, a political leader, a coach, a military genius, a spiritual mentor, an inspiring writer, or a fictional hero.
- Distribute an index card to each student. On one side of the card, have them write the name of the role model (*example: Mother Theresa*) if other students can recognize this leader. Otherwise, ask students to write a brief description (*example: my third-grade teacher*).
- On the back of the card, identify three to five character traits of this individual. Ask students to take on the role of the person they selected. Imagine that a young person is asking this role model for leadership advice. Have students write in one or two sentences on their index card one important piece of advice they would give (in their assumed role) to this young person. The advice may be about leadership styles, characteristics, attitudes, behaviors, or skills.
- Ask each student to turn the card with the name side down and exchange it with someone else. Repeat until all cards have been rapidly and repeatedly exchanged.
- Have each student read the piece of advice on the card they received. Invite them to think about this piece of advice and how it would help them personally to become a better student.
- Ask someone to stand up and read the piece of advice from the card, without revealing the role model.

Process and Reflection:
What?

- Why is it important to reflect upon a role model we may have?

So What?

- Can you guess who could be the role model who gave this piece of advice? Ask the student who read this piece of advice to identify the role model specified on the card.
- Invite other students whose cards contain similar pieces of advice to read them aloud. What are the minor differences among these ideas?

- What similarities do you find between the advices given to a young person?
- Does anyone have different advice?

Now What?
- Select a piece of advice. What is one that you would want to implement in your life?
- What words or phrases would you use to describe someone who is a role model at our school?
- What would be the impact if someone chose you as a role model?

#33   What's on Your Plate?

Learning Objective: To have an understanding of student responsibilities
Materials: Paper plate (one for each student); markers
Instructions:
- Give everyone a plate and some markers.
- Have them write on their plate in pictures, words, or phrases the things and responsibilities in their lives that fill up their time as a student. Math–type students can even make it into a pie graph.
- Students then pair up with another and tell what is on their plate.

Variation: If the group is too big for everyone to explain their plate individually, you can have them raise their plates to various categories. Like: "Who has completing homework on their plate?" "Who has being on time to practice?"

Process and Reflection:
What?
- What is on your plate?

So What?
- Which values are represented in how students fill their day?
- What do choices that one makes have to do with putting values into action?
- How did you decide what goes on your plate?
- What is the most important value to you? Why?

Now What?
- What can you do to live by these core values?
- Why is it hard for everyone to live by the values we desire to see in students at our school?
- Responsibility is more than just a word – it is the outcome of choices made. List all the ways at our school where you see responsibility as an outcome of a choice.
- Can values be taught? What do you think teachers at our school should do if you believe that values can be taught to students?

#34   The Story of Adrian

Learning Objective: To provide an opportunity to practice identifying and determining various levels of responsibility
Materials: Copies of "The Story of Adrian" (one per student)

Instructions:

- Distribute copies of Adrian's story and read it aloud to the group.
- Ask students to list the people responsible for the tragedy, in order from most to least responsible.
- Divide students into groups of three or four. Direct each group to discuss the story and come to a consensus on the responsible characters.
- Have each group write their chosen order on the board or a sheet of chart paper, and explain their reasoning.

Handout:

Adrian is a 15–year–old boy. He has been on probation for a year because he was caught breaking into a neighbor's house and stealing jewelry and a small TV. This was just his first referral to the court. Adrian's father abandoned his mother and two other younger children when he was eight years old.

His mother has not been very effective at disciplining Adrian allowing him to run wild for several years. He is known to skip school, do drugs and now it is common knowledge that he is stealing by breaking into people's homes. But, what has happened after the last break–in is that he was caught and charged with burglary.

At the court hearing, it is learned that Adrian saw his probation counselor only once in the past 11 months. It seems no one really paid attention to whether Adrian showed up and once that became known, Adrian just blew off any planned meetings. The judge, having little confidence in the probation department, commits Adrian to a residential training school. Adrian does not like the school or having to live in a dormitory. One house parent in particular treats him badly, pushing him around and humiliating him in front of the other young people.

Andrew, another boy in Adrian's cottage, is planning an escape. Adrian does not want to run away, but Andrew coerces Adrian into doing it. They escape one night and once outside, Andrew steals a truck. While driving on the highway at a very fast speed, Andrew blows through a red light. The truck smashes broadside into another car that is traveling through the intersection. Adrian, who is not wearing a seat belt, is killed instantly.

Process and Reflection:
What?

- What was the story about?

So What?

- What does stakeholder mean? (anyone with a 'stake' in the decision) Who are the stakeholders in this story?
- Was there any character whom you assigned no responsibility for the tragedy? Who? Why?
- How did you resolve differing opinions about the order of responsibility?

Now What?

- What does our discussion suggest about responsibility?
- What does it mean that as students we are in charge of our choices?
- What did you learn from this process about responsibility, consequences and choices?
- Are there specific conclusions you can draw from this story about responsibility and the impact of our actions on others?
- If you could, what would be a new ending to the story?

FAIRNESS

Touchstone Belief: People deserve to be treated fairly in all situations.

Supporting beliefs that will bring positive results and opportunity for student success:

- There is a need to have pre–established rules that are consistently applied.
- Having a clear system for making decisions promotes fairness.
- I should treat all people equitably based on their merits and abilities.
- I must understand the different perspectives that others have when determining what is fair.

Explain it – Teach what students need to know

Fairness means treating people equitably, without bias or partiality, by actively working to set aside self–interest or group loyalty when rendering a judgment. In everyday life, fairness manifests itself in simple ways, such as taking turns, listening intently, sharing, and not taking advantage of others based on their weaknesses (either perceived or actual).

Students need to understand that impartiality is a key part of fairness. Being impartial does not mean having no biases – rather it means knowing what those biases are, striving to set them aside, and requesting outside perspectives as needed. While inspired by the ideal of justice, fairness is not sameness or always following the letter of the law. Fairness makes room for us to generate solutions and compromises based on reason and circumstance.

The concept of fairness is concerned with actions, processes, and consequences that are morally right, honorable, and equitable. When decisions are made that are fair, they are made in an appropriate manner based on appropriate criteria.

There are two aspects to fairness. They can be categorized as the process of making a decision, and the results of the decision made. In approaching a situation, it is our duty to use a fair process that produces a fair result. This isn't an easy expectation to meet. What must be clear is that fair notice has been given. As the one making a judgment, you can assure others you will act impartially and gather all the facts before a decision is made. Also, opportunity will be provided for a fair hearing should the decision made be disputed, or if the action taken is perceived as being unfair. This process can be called "procedural fairness."

The results side of fairness is called "substantive fairness." It is important for students to become conscious of the various theories that might be used to make a decision. These theories could include having the result of the decision based upon merit, need, might, equality, seniority, or effort. Think of the criteria behind how a set of individuals could be chosen for a team, how scholarships are granted, or how grades are assigned.

Students will have to grapple with a decision that will bring to light the differences in the theoretical frame they each use to make decisions. It is important to note there isn't a 'right' answer. Rather, we need to teach students to become conscious of the personal differences in how a decision is framed, and that people can be given the same information but come up with very different results. The ultimate lesson in this is that when a decision needs to be made, there must be pre–established rules for how it will be made. The student must then be consistent in applying those rules. This does not negate that some decisions will still be found unfavorable, and most likely deemed unfair, by those who do not get the result they anticipated or wanted.

Remember this – when a person says, "That's not fair!" they had an expectation that wasn't met. You need to find out what their expectation was and why they expected it. Their expectation may or may not have been realistic; they could just be upset they didn't get their way, or it could be an instance in which someone wasn't consistent with enforcing the rules. These are all issues that can be discussed at the time as a 'teachable moment.'

The old adage of "life isn't fair, deal with it" does not help students learn about fairness. Inquiring, probing, and having them self–reflect on why their expectation isn't matching the outcome all create the opportunity to teach them a life lesson. They will also learn that this provides a good assessment for the one making the decision, to ensure a fair process was used in producing a fair result.

Explore it – What we can learn from others

1. Expecting the world to treat you fairly because you are a good person is a little like expecting the bull not to attack you because you are a vegetarian. – Dennis Wholey
2. It is not fair to ask of others what you are unwilling to do yourself. – Eleanor Roosevelt
3. Examine what is said, not the person who speaks. – Native American proverb
4. These men ask for just the same thing, fairness, and fairness only. This, so far as in my power, they, and all others, shall have. – Abraham Lincoln
5. If you cannot catch a fish, do not blame the sea. – Greek proverb
6. A single penny fairly got is worth a thousand that are not. – German proverb
7. Though force can protect in emergency, only justice, fairness, consideration and cooperation can finally lead men to the dawn of eternal peace. – Dwight D. Eisenhower,
8. Win or lose, do it fairly. – Knute Rockne
9. Justice knows no friendship. – Estonian proverb
10. Fairness is man's ability rise above his prejudices. – Wes Fessler
11. In a community, it's better for every person to have a little of something than for one person to have everything. – African proverb
12. Let us keep our mouths shut and our pens dry until we know the facts. – A.J. Carlson
13. He who knows only his own side of the case knows little of that. – John Stuart Mill
14. Life may not always be fair to you, but you can always be fair in life! – Author unknown
15. The best index to a person's character is how he treats people who can't do him any good– and how he treats people who can't fight back. – Abigail Van Buren

Engage it – How beliefs and content can be taught at the same time

- Have students role–play a variety of situations in which people are being both unfair and fair to each other. Make lists specifying when people do not play fair. Document how students can respond appropriately.
- As a class, make two lists: a list of things we sometimes do in our personal lives that are unfair, and a list of things we do as a society that are unfair. What could be done to rectify these injustices so we can cross them off the list? Whose responsibility is it to correct the injustices in our society? How could students contribute to the effort?
- Have students bring in articles from newspapers and magazines describing situations in which fairness and justice are issues. Discuss who is acting fairly in these situations, and then discuss who is acting unfairly.
- Have students research attempts that are made to administer fairness or justice in a democracy's legal system.
- Involve students in determining the consequences of violating classroom rules.
- Put literary characters or historical figures 'on trial' to determine appropriate consequences.
- Examine a school rule from the differing viewpoints of students, teachers, parents, and administrators, and why each stakeholder finds it fair or unfair.
- Invite a judge to come and talk to your class about how fair decisions are made in the courtroom.

- One aspect of fairness is equal opportunity. Have students do a research study in your school to see if students feel that they have equal opportunities. Are there groups of students who don't think they do? Is there a group of 'outcasts' in your school who feel that they're being treated unfairly? What could be done to address these complaints?

Enhance it – Learning from stories read, told or viewed
Stories Told

Story 1 – Fairness Is More Rewarding Than Money by Stuart Wolpert[16]

UCLA neuroscience and human–behavior researchers have demonstrated a link between fairness and reward in the brain. "Receiving a fair offer activates the same brain circuitry as when we eat craved food, win money, or see a beautiful face," explained Golnaz Tabibnia.

The experiment utilized the ultimatum game, a test in which money is divided between two parties. The 'proposer' determines how the money will be split. The 'responder' can either accept the offer (in which case both parties keep the cash) or reject it (in which neither party gets anything, thus penalizing the proposer for making an unfair offer). There's no chance for reciprocity because students only play once.

During the test, Tabibnia and her team charted the responders' brain activity with functional MRI. When a proposed offer was fair, such as $5 out of $10, the reward center in the responder's brain was triggered. On the contrary, when a responder received a lopsided offer, like $5 out of $23, the region associated with disgust was aroused.

Even though responders in both examples would get the same amount ($5), most who received a fair deal ($5 out of $10) accepted the offer while nearly half of those who were given a bad deal ($5 out of $23) rejected it. Fewer than 2% accepted offers with a 10% – 90% split. This is significant because logically even 10% of the money would have been a gain.

"We had never thought of ethics or fairness as being tied to neurons," Joy Hirsch. "Certainly money is rewarding, but more and more research is suggesting that our social relations with other people…can be very strong determinants of our happiness and satisfaction."

Story 2 – Wen Wants a Laptop[17]

This story is about two young people, Don and Wen. Don is a boy of 13 and his sister Wen is 12. They live in a small block built house in the suburb of a large city in the Philippines. Their father, Mr. Multi, is a businessman. He works very hard buying and selling foods. He buys in bulk and sells in smaller amounts to the street traders.

When they are not at school they help their father with either delivering food or breaking up the bulk containers and weighing out smaller quantities. Don loves to help with the deliveries. He is a strong lad and can lift and carry quite heavy loads. Wen likes to stay at home and weigh out the food, helping her mother with this important work.

Mr. Multi uses a notebook and pen to record his orders and deliveries. His wife thinks that a computer would be better but he tells her that they cannot afford one, and says he doesn't make mistakes using the old fashioned method of pen and paper.

The children learn how to use the computer in school. They do not have many computers but somehow the children get enough time and instruction to learn how to make files and how to use spreadsheets. For business people spreadsheets are very useful for making complicated calculations. Wen in particular likes using the computer. She gets to be very good at it so that the teacher asks her to write up reports and to make posters to advertise activities to the rest of the school.

One day Wen asks her father, 'Dad, I'm really good at the computer you know. Look at this poster I made, can we buy a laptop now? Please, please, please! I think it would help the business.

80

Wen's dad says, 'That's a really good poster you have made, Wen, but you don't realize how much it would cost me to have a computer. I would have to get a printer too and an internet connection. As you know, we cannot even afford a landline. I don't see how we could afford it all. Anyway I suspect you would spend your time on it instead of helping your mother, then where would we be?'

'Oh Dad, it's not fair! Lots of kids at school have laptops. Well, some do. Surely if they can afford it we can too?'

'You have no idea what other people spend their money on. Everyone has to make his or her own decisions. Life isn't 'fair' as you put it. Everyone is different. Not everyone is lucky enough to have a lovely grandmother and grandfather. We are lucky and we are very happy to look after them. We spend our money on what is important to us, if other people make different decisions that is up to them."

'Oh Dad, I didn't mean we shouldn't look after Grandma and Granddad. I never thought of that!'

'Of course you didn't, Wen, you are still learning about life. Young people have certain ideas about fairness, which can be very useful, like when you are sharing things out with your friends. But when it comes to the bigger picture life can seem very unfair. There is no point in getting upset about it. Sometimes we can change things and sometimes we just can't. How about we weigh out that bag of rice between us now?'

Story 3 – A Teacher's Dilemma About Grades by Michael Josephson[18]

When I was a law professor, I administered multiple–choice tests that I corrected by hand. One day, Ron came to my office informing me I made a scoring error – in his favor.

I was impressed with his honesty and told him so as I was changing my records. Ron was horrified. "You're going to lower my grade?" he sputtered. "Of course" I said, "I'm entering the correct score."

Ron said: "I would have never come to you if . . . ." He stopped mid–sentence. He didn't have to finish – it was obvious. He expected to be praised for his integrity but he thought I would also reward him by allowing him to keep the higher grade. He left my office angry muttering that I punished him for his honesty.

I shared this story with a fellow teacher. He agreed with Ron.

"I have a very high regard for honesty, that's why I had to correct the record. Isn't it dishonest to let him keep a grade he didn't earn? Would that be fair to other students? Integrity is not about seeking advantage; it's about doing the right thing – even if it costs more than we want to pay. If Ron remained silent about the error it would have been as dishonest as keeping too much change."

My colleague said I was missing the big picture. The grade was less important than encouraging honesty.

I protested. "His reward for his honesty was my respect and his self–respect. I didn't punish him or lower his grade – I just corrected my error. A score on an exam is about competency, not virtue. Besides, he wasn't really virtuous. His display of honesty was counterfeit. If he expected praise at no cost it was a calculated tactic not a trait of character. Why would I want to encourage that?"

My friend laughed. "You are really making a big deal out of this. I've got to go to class."

What do you think? What would you have done?

Stories Viewed

From Film Clips on Line

- Glory – Colonel Robert Gould Shaw informs the troops of his all–black company that they are to be paid less than white troops.
- Mighty Ducks – A hockey coach berates the team's captain when he refuses to break the rules in order to win.
- Remember the Titans – Coach Yoast confronts a referee who has been calling the game unfairly.

From Wing Clips
- To End All Wars – After being bombed by Allied troops, Ernest makes the choice to help the injured enemy soldiers.
- Elizabeth: The Golden Age – Elizabeth refuses to punish the Catholics because of their beliefs, even though they pose a threat to her.

From Teach With Movies
- 12 Angry Men – The movie depict jury's deliberations in a murder trial. The first vote is 11 to 1 to convict but through rational argument and persuasion, bias and prejudice are overcome and justice is done.

Susan Boyle – http://www.youtube.com/watch?v=RxPZh4AnWyk
Jonathan and Charlotte – http://www.youtube.com/watch?v=41IS2OKqq1w

Experience it – Using experiential activities to promote learning by self-discovery
FAIRNESS

#35   Where's My Candy?

Learning Objective: To gain an understanding of different ways to look at fairness
Materials: Bags of mixed candy (include at least one piece of chocolate in the mix)
Instructions:
- Divide the students into groups of 6 – 10.
- Tell them they'll have five minutes to divide the candy fairly (do not say 'evenly').
- Without answering any questions, allow the groups to work out their own solutions.

Process and Reflection:
What?
- What is meant by fair?

So What?
- Ask students to raise their hand if they thought their group achieved a fair solution.
- What was your strategy for dividing the candy?
- Did anybody go along with the decision to avoid causing a fuss? If so, how did that feel? How did it feel to the others in their group?
- Did any group make a decision based on Merit? Need? Might? Equality? Seniority? Effort?

Now What?
- Did leadership change during the course of the activity?
- How do you think this activity is related to situations that concern fairness here at our school?
- What strategies do you use to ensure that tasks, benefits, time, etc., expected from members of groups they lead are handled fairly?

#36   Tower Building

Learning Objective: To identify factors in dealing fairly with others
Materials: See the list below (others items could be included – just make sure you have different supplies in each packet)

Label the packets:				
Packet 1	**Packet 2**	**Packet 3**	**Packet 4**	**Packet 5**
• Tape • 13 straws • 1 pack of index cards • 20 sheets of paper • This group has seven minutes	• 13 straws • 1 pack of index cards • Ruler • 20 sheets of paper	• Tape • 20 index cards • 2 sheets of paper	• 10 straws • 10 index cards • 10 sheets of paper	• Tape • Paper clips • Crayons or markers • 20 sheets of paper • Extra points for a colorful tower

Instructions:

- Set up five workstations, each with different supplies and different instructions.
- Say: "We all have a sense of what's fair and what isn't. Think of time when someone treated you unfairly and a time when someone treated you fairly." Take responses from a few volunteers who would like to share.
- The instructions for this tower building contest are at your tables.
- The objective is to build the tallest free–standing tower in five minutes.

Process and Reflection:
What?

- What were you asked to do?

So What?

- How successful was your group?
- Were all groups operating under the same rules?
- Did you have the same supplies? Were all groups treated fairly?
- How did your group handle themselves? Were they respectful and caring of people and their ideas?

Now What?

- Based on this experience, what are some fairness 'don'ts?' Fairness 'do's?'
- Even if everything is done fairly, some will still believe the solution to be unfair. Why is this the case?
- How can we use these 'do's' in everyday life as a student?

#37   Making Fair Decisions

Learning Objective: To evaluate a scenario in which they must apply theories of fairness
Materials: Handout of scenario
Overview:
Say, "Pretend you are a classroom teacher and you have to decide who is going to represent your class at luncheon with the superintendent. Who is the student who fairly deserves to be chosen?"

Distribute the handout and read through the descriptions of each student together. Students are likely to ask you to provide more background information. Instruct them to make their decisions based on the information available.

Scenario

Juan is the smallest, but he is the one who works the hardest and does the best work in class.

Kishara is older than Juan and is competent. She has very few friends and is the one who needs the most praise to help with her poor self-esteem.

Benny is the oldest and is moving on to the high school after this year.

Keara is a natural leader and has the best attitude. She is always willing to help.

Ricky is the principal's son.

Variation: You could have any situation that students face as a member of your school when a selection needs to be made. Just make the descriptions of the students be related to the various theories of substantive fairness. Make sure that students understand the importance of providing pre-established rules, being impartial, and determining facts before a decision is made.

Process and Reflection:
What?
- What made this activity all about fairness?

So What?
- Was your decision easy or difficult?
- Did everyone in your group agree from the start?
- Did you find yourself defending certain students? Why do you think you did that?
- How was your group able to finally arrive at a consensus? Which theory of substantive fairness did your group follow? Equality? Need? Effort? Might? Seniority?

Now What?
- Why do students sometimes say, "that's not fair?"
- How is this example similar to the way decisions are made in our class or school?
- Do you recall a situation in which you think the decision that was made could have been considered unfair?
- What should teachers do to make situations at our school to be considered fair?
- If you are in charge, what would you do to make a situation fair?

#38   That's Not Fair

Learning Objective: To understanding the different perspectives others have while creating a clear system for making decisions that promotes fairness

Materials: Two index cards for each student

Instructions:
- Give each student two index cards. Label the first card with title of 'Unfair.' Have the students write about a time when something was not considered fair or a situation of someone else, where that person was not treated fairly.
- The second card should be titled as 'Fair.' On this card, have the students write about a situation whereby they did believe they or someone else was treated fairly.
- Exchange the unfair labeled cards. What works is to have students trade their cards with someone else and then before reading the card, change with another student.
- Group students and have each student read the 'unfair' situation described on the card.
- When all have read the unfair situation, have them discuss what they found to be in common with how the situation was handled.

- Do a similar process of exchange for the 'fair' labeled cards.
- Have students read the card and then discuss amongst themselves as to what conditions are in place in order to make a situation fair.

Process and Reflection:
What?

- What did this activity have to do with fairness?

So What?

- What makes something unfair? What makes a fair decision?
- What happens when we do not have clearly established rules and a decision or choice is made?
- Can you think of an example when a decision was made without a clear understanding of rules or established procedures?
- Why is it important to not show favoritism when making a decision?
- If I say that for a decision to be considered fair, one must make sure you gather facts. What does that mean?

Now What?

- Why is fairness hard to understand for students?
- Do you think that no matter what you do someone may still think your decision is unfair? Why would this be the case?
- If something is to be fair, one could say there should be pre–established rules that are consistently applied. What does that mean for you as a student? What does that mean for a teacher? For another adult in your life?

#39   The Fair Eggs–periment

Learning Objective: To understand how it feels when you are not treated fairly and what can be done to make sure there is equitable treatment of others
Materials: Clear drinking glass filled with one cup of water; a fresh egg; 1/4 cup salt; tablespoon
Instructions:

- Place the egg in the glass of water telling the students that the egg represents someone who is not being treated fairly. Sinking to the bottom represents how someone who is left out or mistreated would feel – sad, depressed, defeated, unappreciated, and unloved.
- Remove the egg from the water and set it aside.
- One tablespoon at a time, add salt to the water.
- As you stir in each spoonful, explain that the salt represents different ways to show fairness towards others. For example: following the rules when playing a game, taking turns and sharing, treating others with honesty and respect, and taking action to help someone being treated unfairly.
- After you have added all of the salt, put the egg back in the water and it will now float. Explain that the egg is being supported with kindness and 'held up' by the fairness and acceptance of others.

Process and Reflection:
What?

- What happened with the egg?

So What?

- What did the various ingredients in this activity represent?
- What are some things that can make the egg sink to the bottom?

Now What?

- Adding salt to the water changed its composition and allowed the egg to float. What are things that we do as students either in word or action that provides others to be 'lifted up?'
- How do the students in our school benefit from a sense of belonging?
- What do the action of students to include others have to say about fairness?

#40   Who Made It?[19]

Learning Objective: To gain an understanding of what is meant by fairness
Materials: A piece of clothing made in a country with questionable child labor laws (e.g.: Pakistan, India, Thailand, Brazil, Mexico, China, and Indonesia); The Craig Kielburger video clip or story from the organization he founded, *Free the Children* (http://www.youtube.com/watch?v=Fx88LEhNneM)
Instructions:

- Ask students where they think their clothes are made and by whom.
- Students may check tags on their own clothing or on the collar of a classmate's shirt.
- Explain to the students that thankfully due to many determined people that took action when they saw injustice by marching the streets in protest in 1908, the United Stated has laws that protect working conditions and prohibits children from working in factories. Before the workers went on strike, women and children were forced to work in horrible, filthy conditions, for long hours for very little money.
- Unfortunately, there are still countries in this world that do not have laws that protect children. The children that live in these countries may not have schools or the right to an education. They are expected to work in a factory.
- Share the Craig Kielburger video. We see a documentary about a teenage boy who, upon learning of the abuses of child labor in third world countries, felt compelled to take action. He founded an international organization, *Free the Children*.

Process and Reflection:
What?

- What do the labels on one's clothes represent and what does this have to say about fairness?

So What?

- What does treating people fairly mean?
- Does fairness mean everyone gets the same amount, like an equal piece of a chocolate bar?
- In the video one boy said that fairness involves putting yourself in another person's shoes. Is this true? How is it possible to do that? What does the golden rule have to do with fairness?

Now What?

- Is it possible to be fair without considering everyone who will be affected by your decision? Give an example.
- Most people think fairness requires us to treat people equally. What does it mean to treat people equally? Give examples of equal and unequal treatment.
- Can you think of a situation in which it might be right to give someone a special advantage?

- Are there good reasons to give unequal consequences for the same offense?
- What if being fair to others means sacrificing something important of your own, like time, money, or even your job?
- How can you determine what is fair when you have to choose between yourself and others?
- How should you treat people who are not fair with you?
- How did the Craig Kielburger story make you feel? What did you learn from it?

CARING

Touchstone Belief: It is important to show care and concern for others.

Supporting beliefs that will bring positive results and opportunity for student success:

- I can be kind and considerate even when others are not.
- It is important to help find a way to help others.
- I have to show concern for others' well–being.
- I should act compassionately and with empathy.
- I have to be willing to show mercy and forgiveness.

Explain it – Teach what students need to know

Caring is the act of showing love, regard, or concern for the well–being of others. One may also consider caring in the context of both words and actions. Students will be able to relate to caring by the words they use in their interactions with others. These words can either be rude, hurtful, and unkind or affirming, positive, and empathetic. But caring is more than words – it is also action–oriented. In this sense, caring can be defined as a passion for an ideal, belief, or cause. We must have esteem for someone in order to care about them, and how we care about them directly correlates to what we in fact care about.

Students need to understand that caring – including the virtues of compassion, kindness, benevolence, altruism, charity, generosity, and sharing – is the heart of ethics. They should strive to demonstrate concern for the well–being of others by displaying compassion and providing support for those in pain or in need.

From an instructional perspective, we must teach students to understand that they demonstrate caring by: 1) being kind, compassionate, and empathetic to everyone (even those who don't seem to deserve it), 2) expressing support and sympathy at appropriate times and in appropriate ways, 3) being charitable in judging others by assuming good intentions and by being forgiving and merciful, and 4) being charitable to causes and individuals. In their relationships and conversations with others, students should not be cruel, indifferent or apathetic, callous, or unforgiving.

Finally, students should come to the realization that caring frequently interacts with other ethical principles and requires them to be cognizant that:

1. Honesty is not causing them to be unnecessarily hurtful or offensively blunt (e.g., telling a person their speech was absolutely awful).
2. In seeking to impose justice, they do not miss opportunities to be merciful and forgiving.
3. While respecting another's privacy, they do not condone or ignore dangerous and harmful conduct.
4. Their sense of responsibility is proportionate to their actual level of authority and moral duty, and that their own needs are not to be ignored.

Explore it – What we can learn from others

1. People often forget what we say and usually what we do, but they always remember how we made them feel. – Maya Angelou
2. Wise sayings often fall on barren ground, but a kind word is never thrown away. – Sir Arthur Helps
3. The smallest act of kindness is worth more than the grandest intention. – Oscar Wilde

4. Kindness is loving people more than they deserve. – Joseph Joubert
5. Do all the good you can, By all the means you can, In all the ways you can, In all the places you can, At all the times you can, To all the people you can, As long as you ever can. – John Wesley
6. I expect to pass through the world but once. Any good therefore that I can do, or any kindness I can show to any creature, let me do it now. Let me not defer it, for I shall not pass this way again. – Stephen Grellet
7. No act of kindness, no matter how small, is ever wasted. – Aesop
8. There are two ways of spreading light: to be the candle or the mirror that reflects it. – Edith Wharton
9. Real generosity is doing something nice for someone who will never find out. – Frank A. Clark
10. The record of a generous life runs like a vine around the memory of our dead, and every sweet unselfish act is now a perfumed flower. – Robert G. Ingersoll
11. Our prime purpose in life is to help others. And if you can't help them, at least don't hurt them. – The Dalai Lama
12. Forgiveness is a funny thing. It warms the heart and cools the sting. – William Arthur Ward
13. The world is not dangerous because of those who do harm, but because of those who look at it without doing anything. – Albert Einstein
14. You have not lived a perfect day, even though you have earned your money, unless you have done something for someone who cannot repay you. – Ruth Smeltzer
15. Nice words are free, so choose ones that please another's ears. – Vietnamese proverb

Engage it – How beliefs and content can be taught at the same time

- Throughout your discussions and interactions with and between students, a culture of caring should be created in the classroom.
- Model kindness and courtesy, and expect your students to do the same.
- Engage students in service–based projects.
- Have students write a thank–you note to someone in your community who did something very caring.
- Have students write a thank–you note to a historical figure, in terms of nonfiction or biographies they have read as part of the curriculum. An example would be Florence Nightingale, to thank her for what she did.
- Students could write about a real or imagined experience in which they performed a random act of caring, and the results it produced.
- Divide the class into small groups. Have each group develop a list of do's and don'ts for caring behavior. What happens when people live in accordance with these guidelines? What happens when they don't? In what ways do caring and uncaring behavior affect our school?
- Have students brainstorm ways to make the school environment more caring. Create a list of recommendations and then place it in the school newspaper or on a poster.
- Write two headings on the blackboard: Caring and Uncaring. List examples underneath each heading. Then discuss what kinds of efforts could be taken to move all of the items from the Uncaring column into the Caring column.
- Have students write a critique of an uncaring character from a story they have read, suggesting how he or she could have been a more caring person.
- Students could imagine that they have just inherited $20,000, and they want to spend it charitably. What would they do with it, and why? What effect would it have on the people they would be helping?

Enhance it – Learning from stories read, told or viewed
Stories Told

Story 1 – Too Poor to Give by Michael Josephson[20]

The 1992 Olympics are now history, but while they were in progress a few months back, we remembered the story of Henry Pearce of Australia, who was competing in the single scull rowing event at the 1928 Olympics. He was leading when a duck and her string of ducklings came into view up ahead. They were on a collision course and Pearce reckoned that his scull would cut the string in two and sink a few ducklings in the process, so he pulled in his oars. When the ducks passed, Pearce again bent his back to the task. There's a happy ending to the story. Pearce won. Usually, acts of sportsmanship result in defeat. Remember Leo Durocher's pronouncement, "Nice guys finish last"? It happened a couple of years ago in the marathon tandem kayak racing event at the world championships in Copenhagen. Danish paddlers were leading when their rudder was damaged in a portage. British paddlers, who were in second place, stopped to help the Danes fix it. The Danes went on to defeat the British by one second in an event that lasted nearly three hours. But there's a happy ending to this story too.

According to *The Wall Street Journal*, the British kayakers won what many people regard as the highest honor in sports. They became the winner of the Pierre de Coubertin International Fair Play Trophy. The trophy is named for the founder of the modern Olympic Games, and it has been awarded annually for the past 28 years to people in sports who have demonstrated nobility of spirit. It is big news in Europe, but it has not been given much recognition in the United States. In the past, the trophy has gone to a Hungarian tennis player who pleaded with officials to give his opponent more time to recover from a cramp, and to a high school basketball coach who forfeited the Georgia (US) state championship after he found out that one of his players was scholastically ineligible.

The first trophy went to an Italian bobsledder named Eugenio Monti for a gesture that exhibited a touch of class. In the two–man bobsled event at the 1964 Innsbruck Olympics, Monti was the leader after his final run. The only one given a chance to beat him was Tony Nash of Great Britain. As Nash and his teammate got ready for their final run, they discovered that a critical bolt on their sled had snapped at the last moment. Monti was informed of the problem and immediately took the corresponding bolt from his own sled and sent it up to Nash. Nash fixed his sled, came hurtling down the course to set a record and won the gold medal.

Story 2 – Help Needed

A man was driving his car, when he saw an old lady, stranded on the side of the road. He saw that she needed help. So he stopped his Pontiac near her Mercedes and got out.

He smiled, while he was approaching her, still she was worried, as nobody had stopped for hours. Moreover, he did not look safe, as his appearance was so poor and shabby. He could see, how frightened she was, so he tried to calm her: I'm here to help you, don't worry. My name is Bryan Anderson."

The tire was flat, so he had to crawl under the car. While changing the tire, he got dirty and his hands were hurt.

When the job was done, she asked how much she owed him for his help. Bryan smiled and said, "If you really want to pay me back, the next time you see someone, who needs help, give that person the needed assistance, and think of me."

The same evening, the lady stopped by a small, dingy cafe. Inside, she saw a waitress, nearly eight months pregnant, helping an elderly lady with her coat. The waitress had a sweet friendly smile, although she had spent the whole day on her feet. The lady wondered, how someone, who was so little, could be so kind and giving to a stranger. Then, she remembered Bryan.

The lady had finished her meal and paid with a hundred dollar bill. The waitress went to get change and when she came back, the lady was gone. She left a note on the napkin, "You don't own me anything. Somebody once helped me, just like now I'm helping you. If you really want to pay me back, do not let this chain of love end with you." The waitress found four more one hundred bills under the napkin.

That night the waitress came home a little earlier than usual. She was thinking about the lady and the money she left. She was wondering, how the lady could know, how much she and her husband needed it? Especially now, when the baby will soon arrive. She knew, that her husband worried about that, so she was glad to tell him good news. Then she kissed him and whispered, "Now everything will be all right. I love you, Bryan Anderson."

Story 3 – Teenagers Lead the Way by Michael Josephson[21]

Olivia Gardner was a sixth grader in Northern California when she suffered an epileptic seizure in front of her classmates. Immediately, the name–calling began. The hallway insults and ridicule – freak, retard, weirdo – escalated into cyber–bullying as a few nasty students set up an "Olivia Haters" website. One student dragged her backpack through the mud, and another whispered "Die Olivia" in her ear. The taunting was so bold that her tormentors distributed and wore "I Hate Olivia" bracelets.

Neither her parents nor school officials were able to shield Olivia from this sadistic abuse. Even changing schools didn't help. The bullying followed her through two other schools until her parents decided home school was the only option.

Like many teenagers subjected to extreme bullying, Olivia seriously contemplated suicide. Olivia was not a weak girl and she had the love and support of her family, but relentless cruelty inflicted by mean–spirited teenagers and condoned by a much larger group, simply wore her down, leaving her feeling helpless and hopeless.

Fortunately, this is only part one of Olivia's story. Part two is more uplifting.

A story in a local newspaper about Olivia's ordeal caught the attention of two sisters – Emily and Sarah Buder, then 15 and 17 years old. The sisters never met Olivia, but their sense of compassion and justice ignited a desire to offer her personal support so they asked friends to join them in writing nice letters to Olivia to lift her spirits. This genuine gesture of compassion set off a chain reaction of support, encouragement, and love that ended in thousands of letters to Olivia, a worldwide anti–bullying movement, and a successful book, *Letters to Olivia*, edited by Olivia and her new–found friends – the Buder sisters.

This is more than a story about the power of compassion; it's a powerful case study about the nature of leadership and the power of young people to make a difference. Don't ever underestimate the difference you can make when you pursue your values with passion.

Stories Viewed

From Foundations for a Better Life

- Generosity – This message puts the spotlight on young heroes who give from the heart.
- Spread the Love – The easy flow of music and message helps counter the strain of the world's unrest with hopeful encouragement.
- Hockey – A call from a child in the middle of a busy day at work can be awkward. But calling your father between periods during a hockey game–well, it could be embarrassing especially if the request is for a bedtime nursery rhyme. Our father in this case obliges his young daughter.
- Umbrella – In the most challenging weather, one can see what happens when someone cares enough to share.

From Film Clips on Line

- Return of the King – When Frodo collapses before finishing his mission, his friend Sam carries him.

- Charlotte's Web – A rat refuses to help a pig save a dying spider's eggs unless he receive a reward.

From Wing Clips
- Despicable Me – After embracing his new role as a father, Gru reads the girls a new bedtime story that he wrote for them.
- Cinderella Man – Jim pleads with his friends for money so he can pay the utilities and get his children back.
- Ben and Me – A mouse named Amos claims credit for many of Benjamin Franklin's accomplishments and inventions.

From Motivational Media – Character in the Movies
- Frozen – Anna, a fearless optimist, goes on a journey to find her sister, teaming up with a mountain man, Kristoff. Along the way, they encounter a talking snowman.

Power of Words – Change your words – http://www.youtube.com/watch?v=Hzgzim5m7oU
Touching Them All – http://www.youtube.com/watch?v=1PhvXyoGVFw
A Game of Hope – http://www.youtube.com/watch?v=HuxejhBOCOo
Mo Cheeks and Natalie Gilbert –National Anthem
http://www.youtube.com/watch?v=q4880PJnO2E
Power of the Words – http://www.youtube.com/watch?v=2OIfGoNfm4w
Craig Kielburger – http://www.youtube.com/watch?v=Fx88LEhNneM

Experience it – Using experiential activities to promote learning by self–discovery
CARING

#41   Pepper Experiment

Learning Objective: To realize what we say and do makes a difference
Materials: Bowls half full of water; small packets of pepper; sugar packets; pieces of soap
Instructions:
- Put a small bowl half full of water on each table, two packets of pepper, a packet of sugar, and a piece of soap.
- Ask students to sprinkle the pepper liberally on the water. The pepper represents all the people with whom you interact – family, friends, neighbors, teachers, other students, etc. How we get along with these people depends on what we do and say when we are with them. Talk about the power of words and actions and how they can be respectful or hurtful, rude, or unkind.
- The soap represents the hurtful, rude words. Ask students to place and hold the soap in the middle of the pepper. Within three seconds, they are to pull the soap out of the bowl. The soap will repel the pepper and make it move to the sides of the bowl. Relate this illustration to what happens in life with people to whom we are hurtful or unkind.
- Next, have students pour the sugar in the center of the water. The pepper will move towards the sugar. Again, relate this to real life and how others react when we are kind and caring by words and actions.

Process and Reflection:
What?
- What did the pepper, soap and sugar represent related to interactions that occur when dealing with others?

- What is said that can be considered rude, demeaning, hurtful or uncaring?
- "Sticks and stones may break my bones, but words will never hurt me." Is this true? Explain your position.
- Why do some flakes of pepper remain on the outer edge of the bowl? What does that represent? (What has been said, may have a lasting effect).

Now What?

- What happens in life with people to whom we are hurtful or unkind?
- What would our class be like if everyone was aware of the impact of hurtful words?
- What would our school be like if we all were aware and concerned about what it is that we say to others?
- What conclusions can you draw from this activity?

Explanation:

The pepper floats on the surface of the water due to the high surface tension that hydrogen bonds have in water molecules. The piece of soap breaks those hydrogen bonds very easily and as a result the pepper moves away due to the fact it is still on the surface of the water molecules. Hydrogen bonds break very easily as well as reforms easily. This is why the soap can only be added to the water for a few seconds for this to work because the hydrogen bonds will re–bond together.

#42   Paper Heart

Learning Objective: To learn what we say can have a lasting impact on others
Materials: Sheet of red construction paper cut into the shape of a heart
Instructions:

- Hold up a large red construction paper heart.
- Ask students to share words they have heard said which are hurtful and unkind. As each word or phrase is shared, fold down a piece of the heart until it is folded into a small shape. This is how we feel when we have been hurt by the words and actions of others.
- Then, ask students to share words that might be said that are kind and encouraging. As each is shared, unfold a piece of the heart until it is back in shape. Reiterate that we can say encouraging things that make others feel better.
- Ask them what they still see on the heart – the wrinkles or scars that are left. Even if we say we are sorry, we can still leave lasting scars as a result of hurtful words.

Process and Reflection:
What?

- What did the red heart represent and what made changes in its appearance?

So What?

- How do you feel when someone says hurtful or unkind things to you?
- What are the most uncaring words that you have ever heard?
- What are the most caring words you have heard someone say?
- Do words using social media have a similar impact? Why or why not?

Now What?

- Can you think of a teacher you have had that was kind and nurturing? How did it feel to be in that person's room? Then think of a teacher they were pretty sure didn't care about you. What was it like to be in that teacher's room?
- Do you remember what others say to you? Why or why not?
- What do you do to control your language when talking with others?
- What can you do if you see someone else being bullied either physically or verbally?

#43 "Speak No Evil"[22]

Learning Objective: To focus attention on the negative comments that we make while examining how we treat fellow students and adults

Materials: Index cards; "Speak No Evil" stickers

DAY 1

- For the next seven days we will be participating in an activity called "Speak No Evil." We all say and do things that hurt other people's feelings. Sometimes these comments are intended to hurt feelings, but many times we say things that hurt someone's feelings unintentionally. Many times, we make negative comments thinking that they don't bother the other person. Too often they may appear unaffected, but inwardly they hurt very much.
- This is an opportunity to focus on those negative comments we make and try to understand what effect they have on the person receiving them.

CLASSROOM ACTIVITY – Open discussion

Discuss the following questions with your class:

1. Why do people say things to hurt people?
2. What effect does it have on that person?
3. Why do people try to hide the fact their feelings are hurt?
4. How does it affect your friends who see you do this?

Brainstorm: What are some things that people say that hurt others intentionally?

DAY 2 CLASSROOM ACTIVITY – Open discussion and practice run

- Brainstorm things that are said unintentionally that hurt the feelings of others. "What did you do to your hair?" "Why are you so fat?" "You're a real jerk...just kidding!" Or "shut up!" You may also want to discuss how non–verbal cues such as tone of voice, facial expressions, and body language affect the way a message is perceived.
- Introduce the major "Speak No Evil" activity. (Each faculty member should be wearing a "Speak No Evil" sticker). If you make a negative comment about someone during the school day, a teacher or adult will take your sticker. The goal is to become more aware of the things we say and how it affects others.
- "Today we will make a practice run. I will pass out an index card to each of you. You will use this for the first hour. Anytime you make a negative comment either intentionally or unintentionally, you must record it on your card. Write down the comment and the time. Hopefully, you will get through the first hour with an empty card. Be honest! We will do this same trial tomorrow during a designated period."

DAY 3 CLASSROOM ACTIVITY – Writing a favorite expression and continue practice run

- Have students write down a favorite expression learned from parents, grandparents or teacher (i.e.: "If you don't have anything nice to say, don't say anything at all.") If you have been using the

94

"touchstone of character" or supporting beliefs, this would be a good time to include those in the discussion. Have the students share their favorite expression with the class.

DAY 4 CLASSROOM ACTIVITY

- Discuss the trial run. Also, have students share some of the things written on their index cards. Discuss how they thought someone felt when they made the comment. Talk about how students themselves felt when someone made a negative comment to them.
- Have a discussion as to what a day at school would be like if everyone was caring and respectful to others by being considerate of each other's feelings.
- Continue using the index cards through the end of the first period. Remind students that "Speak No Evil" Day is tomorrow.

DAY 5 "SPEAK NO EVIL" DAY

Instructions: Pass out stickers or buttons. Make sure the sticker is in a visible location. Then, discuss the following rules with the students:

1. Be honest
2. After you have 'spoken evil' – any negative comment or action – give up your sticker to an adult when asked or voluntarily give it to a teacher when you find yourself guilty of giving a negative comment. You are on the honor system.
3. Be serious about this. There is nothing funny about hurting another person's feelings.
4. If you still have your badge by the end of the day, write your name on it and I will collect them. These will be your ticket to the special event (or for whatever reward was offered) tomorrow.

DAY 6 CLASSROOM ACTIVITY: Open discussion

- What did you say that made you lose your sticker? How did you feel when you lost your sticker? How do you think the other person felt? What would things have been like if you had made a positive rather than a negative comment?
- For those that survived with your sticker, how did you feel? Is this type of behavior new for you? Will you continue?
- What is good about eliminating negative behavior towards others? (Write ideas on the board).

DAY 7 CLASSROOM ACTIVITY: Writing project

- Have students reflect upon the "Speak No Evil" activity and take out a sheet of notebook paper. Have them write a paragraph beginning with the words, "I learned that..." Give time for the students to write. Have a discussion asking students to volunteer and share their feelings. You could also debrief using the activity, "Circle Within a Circle."

#44   Rotten to the Core[23]

Learning Objective: To decrease name–calling and verbal bullying while increasing the use of positive words
Materials: Two apples; a knife; cutting board
Instructions:

- Before class, the teacher will slightly bruise an apple by rolling/banging it on the floor.
- Ask the students how many of them have heard the saying, "Sticks and stones may break my bones but words will never hurt me." How many of you believe this statement is true? The teacher then states, "Words do hurt us."
- We may be able to tell how a person is feeling by their facial features and body language.

Other times, we may not be able to tell how negative words hurt someone. We are going to see how positive and negative words make a person feel on the inside.

- The students can share a time that someone did or said something mean to them. After the student has made the comment, they drop the apple directly in front of them. After the apple has been dropped, the student will pick up the apple and pass it to their right.
- The teacher then picks up the other apple. This apple will be used for positive statements.
- The teacher then asks students how they feel when a positive statement is made to them. The students say something positive that someone did for them or said to them.
- The teacher then cuts the apple that had negative words to it in half vertically. The other apple, which was given positive words, is cut in half horizontally so the apple looks like it has a star in the middle.

Variation:

The teacher may choose to do this as a large group activity asking students to share the kind and unkind words others say. You may also incorporate the use of cell phones, e-mails, texts, instant messaging, Facebook, etc. Students do not realize the impact such devices may have on another student. Using social media takes out the emotional aspect and when they are joking or teasing, the other person does not realize it and takes the information personally.

Process and Reflection:
What?

- What did the two apples represent?

So What?

- What did the apple that was dropped when negative words were said, look like on the outside?
- How about the apple on the inside?
- What did the inside of the apple look like that was used when we said nice things about each other?

Now What?

- What does that tell us about words others may say to someone else?
- Why is this activity important for students to consider when communicating with others?
- What is the most unkind or uncaring thing that was ever said to you? Why do you remember what was said?
- What kind of apple do you want to represent?
- What kind of community would we have at school if everyone was treated as the apple with the star in the middle?

CITIZENSHIP

Touchstone Belief: I must contribute to my community and fulfill my responsibilities.

Supporting beliefs that will bring positive results and opportunity for student success:

- I am a member of many communities (class, school, neighborhood, and country), and doing my share requires my positive contributions.
- Obeying the law is one way I contribute to society.
- I need to maintain an open mind, a willingness to re–examine my own positions, and the objectiveness to consider the arguments and beliefs of others.
- Everyone must do his or her part to help the environment.

Explain it – Teach what students need to know

Students demonstrate good citizenship by fulfilling their civic and social responsibilities. This means that they contribute to the well–being of their communities, including their class, school, neighborhood, and country.

From our academic content, students will come to understand and appreciate the rights and liberties embodied in the Constitution and Bill of Rights, including freedom of speech and religion, the right to vote and run for elected office, and the right to be treated fairly under the law.

Through direct instruction, students should learn to fulfill the responsibilities of citizenship, including: a duty to abide by the law, respect the rights of others, participate in the democratic process, protect the environment, and volunteer to improve their school and community. They must also understand the additional responsibilities of adult citizenship, including paying taxes and serving on juries.

There are additional ways that students demonstrate good citizenship. Within a school, we would desire students to stay informed about important matters so they can formulate thoughtful opinions, passionately advocate for their beliefs, engage in respectful and informed discussions, vote intelligently, and, if they choose, seek elected or appointed leadership positions.

Finally, students demonstrate good citizenship when they do more than their 'fair' share to help society work. Such a commitment to the public sphere can have many expressions, such as proactively engaging in conduct that conserves natural resources (e.g., reducing, reusing, and recycling, and using water and fuel conservatively). They can also protect the natural environment from unnecessary destruction and all forms of pollution. Whether it is sharing within a classroom, contributing as a member of a community, or participating in a global endeavor, good citizens give more than they take.

We as teachers can exemplify good citizenship by promoting and modeling responsible, respectful, caring, honest, and fair conduct to create and maintain a safe and positive school climate in which all students feel physically and emotionally safe, cared for, and respected.

Explore it – What we can learn from others

1. Never doubt that a small group of thoughtful, committed citizens can change the world. Indeed, it's the only thing that ever has. – Margaret Mead
2. The best way to find yourself is to lose yourself in the service of others. – Mohandas Gandhi
3. What do I owe to my times, to my country, to my neighbors, to my friends? Such are the questions which a virtuous man ought often to ask himself. – Johann Kaspar Lavater
4. Public virtue is a kind of ghost town into which anyone can move and declare himself sheriff. – Saul Bellow

5. Like the body that is made up of different limbs and organs, all moral creatures must depend on each other to exist. – Hindu proverb
6. This country will not be a good place for any of us to live in unless we make it a good place for all of us to live in. – Theodore Roosevelt
7. Provision for others is the fundamental responsibility of human life. – Woodrow Wilson,
8. We can really respect a man only if he doesn't always look out for himself. – Johann Wolfgang von Goethe
9. Cheat the earth and the earth will cheat you. – Chinese proverb
10. If my neighbor is happy, my own work will go easier, too. – Macedonian proverb
11. If you don't believe in working together, watch what happens to a wagon when one wheel comes off. – American proverb
12. Don't let what you can't do stop you from doing what you can do. – John Wooden
13. When spider webs unite, they can tie up a lion. – Ethiopian proverb
14. Having drunk the country's water, one should obey the country's laws. – Tibetan proverb
15. Join the community; the wolf snatches only the stray sheep that wanders off from the flock. – Hebrew proverb

Engage it – How beliefs and content can be taught at the same time

- Explain and illustrate the roles students fulfill in the different communities to which they belong.
- Have students write a speech describing the essential balance of rights and responsibilities in our democracy.
- Students can study how the preservation of our rights depends on our exercise of responsibility in a democracy.
- Design a project that improves the classroom and then moves on to improve the school and community.
- Provide examples of how students of different ages can participate in community projects.
- Examine the effects of following or not following the law.
- Analyze and determine what situations call for civil disobedience.
- Identify some individuals or organizations that are making a positive difference in your community. Work in groups to interview these people and then give class reports on how they got started, why they do what they do, and how they have accomplished everything they have done.
- Have students exercise responsible environmental behavior.
- Examine the effects of protecting (or not protecting) the environment.
- Study the interaction between people and their environment to determine how this may create conflict. Provide specific examples of what can happen for the good of all when people work together.
- Evaluate needs in the school or community and plan a service project to meet those needs. Then, implement the plan and document its activities.
- Have a brainstorming session about ways to improve your school, and develop a comprehensive plan for carrying out these changes.
- Have students write a letter to the editor of your local newspaper about a problem in the community that needs to be addressed, and present a plan for rectifying the problem.
- From a newspaper or magazine, identify an act of poor citizenship displayed by an adult. Students could then write a letter of criticism to this person with the intention of trying to convince him or her to change.
- In ancient Greece, people felt that it was important that they try to leave Athens better than they found it. Apply this principle to your own community.

Enhance it – Learning from stories read, told or viewed
Stories Told

Story 1 – Shopping Carts and Rationalizations by Michael Josephson[24]

When we think about character, we tend to envision really big things, like taking heavy risks, committing bold acts of integrity, being grandly generous, or making tough sacrifices. Such noble choices indicate character, but for the most part, our integrity is revealed in much smaller events, like apologizing when we're wrong, giving to causes we believe in, being honest when it may be embarrassing, or returning shopping carts.

One of my favorite stories is about a father who asked his son to return a cart they had just used. The son protested, "C'mon, Dad. There are carts all over. No one returns them. That's why they hire people to collect them."

After a short argument, mom chimed in, "For heaven's sake, it's no big deal. Let's go."

Dad was about to surrender when he saw an elderly couple walking together to return their cart. He said, "Son, there are two kinds of people in this world: those who put their carts away and those who don't. We're the kind who returns theirs. Now go return the cart."

Which kind are you?

Story 2 – The World is a Wonderful Place – A true story, happened in 1892 at Stanford University[25]

An 18–year–old student was struggling to pay his fees. He was an orphan, and not knowing where to turn for money, he came up with a bright idea. He and a friend decided to host a musical concert on campus to raise money for their education.

They reached out to the great pianist Ignacy J. Paderewski. His manager demanded a guaranteed fee of $2,000 for the piano recital. A deal was struck and the boys began to work to make the concert a success.

The big day arrived. But unfortunately, they had not managed to sell enough tickets. The total collection was only $1,600. Disappointed, they went to Paderewski and explained their plight. They gave him the entire $1,600, plus a check for the balance $400. They promised to honor the check at the soonest possible.

"No," said Paderewski. "This is not acceptable." He tore up the check, returned the $1,600 and told the two boys: "Here's the $1,600. Please deduct whatever expenses you have incurred. Keep the money you need for your fees. And just give me whatever is left." The boys were surprised, and thanked him profusely.

It was a small act of kindness. But it clearly marked out Paderewski as a great human being.

Why should he help two people he did not even know? We all come across situations like these in our lives. And most of us only think, "If I help them, what would happen to me?" The truly great people think, "If I don't help them, what will happen to them?" They don't do it expecting something in return. They do it because they feel it's the right thing to do.

Paderewski later went on to become the Prime Minister of Poland. He was a great leader, but unfortunately when the World War began, Poland was ravaged. There were more than 1.5 million people starving in his country, and no money to feed them. Paderewski did not know where to turn for help. He reached out to the US Food and Relief Administration for help.

The head there was a man called Herbert Hoover – who later went on to become the US President. Hoover agreed to help and quickly shipped tons of food grains to feed the starving Polish people.

A calamity was averted. Paderewski was relieved. He decided to go across to meet Hoover and personally thank him. When Paderewski began to thank Hoover for his noble gesture, Hoover quickly interjected and said, "You shouldn't be thanking me Mr. Prime Minister. You may not remember this, but several years ago, you helped two young students go through college. I was one of them."

Story 3 – Leadership on a Bus by Michael Josephson[26]

Mr. Martin told his English class that leadership was "influencing meaningful change either through your own conduct or by motivating others to act," and he assigned an essay requiring students to write about a personal experience with leadership.

The students groaned, insisting they couldn't think of anything, so Mr. Martin read an essay submitted last semester:

> This year I started taking a bus to work after school. People pretty much keep to themselves. A few months ago, an old guy got on the bus and said loudly to the driver, 'Good morning!' Most people looked up, annoyed, and the bus driver just grunted. The next day the man did it again. He got another grunt. On the third day the driver responded with a semi–cheerful 'Good morning!' "Then the guy said: 'My name is Benny,' and asked the driver, 'What's yours?' That was the first time any of us heard the driver's name.
>
> Soon, Benny offered his cheerful 'Good morning!' to the whole bus. Within a few days, his 'Good morning!' was returned by a whole bunch of 'Good mornings' and the entire bus got friendlier. People started introducing themselves and talking. A man next to me mentioned that the place where he worked was looking for people. He gave me the number and I got a better job.
>
> Things really changed on the bus because of Benny, so I think he was a leader. But about a month ago, Benny stopped getting on the bus. Everyone noticed and lots of people said he may have died. No one knew what to do and soon the bus got awful quiet again.
>
> So last week, I started to act like Benny and say, 'Good morning!' to everyone and they cheered up again. I suppose I'm the leader now.
>
> I learned you don't have to have big titles or lots of power to be a leader. Benny didn't just change the bus, he changed me and lots of others by showing us that just being cheerful can change attitudes, and that changing attitudes can change lives. I hope Benny comes back to see what he started.

Someone in the class asked, "Mr. Martin, whatever, happened to Benny?" Mr. Martin laughed. "Well, he's okay. Benny used to be a teacher here. After he retired, he just keeps riding different buses teaching leadership."

One cynical student said: "Wait a minute, is this all true?" Mr. Martin smiled and said, "Do you mean the story or the lesson?"

Stories Viewed

From Foundations for a Better Life

- Time out – Civility encourages different points of view. This important concept is portrayed in a town meeting that is entertaining and instructive.

From Film Clips on Line

- Ant Bully – After Lucas floods an ant colony with his watergun, he's magically shrunken down to insect size. Here, Lucas learns about democracy from an ant.

From Wing Clips

- Gandhi – After reading about the violence that was performed in the name if his cause, Gandhi decides to go on a hunger strike until the violence stops.

- Fighting Without Violence – Gandhi speaks out to his fellow brethren about the need for non–violent protest in order to gain their equality.
- Equal Citizens – Gandhi creates a public demonstration of civil disobedience where he asks his fellow countrymen to burn their identification passes.

Citizenship – http://www.youtube.com/user/goodcharacter1#p/u/26/9Zx1q1EemvE
Tum Chalo – http://www.youtube.com/watch?v=pFs5vWxW–v
David Levitt – http://www.youtube.com/watch?v=9QpAfZrOtzE
Man in a Red Bandanna – The story of 24–year–old Welles Crowther who worked in the South Tower and died in the 9/11 attacks. Crowther, a volunteer firefighter known for wearing a red bandanna, helped others to safety. https://www.youtube.com/watch?v=NlRTyt6dALM

Experience it – Using experiential activities to promote learning by self–discovery
CITIZENSHIP

#45   Ridiculous Rules

Learning Objective: To realize that part of good citizenship is obeying all rules and laws, even the ones that may be considered ridiculous
Materials: One sheet of colored paper per student (use multiple colors)
Instructions:

- Distribute paper to students and instruct them to write down a rule or law they consider ridiculous (for example, "This pillow tag is not to be removed under penalty of law"). Laws or rules from school, home or community may be used.
- After each person has written a ridiculous rule, instruct students to make a paper airplane out of the paper they wrote on.
- With the group in a circle, have each person sail their airplane, then pick up a landed airplane and sail it.
- Repeat one more time; then have the students choose a plane of a color different than their original, and take it to their seats.
- Ask students to open up the plane they have and read the rule written on the paper.
- Develop the thought that we do not have the option of only following the rules we think make sense. If, by chance, everyone agrees that all the laws written down are 'dumb,' challenge students to imagine why such laws or rules were created.

Process and Reflection:
What?

- What was meant by 'ridiculous rules?'

So What?

- Why do you think the person or people made the rule?
- The rule was written because it makes no sense. In reflecting upon the various rules that were shared, would you agree or disagree with this statement?

Now What?

- Do we have ridiculous rules in our class or school? If you think that is the case, how would you support your answer?

- How can you contrast the necessity to obey just laws with the practice of civil disobedience, in which someone disagrees with the fundamental morality of a law and disobeys it as a form of protest, in order to bring attention to the law and hopefully change it?

#46   See Ya

Learning Objective: To build a sense of belonging and connectedness

Instructions:
- Divide the class into groups of three or four students. As the teacher, call out some qualities or specific characteristics. The person in the group who matches the quality or characteristic will be leaving the group and finding another.
- Tell each group to remember the size group they are in when they start – this group must always stay this size.
- Explain to the group that you will all be sending off the players in this way – when you hear the word, 'READY' we will all announce, "SEE YA!"
- The teacher might say, "The player with the longest hair." Each small group decides who the player with the longest hair is. After a few seconds, the teacher says, 'READY?' Everyone says, "SEE YA!" Then the player with the longest hair has to go and find another group to be with. This is where remembering the size of your group comes in. Each small group will want one new person to join them.
- After everyone has found a new home, call out another quality like: The oldest student, the youngest, darkest eyes, longest nails, most jewelry, closest birthday to today.
- After the new group is formed, the student who was just added must share the value that best describes him or her and why. Or, write a starter character question on the board that the student must finish and then he or she can pick someone in the group to answer. Character questions could include:

How would you describe…?
Does character…?
How do you decide…?
How would you feel if…?
Do your actions…?

What role does character…?
How honest…?
What would you do if…?
What is the importance of…?
Who deserves…?

Process and Reflection:
What?
- What were you asked to do?

So What?
- What did you notice after each instruction was given?
- Why didn't the teacher stop after the first grouping was made?
- Why were more groupings created?

Now What?
- What does this activity say about how we should treat others?
- Compare the results of creating different groups from the varied instructions of the teacher to what school is like?
- How should you treat those who are different than you?
- What do most of the students at our school do?
- How can you intervene if you see someone being mistreated, harassed or bullied?

#47   Have You Ever?

Learning Objective: To explore and celebrate the rich diversity of experiences different students bring to any group

Instructions:

- Have students form a circle.
- Call out different things that may or may not apply to each student. If the item does apply, the student will run into the middle, jump in the air, and do a high–five with anyone else who runs into the circle.
- A list of about 20 items should be tailored to the group, but some suggestions are below. Items should be carefully considered in order to prevent embarrassment, ridicule, etc.

List of Possible "Have You Ever?" Items:

1. Have you ever traveled overseas?
2. Have you ever sung karaoke?
3. Have you ever been without a shower for more than two weeks?
4. Do you have both a brother and a sister?
5. Have you ever ridden a horse?
6. Have you ever eaten frogs' legs?
7. Have you swum in three or more different oceans?
8. Have you broken a bone in your body?
9. Have you done volunteer work sometime in the last month?
10. Have you ever had a close relative who lived to over 100?
11. Have you ever cooked a meal by yourself?
12. Can you not click your fingers on your non–dominant hand?

Process and Reflection:

What?

- What did you need to do?

So What?

- How often do we categorize people either by race, national origin, background, or academics and then make assumptions as to what they are like?

Now What?

- What does this say about how we should treat others, particularly those we do not know well, or pre–judge?
- How should we respond to those who are different than us?

#48   Sneak a Peek and Build[27]

Learning Objective: To help in understanding what it means to share and be a contributor to a solution

Materials: Building blocks or something similar (Lego's, Popsicle Sticks, etc.)
Prior to the activity, build a small sculpture or design with some of the building material and hide it from the class.

Instructions:

- Divide the class into small teams of four – six students each. Give each team enough building items to duplicate what you have already created.

- Place the original sculpture in a place that is hidden but that is at an equal distance from all the groups. Ask one member from each team to come at the same time to look at the sculpture for five seconds in order to try to memorize it as much as possible before returning to his or her team.
- After they run back to their teams, they have 30 seconds to instruct their teams how to build the structure so that it looks like the one that has been hidden. After the 30 seconds, ask each team to send up another member of their group who gets a chance to 'sneak a peek' before returning to their team. Continue in this manner until one of the teams successfully duplicates the original sculpture.

Process and Reflection:
What?
- How did this activity involve working cooperatively with others?

So What?
- What did each person in your group do to help?
- Why is it important to be a contributor to solving a problem than one who only sits back to complain?
- What are some important parts of sharing with others?

Now What?
- Is sharing and doing your part important in your daily life? How?
- Describe what makes a successful team experience for you as a student.

CHAPTER 5:
SOCIAL AND EMOTIONAL BELIEFS
Action Steps to Instill the Key Beliefs

Touchstone Belief	
Collaboration	*Working productively with others, as being part of a team or group, will allow me to accomplish more than I could alone.*
Communication	*It is my responsibility to communicate clearly with others and express my views effectively and respectfully.*
Gratitude	*I consistently identify, experience and express thankfulness for the good things in my life.*
Perseverance	*When something doesn't work right, try again and again.*
Resilience	*Even when life is tough, I know I can survive.*

COLLABORATION

Touchstone Belief: Working productively with others, as being part of a team or group, will allow me to accomplish more than I could alone.

Supporting beliefs that will bring positive results and opportunity for student success:

- I should work effectively and respectfully with diverse teams.
- I have to exercise flexibility and willingness to be helpful in making necessary compromises to accomplish a common goal.
- I need to assume shared responsibility for collaborative work, and value the individual contributions made by each team member.
- It is important to demonstrate the ability and willingness to pursue common goals as part of a team, constructively participate in cooperative learning, and communicate effectively with people who have diverse styles, views, and backgrounds.

Explain it – Teach what students need to know

Working effectively with others is an extremely complex endeavor. Collaboration skills are complicated to learn because they are actually people skills. Learning these skills takes guided practice and quality feedback.

The importance of collaboration and working as a team is a necessary skill for students to master, not only for use in the classroom but also in the workplace environment. James Surowiecki explains how we use the 'wisdom of crowds' in the new economy by saying that "under the right circumstances, groups are remarkably intelligent, and are often smarter than the smartest people in them."[1] Surowiecki underscores the importance of collaboration by remarking that "a large group of diverse individuals will come up with better and more robust forecasts and make more intelligent decisions than even the most skilled 'decision maker.'" Not only does a collaborative effort create better results than individual efforts, but it also creates knowledge for a greater number of people.

While teaching the key belief of collaboration to students, an emphasis must be placed on the fact that collaboration is the act of working together for a common goal. As a result of students learning how to work together, there comes the realization that a group of people can generate more knowledge than one person operating in isolation. This makes collaboration a key ingredient for student success in today's global society. The Partnership for 21st Century Skills says that mastering collaboration skills requires the ability to work effectively with diverse teams. It also requires the ability to "be helpful and make necessary compromises to accomplish a common goal."[2] Advocates point out that more and more projects in the workplace are team efforts, and businesses need individuals who know how to work well with others.

Making time for productive collaboration is a must in today's classrooms. The techniques a teacher uses to engage students, such as affiliation (the opportunity to work with others), can be a positive influence in engaging students in the learning process.

Teachers must explicitly teach and model collaboration skills to students before expecting them to work together effectively. The skills that a teacher can demonstrate include:

1. Active listening.
2. Respect for others.
3. Having a positive attitude by being uplifting to team members.
4. The ability to be focused on the task at hand.
5. Contributing toward a solution.
6. Positive interdependence; we swim or sink together. This includes face–to–face interaction, because by so doing we help each other to learn.
7. Individual and group accountability in order for goals to be reached.
8. Interpersonal and small group skills, which allow for practice in making decisions and sharing leadership.
9. Group processing, which provides the opportunity to reflect on how well students did and how they could do better.

As an implementation strategy, teachers could set aside a 15 or 20–minute block of instructional time each week for initial instruction on collaborative skills. The goal is to introduce one new skill each week. One or more daily interactive activities (partner activities, small group activities) can also be identified, during which the students can practice using the collaborative skill. Many of the experiential learning activities in this book would assist in providing students the opportunity to practice the collaborative skill.

Explore it – What we can learn from others

1. Alone we can do so little; together we can do so much. – Helen Keller
2. If everyone is moving forward together, then success takes care of itself. – Henry Ford
3. I never did anything alone. Whatever was accomplished in this country was accomplished collectively. – Golda Meir
4. The secret is to gang up on the problem, rather than each other. – Thomas Stallkamp
5. Individually, we are one drop. Together, we are an ocean. – Ryunosuke Satoro
6. The strength of the team is each individual member. The strength of each member is the team. – Phil Jackson
7. Coming together is a beginning, staying together is progress, and working together is success. – Henry Ford
8. The lightning spark of thought generated in the solitary mind awakens its likeness in another mind. – Thomas Carlyle

9. Your corn is ripe today; mine will be so tomorrow. 'Tis profitable for us both, that I should labour with you today, and that you should aid me tomorrow. – David Hume
10. Individual commitment to a group effort–that is what makes a team work, a company work, a society work, a civilization work. – Vince Lombardi
11. No one can whistle a symphony. It takes a whole orchestra to play it. – H.E. Luccock
12. Teamwork is the ability to work together toward a common vision. The ability to direct individual accomplishments toward organizational objectives. It is the fuel that allows common people to attain uncommon results. – Andrew Carnegie
13. If two men on the same job agree all the time, then one is useless. If they disagree all the time, both are useless. – Darryl F. Zanuck
14. Many ideas grow better when transplanted into another mind than the one where they sprang up. – Oliver Wendell Holmes
15. If you have an apple and I have an apple and we exchange these apples then you and I will still each have one apple. But if you have an idea and I have an idea and we exchange these ideas, then each of us will have two ideas. – George Bernard Shaw

Engage it – How beliefs and content can be taught at the same time

- Assign clear and specific roles and responsibilities during group work.
- Practice group or class activities that require working together.
- Illustrate techniques for compromise when it is evident in the discussion of specific content.
- Focus on and evaluate the process of group projects, in addition to their final products.
- Examine careers based on your subject matter and look at the roles collaboration and team skills would play.
- Have students team up with another class in a target language country to identify and compare endangered species in both countries and produce a multimedia informational presentation.
- While rehearsing a piece in music class, have students discuss as a group how each individual part (melody, descant, harmonic or rhythmic accompaniment) contributes to the musical effectiveness of the overall performance, and how every musician must work together to create a satisfying whole.
- After studying an environmental community issue (landfills, water quality, maintaining open space, recycling), have students compose e–mail messages to various local, state, and national officials, stating their opinion and offering alternatives to current methods of dealing with the issue.
- Working in groups, students could survey favorite forms of recreation among local teens.
- Have students research the local history of recreational facilities for teens and the potential sources of political and economic support. Graph and analyze the information, and then have each group create a business plan for developing a local recreation center/club for teens.
- Students could collaborate with senior citizens in a digital storytelling workshop. Assign different groups of students to a different senior citizen. Then have each group bring to life a story from their senior's history as they collaborate on writing and creating a video, including recording the narration and selecting images and music.

Enhance it – Learning from stories read, told or viewed
Stories Told

Story 1 – The Bee Team

Bees can show you something about teamwork. On a warm day about half the bees in a hive stay inside beating their wings while the other half go out to gather pollen and nectar. Because of the beating wings, the temperature inside the hive is about 10 degrees cooler than outside. The bees rotate duties and the bees that cool the hive one day are honey gatherers the next.

Story 2 – A Mousetrap

One sunny morning something caught the mouse's eye through a crack in the wall. It was a package the farmer's wife was opening. The mouse wondered what kind of delicious food it might contain. To his surprise it wasn't food, but a mouse trap!

As the mouse scurried out to the yard he shouted a loud warning to all. "Watch out for the mousetrap in the house! Watch out for the mousetrap in the house!"

The chicken raised his head and said, "I can tell my friend that this causes you great worry, but it is of no worry to me. Please don't bother me with it!"

The mouse then turned to the pig who said, "Sorry Mr. Mouse, it has no consequence to me either."

The mouse then turned to the bull who said, "Sounds like you have a problem friend, but it really doesn't concern me... sorry, I will keep you in my thoughts and prayers."

The mouse went back to the house to face the mousetrap alone. He felt down and dejected. That night the sound of the trap was heard throughout the house – Snap! The farmer's wife rushed to see what was caught, but couldn't see in the darkness that it was a venomous snake. She was bitten!

After rushing his wife to the hospital, the farmer returned home with her. She had quite a fever. The farmer knew the best way to treat her fever was with chicken soup so he took his hatchet to the farmyard to get his main ingredient.

The wife grew sicker by the day and friends kept visiting her throughout the days and around the clock. The farmer felt he had to feed them so he slaughtered the pig.

The farmer's wife unfortunately didn't get better and eventually died. There were many, many people who came to pay their final respects. The farmer had the cow butchered so he could feed them all.

Each member of the team plays an important role in the team's success. You may think that because someone on the team is struggling that it doesn't concern you, but it does. When everyone pulls together the team wins.

Story 3 – I Just Have to Outrun You by Michael Josephson[3]

During a camping trip, Marie and Jessica were hiking in a trail when they saw a big black bear. Marie started to take off her backpack. Jessica whispered, "What are you going to do?"

Marie answered, "I'm going to run for it."

"You can't outrun a bear," Jessica replied.

Marie just looked at her friend and said, "I don't have to outrun the bear. I just have to outrun you."

Sadly, this self–centered "look–out–for–number–one" mentality is common in today's society, even on a lot of school campuses.

Everywhere, basically good people engage in – and justify – selfish, short–sighted conduct that treats classmates, teammates and even their so–called friends as competitors rather than comrades.

A very different vision is suggested by a story about nine youngsters in the Special Olympics. Right after the start of a race, a young boy stumbled badly and fell down. A girl just ahead of him noticed and turned around to help him up. As the other runners saw this, one by one they all went back to help their fallen comrade. Then, all nine linked arms and triumphantly ran together to the finish line.

When I think of the bullying problems at most schools in relation to this story I realize how powerful it is when kids, like the first girl to help the fallen runner, see a problem and take it on themselves to deal with it.

Teachers, parents and other adults can make rules and try to enforce them, but the only way school is going to be a safe place is if the majority of students stand together, united in a commitment to create a culture of caring where students like you support, help and protect classmates who are the victims of mean and nasty conduct.

It's your choice – run together arm in arm or keep trying to outrun each other.

Stories Viewed

From Foundations for a Better Life

- The Race – The clip teaches us that sometimes, caught up in the heat of the moment, we may find the richest rewards in life by just pausing and realizing something important may be happening right in front of us.

From Film Clips on Line

- Ice Age – A saber–toothed tiger tells a wooly mammoth and a sloth that he has betrayed them. Nevertheless, they must trust him now or die.

From Wing Clips

- World Trade Center – John McLoughlin rounds up a volunteer team of police officers to evacuate one of the towers.
- Friday Night Lights – As his lethargic team is getting pummeled in the championship game begins, Coach Gaines tells his team to wake up and get their heads in the game.

From Teach With Movies

- Apollo 13 – The movie shows men solving problems with intelligence, skill, teamwork, and bravery as they prepared for space travel in the 1970s. It raises issues of loyalty to individuals on the team against the need for loyalty to the team as a whole.

Experience it – Using experiential activities to promote learning by self–discovery
COLLABORATION

#49   Gear Simulation

Learning Objective: To build relationships and create a sense of community
Materials: For groups of 15, 24 or 35
For a group of 35 – Three scraps of paper with the number 3 written on it, five scraps with the number 5 on it, seven scraps with the number 7 on it, nine scraps with the number 9 on it, and eleven scraps with the number 11 on it. If you only have 24 in the class, do not do 11 scraps with the number 11. For a group of 15, skip the number nine.
Instructions:

Show the Gears Drawing handout and tell them: "Just as well–functioning gears keep machinery going, collaboration keeps our schools and communities going. To examine how this works each of you will become a tooth on a gear."

- Distribute the scraps of paper and ask students to form groups according to the number on their paper.
- Ask all the 3's to form a tight circle by holding hands facing outward with their arms parallel to the floor. Tell them their arms are the teeth on the gear.
- Tell the 5's to form a circle in the same way next to the 3's in such a way that the two circles will interlock and touch at only one single point when they rotate. In that way, when one gear moves, it will turn the other.
- Have the 7's form their circle and interlock with the 5s. Have the 9's circle and interlock with the 7's, and have the 11's circle and interlock with the 9's.
- Once they're all lined up interlocking at one point with one or more circles, have the 3's start moving very slowly. This should start a chain reaction where all the gears will begin moving.
- Once they're successfully moving at a slow pace, have the 3's speed up.
- Then say: "Everyone stop! Reverse and go in the opposite direction."
- Let them try this three to four times.

Process and Reflection:

What?

- What did you have to do with the concept of interlocking gears?

So What?

- What worked well? What could have been improved?
- What did you see happening, especially when you sped up or changed direction?
- Who was the leader in this activity? (They may say you or the 3's. Probe more. Ask if there was a leader in each gear).
- Did that leadership shift during the course of the activity?

Now What?

- How does this activity apply to student leadership?
- What happens if one gear, or one tooth on a gear, isn't paying attention or isn't doing its share to help the whole?
- What happens when people don't take responsibility for their role in the overall effort? Discuss how groups sometimes compensate for such individuals so much that the person eventually doesn't need to be responsible. Is this a good thing? What are the alternatives?
- What are strategies you can do to help our classroom or school work together more smoothly?

#50   Circle Within a Circle

Learning Objective: To learn how to be a respectful listener

Instructions:

- Have students form two circles, one inside the other. The inside circle should face out and the outside circle should face in.
- Each student should be facing a partner. Give a topic for each pair to discuss.
- Below are a few topics, but any will work.
  1. Name something fun you have done this week.
  2. What character trait best describes you and why?
  3. Who has influenced your life positively and why?
  4. What is character?
  5. If you could change one thing in your school or community, what would it be?

6. What legacy would you like to leave for future generations? What would you like to have remembered about you after you leave our school?

- At the end of one minute, have either the inside or outer circle move so there will be different parings for the next topic.

Process and Reflection:
What?

- What was the purpose of the activity?

So What?

- What is the benefit of this activity related to discussion amongst students?
- What was the level of participation?
- Contrast the discussion with partners in this activity to a class discussion we might have with the large group.
- What did you learn from your partners?

Now What?

- How can this activity be used in our class for other topics?
- What kind of questions would students ask if they planned the activity?
- How could this activity be used to prepare students for a discussion of academic subjects?

#51   Add a Word[4]

Learning Objective: To demonstrate diversity and opportunities to work together
Concept: When there is a problem to solve, the more people that provide input the better the outcome as a wide variety of experiences is then brought to a given situation. These experiences can help to see things in a different light or provide a changed viewpoint. If everyone works alone with only their own experiences to draw upon, then they have a very narrow reservoir of knowledge.
Material: Paper; /pencil
Instructions:
Part 1

- Divide your class into teams of four.
- Explain that the object of this activity is for each team to create the longest sentence they can. You will give them the first few words to the sentence.
- Each person will then take turns adding one word at a time to the sentence. The sentence must make sense and it has to come to a logical ending. They may not talk at all during this part of the activity.
- They have one minute to complete their sentence.

Part 2

- After you have called time, have each group count up the number of words that they used including the words that you gave them to start with. Have each group tell how many words they used. Ask for volunteers to read their sentence aloud.

Here are examples of sentence starters:
When I think about integrity…
People who are…
At our school…

A loud crash…
The next time I need to make a decision…
The adults in my life…

When someone lies to me...
One dark night...
I hope you care...

Treating others...
I am in control...
I would like to see our class...

Part 3
- This time the paper is still passed and each person may still only add one word at a time, but the group may talk among themselves to make suggestions on what the sentence will say.
- Once again only give them one minute to create their sentence.
- When time has ended, have them read their sentence aloud and tell how many words they used. Repeat this twice. You should notice an increase in the number of words that they were able to write compared to when they couldn't talk.

Process and Reflection:
What?
- What were the two tasks you were asked to do as a group?

So What?
- How easy was it to figure out which word to use next?
- How well did your team do when you couldn't talk?
- How much pressure did you feel when it was your turn? Explain.
- How did the activity change for you when the group could talk?
- Was your team able to create longer sentences when they could talk? Why or why not?
- How much pressure did you feel when the group could make suggestions? Explain.

Now What?
- When you have a problem to solve, how much help is it to have someone else give you suggestions?
- Will a greater number of people always make it easier to solve a problem? Why or why not?
- How can students with different backgrounds than yours help you solve a problem?
- How do different viewpoints help solve problems?

#52 Human Knot

Learning Objective: To understand that everyone must work together to accomplish an identified goal
Instructions:
- Ask a group of about six to eight students to face each other in a tight circle. This activity works best with an even number in each group.
- Each student holds out his or her right hand and grasps the right hand of someone else as if shaking hands. Each person then extends the left hand and grasps the hand of someone else so that each person is holding hands with two different people. The result should be a confusing configuration of arms and bodies – a human knot.
- The group must untangle the web of arms into a hand–in–hand circle. Students may not let go of hands as they work together as a group to untangle themselves.

Process and Reflection:
What?
- What did it take to get everyone to work together?

So What?

- What were the challenges you faced? How did you address them?
- How many options did your group consider to get yourselves untangled?
- Did your group discuss the options before making an attempt to untangle the web of arms? If so, was that a help to your group? Explain your answer.

Now What?

- What are examples of how well we work together as a class?
- How do you develop strategies to work together as a team?
- How does this activity represent something we do when working with others on a team or in a group situation here at school?

#53   Tag Team Tic – Tac – Toe

Learning Objective: To help students understand the concept of collaboration and the benefit of working well with others

Materials: Tic – Tac – Toe game sheet

TAG TEAM TIC –TAC –TOE

	1	2	3	4	5	6
A						
B						
C						
D						
E						
F						

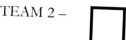

TEAM 1 – △   TEAM 2 – ☐   TEAM 3 – ◯

Instructions:

- Pair students up as a team. There are three teams that work on a single Tic–Tac–Toe sheet.
- The objective is to achieve the highest score.
- Play is conducted by placing a team's symbol in one of the 36 squares to achieve four to six in a row, horizontally, vertically or diagonally.
- Rotate players within a team.
- Maintain silence during other team's turn.
- Each cell counts once for scoring.
- No more than 30 seconds to strategize and 10 seconds for each team to move.

Scoring

Six in a row = 50 points   Five in a row = 40 points   Four in a row = 30 points

Observe to see if any team simply collaborates and works together to achieve points.

Process and Reflection:

What?

- What were you told was the objective of the activity?

So What?

- How many points did you get?
- How did you play the game?
- Did anyone play the game cooperatively?
- If so, what point total did you achieve?

Now What?

- What does this activity have to say about working together?
- What are the benefits of working collaboratively?
- Do the students look upon activities, group projects, games or other educational experiences as competition rather than collaboration? Explain.
- Where on a job are employees asked to work with others?

#54   Partners

Learning Objective: To help students see the benefit of working together

Materials: Paper; newspaper sheets; rubber bands; pieces of string cut into 12 inch lengths; balloons (per team)

Instructions:

- Have everyone in the group find a partner. Each of the following five tasks must be accomplished while holding one of their partner's hands.

Task one:	Make a paper airplane with the sheet of paper
Task two:	Tie a bow with the piece of string
Task three:	Roll up a newspaper and put a rubber band around it
Task four:	Inflate a balloon and tie the end
Task five:	Both of you do a somersault at the same time, remembering that you can't let go of your partner's hand.

Process and Reflection:

What?

- What did you have to do?

So What?

- How easy was it to do the tasks that you were given?
- What problems did you experience when completing the task?
- Would the tasks have been easier to complete if you were doing it without your partner's help? Why or why not?

Now What?

- What can this activity teach us about working together?

- How hard is it to do some things as a group rather than by yourself?
- When working as a group, how can you avoid having problems?

#55   Link Up

Learning Objective: To generate a student's connection to the class or school
Instructions:

- One student stands and shares something with the class.
- When someone in the group has something in common with what was said, he or she gets up to link arms with the student speaking. Only one student at a time.
- The two linked students declare the thing that they had in common and then begin talking about themselves until someone else comes up with something in common with them.
- The activity continues until all group members are 'linked up.'

Process and Reflection:
What?

- What is meant by 'linked up?'

So What?

- What did you learn about your fellow students?
- What does this activity have to say about respect?
- Who should we respect in our class?

Now What?

- What makes it so easy to focus on differences amongst students rather than what it is that we have in common?
- When you have to do something in collaboration with someone else here at school, do you want to have the opportunity to choose whom you work with or are you willing to accept an assigned partner or group? Give reasons for your choice.
- Why don't we at times value each other even though we have the same worth?

#56   Popsicle Stick Teamwork

Learning Objective: To engage students in learning the benefits of working as a team and accepting the ideas of others
Materials: Popsicle sticks; masking tape; markers
Instructions:

- Have students take a Popsicle stick and write with a marker a key challenge in making character education a part of their class.
- Then have students throw their Popsicle stick as far as they can. Typically, it doesn't go very far.
- Have students pair up, read what they wrote on the stick, tape the sticks together and throw. Again, it doesn't go far.
- Create groups of four students with the assigned task to make a flying object using four Popsicle sticks and 12 inches of masking tape. Before assembling the sticks, students will read what they wrote.
- After the groups have completed the building of their flying object, have them line up behind a clearly defined line, and throw their creation.

- After this, have three groups get together to form a larger group of 12. Instead of reading what they wrote, students verbally share their ideas on making character education a part of the class while providing specific examples of when the intentional teaching of character has occurred.
- One person in the group will then tape the 12 sticks together in one big brick. Then, standing at the line, one student throws this tightly wrapped bundle. This pack of 12 sticks should fly the farthest.

Process and Reflection:
What?
- What does this activity have to do with working together as a team?

So What?
- What does it look like to work together as a team?
- How do team members contribute?
- What was the difference between throwing one stick, four sticks, and the bundle of twelve?
- Share a few examples of where you specifically see character being taught in this class or throughout our school.

Now What?
- What similarities do you see between this activity and situations you encounter at school or in any after school activity in which you participate?
- What symbolism is represented in the bundle of sticks, and the words on them, that should be remembered? (The answer you are looking for might be something along the lines of, "Just like the sticks you threw the greatest distance, we might be able to have greater performance by coming closer together and sharing our hopes, dreams and what we've learned with each other. The closer we become, the greater the trust and the greater the performance.")
- What was the most valuable part of this activity for you personally and why?

#57   Bid and Build[5]

Learning Objective: To work together as a team to build a bridge out of objects your team obtains
Materials: A large sheet of paper (or chalkboard, dry erase board, etc.); various items that can be used or not used to get a group from point A to point B (i.e. Frisbees®, sheets of paper, rope, hula hoops, pieces of wood or cardboard, an old garbage can, a tumbling mat, or anything else you can find)
Instructions:
- For the first part, list all the items that you have gathered on the large sheet of paper, display it for the group to see, and show them the items listed.
- Divide the group into at least two smaller teams of two or more and give each group a piece of paper and a pen or pencil.
- Explain to the groups that their task is to attempt to get their entire team from one side of an open area to the other side (at least ten yards apart) using any of the items listed and without anyone on their team touching the ground at any time.
- First the teams must bid for the items listed. Each team gets 100 points (or $100 in play money) that they may spend however they wish on the items.
- They must divide up the points based on what they think will help them the most and write down their bids on the paper given to them. For example, one team may bid 75 points on the

Frisbees, and 25 points on the rope. Another team may bid 50 points on the rope, 25 points on the Frisbees, 10 on the paper, and 15 on the cardboard.

- After all the bids are completed, collect them and divide up the materials based upon the highest bid. In the example, the first team would end up with the Frisbees and nothing else, but the second team would get the rope, paper, and cardboard. If there is a tie for any item, you may have the teams bid again on certain items or divide the items up if possible.

- Once the teams have their items, the second part of this teamwork activity occurs. They must now work together to get their entire team across the open area without any of the team members touching the ground in the process.

Process and Reflection:
What?

- What were the various elements of this activity?

So What?

- Was it hard for your team to agree on what numbers to bid? Why or why not?
- What did you do to come to an agreement?

Now What?

- When you disagree with others how do you handle it?
- How do you feel about your ability to work with others after this activity?
- What role do you usually take when in a group that is making decisions? Do you feel this is a good role for you? Why?

COMMUNICATION

Touchstone Belief: It is my responsibility to communicate clearly with others and express my views effectively and respectfully.

Supporting beliefs that will bring positive results and opportunity for student success:

- I know when and how to use different forms of communication, including technology.
- I need to articulate thoughts and ideas effectively using oral, written, and nonverbal communication skills in a variety of forms and contexts.
- It is important to listen effectively to decipher meaning, including knowledge, values, attitudes, and intentions.
- I understand how to use communication to inform, instruct, motivate, and persuade.

Explain it – Teach what students need to know

Students must be able to effectively analyze and process the overwhelming amount of communication in their lives today. Which information sources are accurate? Which ones are not? How can they be used or leveraged effectively?

The power of modern media and the ubiquity of communication technologies in all aspects of life make teaching students strong communication skills even more important than ever before. While education has always emphasized fluent reading, correct speech, and clear writing, there is evidence that students are not mastering these most basic skills. In the report *Are They Really Ready to Work?*, employers note that although oral and written communication are among the top four skills they seek in new hires, all graduates are lacking in these areas. High school graduates fare the worst, with 72 percent of employers citing this group's deficiency in writing in English, and 81 percent citing their deficiency in written communications. Almost half of employers said employees with two–year degrees were still lacking skills in these two areas, while over a quarter of employers felt four–year graduates continued to lack these skills.[6]

For the classroom teacher, instruction should include teaching students the importance of sending, receiving, and correctly interpreting information, ideas, thoughts, desires, and needs by both verbal and nonverbal communication. In responding to others, a student needs to be able to demonstrate assertiveness without being offensive or arrogant.

An important aspect of learning is for students to be able to communicate what they know, or think they know. The best way for teachers to encourage communication from all students is through classroom discussion or small group work. There has always been the notion that you learn best when you actually have to teach or explain a concept to someone else, because it requires verbalizing what you know. So teachers need to encourage their students to verbalize their own knowledge so that they can learn more efficiently.

Students also benefit from hearing their classmates' explanations, because more often than not, the concepts being explained are from different viewpoints, and are presented in a way that might be closer to the students' ways of thinking. When students listen effectively, they generate questions to further everybody's thinking and learning.

Debate is another way teachers can provide their students with the opportunity to practice their communication skills. Research suggests that debate encourages different types of responses, helps students to develop convincing arguments, and allows teachers and students to learn from one another.[7] This also encourages students to support what they believe, and it allows teachers to really get a good idea of what kind of conceptual knowledge students have about certain topics.

As a 21st century skill, there is agreement that this ability to communicate well – to express oneself clearly and concisely to others and the ability to understand, analyze, and use information communicated by others – is vital to academic and personal success.

Explore it – What we can learn from others

1. The single biggest problem in communication is the illusion that it has taken place. – George Bernard Shaw
2. We have two ears and one mouth so that we can listen twice as much as we speak. – Epictetus
3. The most important things are the hardest to say, because words diminish them. – Stephen King
4. The two words information and communication are often used interchangeably, but they signify quite different things. Information is giving out; communication is getting through. – Sydney Harris
5. Communication is everyone's panacea for everything. – Tom Peters
6. Two monologues do not make a dialogue. – Jeff Daly
7. Wise men talk because they have something to say; fools, because they have to say something. – Plato
8. The difference between the right word and the almost right word is the difference between lightning and a lightning bug. – Mark Twain
9. Who you are is speaking so loudly that I can't hear what you're saying. – Ralph Waldo Emerson
10. If you don't have something nice to say, don't say anything at all. – Thumper from Bambi
11. I speak to everyone in the same way, whether he is the garbage man or the president of the university – Albert Einstein
12. The most important thing in communication is hearing what isn't said. – Peter Drucker
13. The way we communicate with others and with ourselves ultimately determines the quality of our lives. – Anthony Robbins
14. Communication is the solvent of all problems and is the foundation for personal development. – Peter Shepherd
15. Blessed are they who have nothing to say, and who cannot be persuaded to say it. – James Russell Lowell

Engage it – How beliefs and content can be taught at the same time

- While reading a story or discussing the content of your subject matter, explain and illustrate the core components of effective communication and how it impacts others.
- Have students prepare and deliver explanatory and persuasive arguments and presentations.
- Have students research a recent world/local event (hurricane, volcanic eruption, flood, war, famine, mass migration, earthquake, etc.) and adopt a perspective of someone directly involved in what has happened or in the response.
- Ensure that students are able to articulate thoughts and ideas clearly and effectively through speaking and writing.
- Have students conduct an interview with someone from the local community.
- Students can organize a storyboard on a person/place/event, and use digital tools to create a presentation that teaches their topic to the remainder of the class.
- Have students research, organize, and present historical information in clear, complete, and effective formats.

- Have children 'retell' a story they have read in their own words to encourage them to summarize the main ideas of the story, instead of just responding to specific questions with facts.
- Identify strengths and weaknesses, and constructively express criticism concerning the merit of oral communications, writings, performances, and artistic works.
- Debates can help provide relevancy of course material to everyday issues, which can improve student learning.

Enhance it – Learning from stories read, told or viewed
Stories Told

Story 1 – What You Say Will Give You Away
Aesop, the ancient storyteller, told this fable: Once upon a time, a donkey found a lion's skin. He tried it on, strutted around, and frightened many animals. Soon a fox came along, and the donkey tried to scare him, too. But the fox, hearing the donkey's voice, said, "If you want to terrify me, you'll have to disguise your bray." Aesop's moral: Clothes may disguise a fool, but his words will give him away.

Story 2 – The Challenger Disaster[8]
The Challenger shuttle crew of seven astronauts died tragically in the explosion of their spacecraft during the launch of STS–51–L from the Kennedy Space Center on January 28, 1986. The explosion occurred 73 seconds into the flight as a result of a leak in one of two Solid Rocket Boosters that ignited the main liquid fuel tank.

The NASA investigational commission's report on the incident cited the cause of the disaster as a failure of an O–ring seal in the solid–fuel rocket. The faulty design of the seal coupled with the unusually cold weather of the launch date, let hot gases leak through the joint. This allowed booster rocket flames to pass through the failed seal, further enlarging the small hole.

The commission not only found fault with a failed sealant ring but also with the officials at the NASA who allowed the shuttle launch to take place despite concerns voiced by engineers regarding the safety of the launch. One of the major factors to the Space Shuttle Challenger disaster was a lack of effective communication between the NASA engineers and management. Communication between the company that designed the Solid Rocket Boosters and NASA management was also very poor.

The environment was such that it was not conducive to creating an atmosphere where everyone was comfortable expressing their opinions and making thoughtful decisions. The truth of the matter is that Morton Thiokol did not have any data on how its Solid Rocket Boosters and O–rings would perform at temperatures lower than 51 °F. The night before the launch, the temperature outside fell to 18 °F, and the morning of the launch the temperature was at 36 °F. While some engineers believed that the boosters would still be able function safely under these conditions, many were very worried that the temperature would cause a failure. The inability of the Morton Thiokol engineers to effectively convey their concerns to the NASA management and convince them to postpone the shuttle's launch is one factor that ultimately led to the disastrous outcome.

Another interesting failure in communication occurred between grounds crew and NASA management. The grounds crew was out measuring the thickness of the ice on the shuttle the morning of the shuttle's launch. In order to do this, they used infrared cameras that also allowed them to record the temperature of each part of the shuttle. They recorded a temperature of only 8 °F on the right Solid Rocket Booster only hours before the launch. This is far below the temperature range that the O–rings were designed to be used in. However, this vital information was never conveyed to NASA's managers or the engineers because the grounds crew was only instructed to report on the thickness of the ice on the shuttle.

Story 3 – A Bridge or a Fence

Once upon a time two brothers, who lived on adjoining farms, fell into conflict. It was the first serious rift in 40 years of farming side by side, sharing machinery, and trading labor and goods as needed without a conflict.

Then the long collaboration fell apart. It began with a small misunderstanding and it grew into a major difference, and finally it exploded into an exchange of bitter words followed by weeks of silence.

One morning there was a knock on the older brother's door. He opened it to find a man with a carpenter's toolbox.

"I'm looking for a few days' work." – he said. "Perhaps you would have a few small jobs here and there I could help with?"

"Yes." – said the older brother. "I do have a job for you. Look across the creek at that farm. That's my neighbor; in fact, it's my younger brother. Last week there was a meadow between us and he took his bulldozer to the river levee and now there is a creek between us. Well, he may have done this to spite me, but I'll do him one better."

"See that pile of lumber by the barn? I want you to build me a fence –an 8–foot fence – so I won't need to see his place or his face anymore."

The carpenter said, "I think I understand the situation. Show me the nails and the post–hole digger and I'll be able to do a job that pleases you."

The older brother had to go to town, so he helped the carpenter get the materials ready and then he was off for the day.

The carpenter worked hard all that day measuring, sawing, nailing. About sunset when the farmer returned, the carpenter had just finished his job.

The farmer's eyes opened wide, his jaw dropped. There was no fence there at all. It was a bridge – a bridge stretching from one side of the creek to the other! A fine piece of work, handrails and all – and the neighbor, his younger brother, was coming toward them, his arms outstretched – "You are quite a fellow to build this bridge after all I've said and done."

The two brothers stood at each end of the bridge, and then they met in the middle, taking each other's hand.

They turned to see the carpenter hoist his toolbox onto his shoulder.

"No, wait! Stay a few days. I've a lot of other projects for you," said the older brother.

"I'd love to stay on," the carpenter said, "but I have many more bridges to build."

Stories Viewed

From Film Clips on Line

- Babe – When Babe, the pig, is instructed by his stepmother to herd sheep, he learns the right way from the sheep themselves.

From Wing Clips

- Fireproof – After a bitter argument, Catherine tells her husband that she wants out of their marriage.

Experience it – Using experiential activities to promote learning by self–discovery
COMMUNICATION

#58   Back Draw

Learning Objective: To experience how a message may change as it goes from person to person
Materials: Five pieces of paper for each small group and a marker; a sheet for each group with the five drawings (see diagram)

Pass it On Activity Shapes

Pass it On Activity—Shape #1 Pass it On Activity Shape #2

Pass it On Shape #3 Pass it On Shape #4

Pass it On Shape #5

Instructions

- Have groups of six to eight sit in a line facing one direction – front to back (so they can 'draw' on the person's back in front of them).
- Give the person at the front of the line five pieces paper and a marker.
- A simple drawing is shown only to the person at the back of each line.
- Instruct the students that the person in the last seat will look at the drawing and will use their finger to 'draw' what they see on the next person's back. Each person passes it on by drawing what he or she felt on their back with their finger on the back of the individual sitting in front of them.
- When it gets to the front person, he or she draws it on one of the blank sheets of paper.
- Do the remaining drawings in the same way.
- Comparing each group's final drawings with the original completes the activity.

Process and Reflection:
What?

- What did you have to do?

So What?

- How did your group do with keeping the message correct all the way through?
- What happened when the message was easy? How about when it got more complicated?
- What was your confidence level that you perceived the message correctly and passed it on correctly?
- Where was the most responsibility in this activity?

Now What?

- How is this activity related to communication?
- As a student, what are the kinds of things you need to communicate?

- Often we are in a position to pass on information that we were given from someone else. How did it feel to have to pass on something you weren't sure was accurate?
- How does this activity relate to the choice of whether or not to share something you hear? (i.e. gossip) How did the message change as it went from back to front?
- What is the importance of respect and responsibility when communicating with others and the danger of gossip?
- Knowing that messages change through multiple people and that the more complicated the message the more likely it will not be shared correctly, what are some strategies that you could use when you need to communicate something to someone else?

Summary Drawing  **Message Learned**

Smiley face drawing – Keep it simple
Sun and the moon – Sometimes we receive conflicting information and must decide what is more likely to be the truth
Star – Lines of communication are straight
Two triangles – Two–way communication is best
House drawing – What we say can be complicated and must be made as clear as possible.

#59   Wright Family[9]

Learning Objective: To divide attention between two tasks with one being so overwhelming that students forget the details of the story being told
Materials: Poker chip, penny, or similar object (one per student); copy of the Wright Family Vacation story for the reader
Instructions:

- Ask students to stand in a circle close enough to reach and touch the student next to them.
- Distribute one chip/penny to each student. Tell them you are going read a story.
- When they hear the word *right*, they are to pass the chip to the person on their right. When they hear the word *left*, they are to pass the chip to the person on their left.
- Tell them you will not repeat or stop reading.
- Begin reading the Wright Family Vacation story.

Process and Reflection:
What?

- What were you asked to do?

So What?

- How successful were we as a group in completing the activity?
- How did the activity reflect responsibility?
- Is a value of responsibility about each of us or about what others do?
- How would you reframe the comment so they accept the responsibility: "I was responsible to take/pass the object to the person on the other side." It's important that students understand that the responsibility to conduct themselves appropriately is on their shoulders.
- What about the person reading the story?
- What does this activity have to do with communication?
- What happens when we get caught up in the 'rights and lefts' of what we need to do?

Now What?

- How does it feel to collaborate on a project that requires everyone's participation?
- How could this activity be done differently to allow for you to remember the details of the story and still follow the directions of right and left?
- There are times we get so caught up in the academics of school that we fail to realize that it is our values being put into action that allows us to be successful. What does this mean for you as a student? In what ways did the activity reflect this?

The Wright Family Vacation

One day the Wright family decided to take a vacation. The first thing they had to decide was who would be left at home since there wasn't enough room in the car for all of them. Father Wright decided Aunt Linda Wright would have to stay home. This made Aunt Linda Wright so mad, she left the house, saying, "It'll be a right cold day before I return."

The family bundled up the children –Tommy Wright, Susan Wright, Timmy Wright, and Shelly Wright – got in the car, and left. Unfortunately, someone had left a trashcan in the street that blocked them, so they had to stop the car. Tommy was told to move the trashcan, but he took so long they almost left him.

Once the family got on the road, Mother Wright wondered if she'd left the stove on. Father Wright told her not to worry; he'd checked the stove and it was off. As they turned the corner, everyone started to worry about other things they might have left undone.

When they stopped at the gas station, Father Wright discovered he'd left his wallet at home. So Timmy had to run home to get it. After Timmy left, Susan started to feel sick. She got out and said she had to throw right up. This got Mother Wright's attention, and she left the car to take care of Susan. Shelly wanted to watch Susan get sick, so she left, too. Father Wright remained with Tommy, who was playing a game in the backseat.

With all of this going on, Father Wright decided it wasn't the right time to take a vacation, so he gathered up the family and left to go home. When they arrived, he turned into the driveway and said, "I wish the Wright family had never left the house!"

#60   Student Voice Carousel

Learning Objective: To identify and agree upon value–based rules while giving students a voice in creating a safe environment that is conducive to learning

Materials: Six large sheets of paper, each should have one of the six questions (see below) written at the top; six markers, each one a different color

Questions:

1. What makes a class/school safe?
2. What makes for good learning?
3. What makes a good teacher/coach?
4. What makes a good principal/leader?
5. What should students learn to equip themselves for life in the 21st century?
6. What would you like to see in our school?

Instructions:

- Divide the class into six groups and give each group a different color marker.
- Spread the question sheets out on the walls and place one group at each sheet.

- Ask each group to nominate a recorder to write ideas down.
- Explain how a Carousel works:
  1. Each group has a different color marker that stays with them throughout the activity.
  2. They will have two to three minutes at each station to read the question, any ideas that are already there and then add their own answers to the sheet.
  3. They are trying to come up with as many ideas as they can; no criticism of their own or others ideas.
- Once they have visited all six stations explain that they are going to do a second Carousel to decide what are the most important ideas on each sheet.
- Ask them to consider all the responses on the sheet and check the two that they think are the most important answers to the question at the top.
- Once they have checked all six sheets and are back at their starting point ask them to identify which two responses have the most checks. If there is a 'draw' between two or more ideas, ask them to make a decision that they consider to be in the best interests of the class.
- Have groups report on the outcome from their group.
- The reason for the double carousel is so that the class can make decisions based on all the ideas rather than just check as they go round the first time.

Process and Reflection:
What?
- Why is the activity called "student voice carousel?"

So What?
- What did you learn?
- What ended up for your group being the most important responses?
- Why do you think we did the double carousel?

Now What?
- How can we use what was created to benefit our class? Our school?
- Can you compare and contrast our responses with what a student at a lower grade may have said in response to the questions? How about a student in a higher grade?
- What will have to be done to initiate or implement the responses you generated to the question, "what would you like to see in your school?"

#61   Miss – Understanding[10]

Learning Objective: To demonstrate what we might miss when we jump to conclusions
Materials: Handout; a PowerPoint slide that highlights each time the letter 'e' appears in the text
Instructions:
- Distribute the handout. Ask each student to independently read through the handout and circle each time the letter 'e' appears in the text.
- Call time after one minute. Ask the students to count the number of times they found the letter 'e.
- Display the answer. Show the PowerPoint slide to reveal that the letter 'e' appeared a total of 58 times. Ask if anyone found all 58 appearances.
- Review the handout. Ask students to check their handout and count the number of times they circled the letter 'e' when it appeared at the beginning of a word. Ask them to count each time they missed finding the letter 'e' when it appeared at the end of the word. Also ask them to count the number of times they missed the 'e' in a familiar word like 'the.'

Process and Reflection:
What?

- What were you asked to do?

So What?

- Explain that the more familiar we are with a word, the less likely we are to read it letter by letter. Instead, we pay attention to the first few letters, consider the context, scan and look for patterns, and then make assumptions about how the word ends. Why do you think this happens?
- What kind of words were you able to find the letter 'e?'
- What made the activity a challenge for you?
- What does this activity have to do with the idea of mindsets?

Now What?

- What are other areas of our lives where our attention is not always equally distributed?
- How often do our assumptions cause conflicts?
- How often do we make decisions based on assumptions? What happens when we do this?
- What can we do to reduce our natural tendency to jump to conclusions?

Handout

As educators we often rely on text–based resources, and this often requires the need for a professional proofreader. Proofreaders are sometimes called typesetters or copywriters, but whatever you call them you will quickly come to realize that these people are professionals who take pride in their work. Your trusted proofreader will do their level best to catch every spelling or grammar mistake and make sure your work is error free.

PowerPoint Slide – need to identify the letter 'e' in red.

As educators we often rely on text–based resources, and this often requires the need for a professional proofreader. Proofreaders are sometimes called typesetters or copywriters, but whatever you call them you will quickly come to realize that these people are professionals who take pride in their work. Your trusted proofreader will do their level best to catch every spelling or grammar mistake and make sure your work is error free.

#62   Leaving a Mark

Learning Objective: To understand what we say matters and even on the Internet words can hurt
Materials: Pencil; paper (for each student)
Instructions:

- Students will rub a graphite pencil on a piece of paper.
- Students will then rub their finger in the graphite until their finger is coated with the graphite.
- They will then place their finger, which is coated with the graphite, on a plain piece of paper.
- The students will look at their fingerprint and compare their fingerprint to others in the class realizing that their fingerprint is different.
- The students are then asked to erase the fingerprint so that it can't be seen. They come to the conclusion that this cannot be done.

Process and Reflection:
What?

- What was the objective of this activity?

So What?

- How does this activity connect with what some students do when posting information on the Internet, texting or using social media?
- Which value is violated when we say hurtful words on–line?
- Why would a student intentionally hurt someone else with the words they write on–line?

Now What?

- How do you want to be treated by others?
- Does what one say hurt less if it is on–line rather than in person?
- How should we respond when we determine what was said about us was unkind or hurtful?
- What are ways we can respond when we read or hear unkind things said about someone else we know?

Summary:
You can then discuss how every source of the Internet connection leaves a 'fingerprint.' Every time students communicate on–line, they leave a 'fingerprint' that cannot be erased.

#63   The Three Question Interview

Learning Objective: To prepare critical questions that can be used to effectively determine one's contribution to a team or job that needs to get done
Materials: Index cards
Instructions:

- Have student pair up with a partner.
- Share either a specific situation for the whole class to discuss or have the pairs work from a variety of scenarios. Situations could include:
  o   Running for student council
  o   Being the captain of the basketball team
  o   Being hired for a part–time job
  o   Auditioning for a part in honor's chorus
  o   Selection as a peer–tutor
- Each student in a two–person team would come up with three questions that would help him or her discover whether or not the partner was suitable for the position or assignment.
- Students should write their three questions on an index card.
- After each has determined the questions, turn the index card over and exchange your cards with another pair.
- With the cards you now have, each student will read the interview questions to the other person.
- When the question is read, the student will respond.

Process and Reflection:
What?

- What types of questions asked can best be used to determine the choosing of someone for a position or assignment?

So What?
- How difficult was it to come up with just three questions?
- What conclusion can you draw from the similarities in the questions you thought of and those of others?
- What were the differences that you found?
- Why do you think there were similarities? Differences?

Now What?
- What role did character play in the kinds of questions asked?
- Someone once said about hiring an individual for a job: "Hire for character and if you have to, train for skills." What does the statement mean and why do you think it is important when considering someone for a job?
- If you are hired for a job, assume an assignment in an organization or get selected for a leadership role, can you identify and describe where character will play a role?

#64   M&M Questions[11]

Learning Objective: To practice and apply effective communication and listening skills
Materials: A bowl of M&Ms, Starburst, or other multi colored candy
Instructions:
- Pass around a bowl of the candy.
- Ask each student to take three pieces of candy. Explain that for each colored candy they must relate to the group something from the topic you have assigned to the color.
- Suggested questions or statements based on the color of the candy:
  - Red: A memorable moment as a student in our school
  - Orange: The character trait that best describes you and why
  - Yellow: A thank you to someone in your life for something he or she has done to strengthen your character
  - Green: A feeling or emotion the student is experiencing and why
  - Brown: Explain in your own words: "Character is who you are when no one is looking."
- Continue around the group until all have discussed each candy and the topic that goes with it.

Variation:
Feel free to change the topics to items that your class might need to work on or for the beliefs you are seeking to instill in your students. For example, you could have a color mean something that students would like to improve about your school or identifying what it is that they like about school.

Process and Reflection:
What?
- Why did we have different colors of candy?

So What?
- What did you have to think about before you responded to the question you were assigned based upon the color of the candy you chose?
- Would it have been easier if you knew the question prior to choosing the candy?
- Were any of the questions harder than the others?

Now What?

- What communication skills did you have to use to be successful with this activity?
- Compare your responses to the question asked with what the majority of students might say who are in our school?
- Does it make a difference how someone would respond based upon whether they were a good student? One who did not get in trouble? Someone who makes poor choices?
- My responses today would have been different than what I would have said last year. Yes or no? Explain your answer.

#65   Happening Handshake

Learning Objective: To have students become aware of non–verbal communication skills and its potential impact

Instructions:

- Create groups of six to eight students
- Have a leader greet each member of the group with a handshake. Be sure to provide the very same greeting to each member of the group.
- Vary the intensity of the grip of the handshake from strong to weak to nonexistent.
- After the group is seated, ask for a volunteer to come to the front of the room.
- As the teacher, shake the volunteer's hand with a very limp grasp. Then invite another student of the opposite gender of yourself to the front of the room. Ask him or her to shake your hand but this time provide a 'regular' strength hand shake. Now ask a third student to the front of the room, but this time keep your hand to your side or place it into your pocket.

Variation:

Divide the students into three groups. Instruct one group that they will give strong handshakes, another weak handshakes and the third group will not extend their hand. Now, invite the students to mingle and greet students from the other groups.

Process and Reflection:
What?

- What did you do?

So What?

- What did you notice?
- What emotional impact would these handshakes have on you?
- What signals did you receive from the verbal and non–verbal greeting that you received?

Now What?

- What did you see and hear?
- What did you think the person's intent was?
- Might this emotional impact affect future interactions with that person? How?
- Are there other reasons for someone to give a handshake like the one you received other than what you initially thought?

#66   Barnga[12]

Learning Objective: To have students learn more about non–verbal communication, teamwork, personal biases, and intercultural awareness/diversity

Materials: (for each table): Copy of rules; deck of cards (no face cards), poker chips or other 'token' (paper clips; toothpicks; popsicle sticks, etc.)

Instructions:

- Arrange the room so that there are separate places for each group (approximately four to five students per group) to play cards.
- Set a copy of the rules and a deck of cards (Ace –10 only, no face cards) at each table.
- Let the students play a few rounds to get used to the rules at the table, with talking allowed at each table.
- Then remove the rules from each table, but continue to allow talking. Walk around to each table, ensuring that each group understands the rules at that table. From now on, the winner of each trick will receive one poker chip (or token of your choice) but talking is now prohibited.
- After allowing a few rounds without talking, make the student who won the most tricks move clockwise to the next table, and the student who won the least number of tricks move counter–clockwise to the next table.
- Play continues at the new tables for a set number of minutes or rounds (with no talking). It is up to the students at the tables to figure out how to communicate to each other and which rules are correct.

What the players do not know, is that each table has been playing with a different set of rules (see below). Depending on the number of groups, you may choose to discard or alter the rules as you see fit.

    Table 1: Ace high, no trump
    Table 2: Ace low, diamonds trump
    Table 3: Ace low, clubs trump
    Table 4: Ace high, hearts trump
    Table 5: Ace high, spades trump
    Table 6: Ace low, no trump
    In all cases, other cards will be worth face value–10 high, 2 low

Each table shares the following rules (add the table–specific rules to each table's set of rules; remember– they don't know it's different at each table):

- Players are dealt five cards each
- Whoever wins the most tricks will move clockwise to the next table
- Whoever loses the most tricks will move counter clockwise to the next table
- Everyone else stays at the same table
- Ties are resolved by paper rock scissors
- Each round will be about five minutes long (longer if time allows) and each round will consist any number of games that the time allows.
- After the initial round, players will not be allowed to see the rules or speak to each other. Gestures and pictures are allowed, but players are not allowed to use words.
- The game 'winner' will be the person who has won the most tricks in total. (Of course, once game play starts, winning will likely take a back seat to trying to figure out what everyone else is doing, as they are playing by different rules).
- Players can keep track of scores with popsicle sticks (one stick per trick won).
- The dealer can be anyone at the table, the person who plays first will be to the right of the dealer.

- The first player for each trick may play ANY suit. All other players must follow suit (play a card of the same suit). For each round, each player plays one card.
- If a player does not have that suit, a card of any suit must be played. The person wins the trick with the highest card of the original suit (players will begin to become confused when some players believe their card is trump, and others disagree or contradict this).

Process and Reflection:
What?
- What was the objective of the activity?

So What?
- If you could describe the game in one word, what would it be?
- What did you expect at the beginning of the game?
- When did you realize that something was wrong?
- How did you deal with it?
- How did not being able to speak contribute to what you were feeling?

Now What?
- What are the ways our school or class is like playing Barnga?
- What does this game suggest when we face situations in the real world?
- How does this activity focus our attention on the hidden aspect of school culture?
- How is this simulation similar to real life scenarios?
- What does the game demonstrate about communication?

GRATITUDE

Touchstone Belief: I consistently identify, experience and express thankfulness for the good things in my life.

Supporting beliefs that will bring positive results and opportunity for student success:

- I see the glass as half full and am thankful for the half I have rather than resentful about the half I don't.
- I express appreciation for the meaningful experiences and kindness shown by others.
- My capacity and feeling of gratitude is inversely related to how much I take for granted.
- I invariably and graciously express gratitude for gifts, favors, compliments, and services received.

Explain it – Teach what students need to know

Students demonstrate gratitude by consistently appreciating and expressing thanks for the good things in their lives. They consciously and intentionally count their blessings. While positive people see the glass as half full, grateful people are thankful for the half they have, rather than resentful about the half they don't. There is nothing more crippling to the growth and development of young people than the inability to recognize what is good in their lives.

The biggest difference between people who are generally happy and people who are generally not, is this: Happy people recognize, focus on, think about, talk about, and attribute value to what is good in their lives. Unhappy people don't. It really is that simple.

Adults, regardless of whether they are a teacher or a parent, should strive to help students become gracious, considerate, and thoughtful human beings. We want our students to genuinely feel and express appreciation for the happy moments, meaningful experiences, and the kindnesses shown to them by others. We want them to experience the peace and joy that comes with being truly thankful.

I have reached the conclusion that we have taken gratitude for granted for too long. Yes, 'thank you' is an essential, everyday part of family dinners, trips to the store, business deals, and political negotiations. That may be why so many people have dismissed gratitude as simple, obvious, and unworthy of serious attention. But I believe that is starting to change. Recently, scientists have begun to chart a course of research aimed at understanding gratitude and the circumstances in which it flourishes or diminishes. They are finding that people who practice gratitude consistently report a host of benefits:

- Stronger immune systems and lower blood pressure;
- Higher levels of positive emotions;
- More joy, optimism, and happiness;
- Acting with more generosity and compassion;
- Feeling less lonely and isolated.[13]

Summarizing the findings from studies to date, Emmons says that those who practice grateful thinking "reap emotional, physical, and interpersonal benefits." People who regularly keep a gratitude journal report fewer illness symptoms, feel better about their lives as a whole, and are more optimistic about the future. Emmons's conclusion is that gratitude is a choice, one possible response to our life experiences.[14]

We should strive to instill in students the understanding that gratitude is a way for people to appreciate what they already have, rather than always reaching for something new in the hopes that it will make them happier. Students must realize that gratitude is demonstrated by being happy with what they've been given, not by feeling unsatisfied until every physical and material need is met. Gratitude helps students refocus on what they have instead of what they lack. And, although it may feel contrived at first, this mental state grows stronger with use and practice.

Explore it – What we can learn from others

1. We often take for granted the very things that most deserve our gratitude. – Cynthia Ozick
2. Let us be grateful to people who make us happy; they are the charming gardeners who make our souls blossom. – Marcel Proust
3. As we express our gratitude, we must never forget that the highest appreciation is not to utter words, but to live by them. – John F. Kennedy
4. At times our own light goes out and is rekindled by a spark from another person. Each of us has cause to think with deep gratitude of those who have lighted the flame within us. – Albert Schweitzer
5. He is a wise man who does not grieve for the things which he has not, but rejoices for those which he has. – Epictetus
6. Silent gratitude isn't much use to anyone. – G.B. Stern
7. If a fellow isn't thankful for what he's got, he isn't likely to be thankful for what he's going to get. – Frank A. Clark
8. Gratitude is the best attitude. – Author unknown
9. Two kinds of gratitude: The sudden kind we feel for what we take; the larger kind we feel for what we give. – Edwin Arlington Robinson
10. Gratitude is a quality similar to electricity: it must be produced and discharged and used up in order to exist at all. – William Faulkner
11. Gratitude is the least of the virtues, but ingratitude is the worst of vices. – Thomas Fuller
12. Gratitude is an opener of locked–up blessings. – Marianne Williamson
13. Who does not thank for little will not thank for much. – Estonian proverb
14. The hardest arithmetic to master is that which enables us to count our blessings. – Eric Hoffer
15. When eating bamboo sprouts, remember the man who planted them. – Chinese proverb

Engage it – How beliefs and content can be taught at the same time

- Have students keep some form of "Gratitude Journal."
- Openly appreciate and sincerely thank your students by finding things they've done that are worthy of appreciation.
- Involve students in activities in which they can earn the appreciation of others.
- Engage students in service activities.
- Create routines that promote appreciation. Ask students, "What is the best thing that happened today?"
- Initiate a community appreciation bulletin board or newsletter, or set aside a time in the classroom when students can publicly express appreciation for each other and the adults in their lives.
- Point out how happy someone looks when they are being thanked, and talk about how much more enjoyable it is to be around people who are gracious and grateful.
- Explain how much it means to you and to others when someone expresses appreciation.
- Have students write what they are thankful for on a large piece of paper.

- Have students cut out pictures of things they're grateful for and then have them use the pictures to create collages, or to decorate a classroom gratitude bulletin board.
- Have students write what they're thankful for on strips of paper, and then use the strips to make a gratitude chain to hang up in the classroom.
- Have each student write one thing that he or she is grateful for on a Post–it note and then plot it on a classroom gratitude graph.
- If using classroom meetings, set aside time to have each student share one thing that he or she is grateful for and why.
- Write letters of gratitude and deliver them to people in the greater school community (e.g., janitors, food staff, secretaries, and administrators).
- Have students think of something they're grateful for and then re–frame it in their minds as a gift they've been given. Then ask students to 1) notice that someone recognized they had a need and acted upon it; 2) appreciate the cost incurred by the person extending the gift; and 3) recognize the personal value of the gift they received.

Enhance it – Learning from stories read, told or viewed

Stories Told

Story 1 – Gifts From the Heart Are Gifts of the Heart by Michael Josephson[15]

According to legend, a young man roaming the desert came across a spring of delicious crystal–clear water. The water was so sweet he filled his leather canteen so he could bring some back to a tribal elder who had been his teacher.

After a four–day journey, he presented the water to the old man, who took a deep drink, smiled warmly, and thanked his student lavishly for the sweet water. The young man returned to his village with a happy heart.

Later, the teacher let another student taste the water. He spat it out, saying it was awful. It apparently had become stale because of the old leather container. The student challenged his teacher: "Master, the water was foul. Why did you pretend to like it?"

The teacher replied, "You only tasted the water. I tasted the gift. The water was simply the container for an act of loving–kindness and nothing could be sweeter. Heartfelt gifts deserve the return gift of gratitude."

I think we understand this lesson best when we receive innocent gifts of love from young children. Whether it's a ceramic tray or a macaroni bracelet, the natural and proper response is appreciation and expressed thankfulness because we love the idea within the gift.

Gratitude doesn't always come naturally. Unfortunately, most children and many adults value only the thing given rather than the feeling embodied in it. We should remind ourselves and teach our children about the beauty and purity of feelings and expressions of gratitude. After all, gifts from the heart are really gifts of the heart.

Story 2 – Global Village[16]

If we could shrink the earth's population to a village of precisely 100 people, with all the existing human ratios remaining the same, it would look something like the following.

There would be:

- 57 Asians
- 21 Europeans
- 14 from the Western Hemisphere, both north and south
- 8 Africans
- 52 would be female

- 48 would be male
- 70 would be non–white
- 30 would be white
- 70 would be non–Christian
- 30 would be Christian
- 89 would be heterosexual
- 11 would be homosexual
- 6 people would possess 59% of the entire world's wealth and all 6 would be from the United States.
- 80 would live in substandard housing
- 70 would be unable to read
- 50 would suffer from malnutrition
- 1 would be near death; 1 would be near birth
- 1 (yes, only 1) would have a college education and 1 would own a computer

When one considers our world from such a compressed perspective, the need for both acceptance, understanding and education becomes glaringly apparent. The following is also something to ponder:

- If you woke up this morning with more health than illness... you are more blessed than the million who will not survive this week.
- If you have never experienced the danger of battle, the loneliness of imprisonment, the agony of torture, or the pangs of starvation ... you are ahead of 500 million people in the world.
- If you have food in the refrigerator, clothes on your back, a roof overhead and a place to sleep... you are richer than 75 percent of this world.
- If you have money in the bank, in your wallet, and spare change in a dish someplace... you are among the top 8 percent of the world's wealthy.
- If you hold up your head with a smile on your face and are truly thankful... you are blessed because the majority can, but most do not.
- If you can read this message, you are more blessed than over two billion people in the world that cannot read at all.

We're a fortunate group of people.

Story 3 – Is This Generous or Just Dumb? by Michael Josephson[17]

Jack was excited when he was given an unexpected bonus check of $1,000 from his employers. He was anxious to rush home to tell his family, but before he got to his car, a desperate–looking woman holding a baby who looked quite sick asked him for a few dollars. She said her child was dying and she showed him a letter from a hospital saying they could not give her the very expensive medicine he needed.

Jack looked at his check and then at the baby. Acting on impulse, he endorsed the check to the woman, saying, "Use this to do what you can for your baby."

When he told his family what he'd done, his wife was silent but his teenage son ridiculed him. Deflated, Jack said, "We don't need the money. It felt like the right thing to do."

A week later, his son waved a newspaper article in his face reporting that a woman with a baby was arrested for scamming people. "This is the lady you gave the money to, isn't it?" he asked contemptuously.

"Yes," Jack replied quietly and then he suddenly beamed with joy.

"What are you smiling about?" his son demanded. "She made a fool of you."

"Yes, but there's something much more important," Jack said, "This means the baby's not dying."

His son declared, "You're an even bigger fool than I thought."

After a long pause, Jack's wife embraced her husband lovingly. "There are two ways to look at this and I choose to be awfully proud to be married to a man with such a generous heart. You're lucky to have him as a dad."

Who was right – the son or the wife?

Stories Viewed

From Foundations for a Better Life

- Gratitude – Looking back on the milestones of our lives, it is important to recognize those who have made our path a little easier. Perhaps it was a parent, a teacher, a coach, a mentor or someone we simply call 'friend.'
- Biker – This clip goes to show we can make a difference if we only care.

From Wing Clips

- Tears of the Sun – After Lt. Waters and his team successfully fought off the militia and brought the refugees to safety, a woman thanks Lt. Waters and tells him that he will not be forgotten.

From Motivational Media – Character in the Movies

- Les Miserables – Eponine, a young, but ragged, lady living in poverty in Paris in 1832, has a secret love for Marius and she mourns her unrequited love. Students will see the importance of people evaluating how grateful they are for friendship or other blessings.

Experience it – Using experiential activities to promote learning by self–discovery
GRATITUDE

#67   Gift of Happiness

Learning Objective: To help see the good in others and to express uplifting words to someone else
Materials: A large envelope and a piece of masking tape (one for each student); index cards
Instructions:

- Each student receives a legal–size envelope and a piece of masking tape.
- Students write their names on the backs of the envelopes and decorate them any way they wish.
- Students are to write positive messages to the members in their group expressing a specific appreciation to each person.
- When all have finished writing their messages, they wait to deliver them until instructed to do so.
- Students tape their envelopes to their backs with the name showing outward.
- After all have finished writing a message to each student in their group and all have taped envelopes to their backs, students walk around the room depositing the messages.
- When all have received their messages, allow them to read their messages.

Process and Reflection:
What?

- What were you asked to do throughout this activity?

So What?

- What were the words or phrases that your classmates used that made you feel good?
- Can you identify the emotions you felt when you read what others wrote?
- How should we respond?

Now What?

- Why is it important to use kind word when we communicate with others?
- What words or phrases had the most powerful effect on you?
- What would be examples of what students say at our school when communicating with classmates? The good things said? The not so good things students say?
- How would our class or school be different if what was said to others was kind and caring?

Note: As the teacher, consider participating in this activity. Try and pay close attention to which student are receiving messages. Make sure every student receives a message either from you or a member of the class.

#68   Saying Something Nice

Learning Objective: To support social and emotional development and provide positive guidance
Materials: A ball of thick white yarn
Instructions:

- Introduce the activity by suggesting that we should try to spin a web as a group.
- Have the students form a large circle (sitting down) and show them the white yarn.
- Explain that you will begin spinning the web by holding the end of the yarn ball tightly in your lap and then picking a friend to toss the remaining ball.
- "I pick Jackson to help spin our web."
- When Jackson catches it, share something you like about him (i.e., "I like how Jackson shares with his friends").
- Remind Jackson to hold the yarn string tight in this lap, as he picks the next friend to toss the ball of yarn to.
- The activity proceeds until the ball is complete, and the number of times a child is picked doesn't matter, unless of course the circle has gone through everyone (with teacher assistance, "I think Mia would like to join our web").
- It's fun to see how huge your life size web has become. Sometimes it's fun to see if the group can stand up together without getting tangled in it too.

Process and Reflection:
What?

- What does nice mean to you?

So What?

- How did you feel when someone said something nice about you?
- Why aren't we always nice to others in our class?
- What words should we use when we talk to others in our class?
- Describe how you feel when you are recognized by others for something you have done or for how you have handled a situation.

Now What?

- How do you like others to treat you?
- What did we create with our kind words?
- What do you think it means to have created a web with the kind words we used in talking about the students in our class?

#69   I Think You Are Great

Learning Objective: To help students see the impact that kind words have on how others feel
Materials: Piece of construction paper for each student; individual student pictures; sheets of $8^{1/2}$ x 11 paper with a double–sided arrow drawn on each

Instructions:

- Prior to the activity, make a poster using construction paper for each student with his or her name, maybe a picture that has been taken and the words, "I think you are great because…"
- Brainstorm positive words that we can use to describe others. What are uplifting and kind words we can say to someone else? Record the words on the board for reference.
- Place the posters around the room and assign a student to each poster (not their own).
- Have the students write a positive statement on the poster about the fellow classmate.
- Then, have the students rotate around the room to make sure they get to write something on each poster. This could be done at intervals throughout a month period of time. It could be a great way to begin each week with students having to choose another couple of students to write something positive about.
- As we know, caring is expressed not only in words but also actions. As a part of this activity, create mini–posters that have a double arrow. Ask students to share ways that they can demonstrate caring to their fellow classmates (letting others play, sitting by someone you may not know well at lunch, not fighting, helping someone when they are in trouble).
- Write each of the ideas given by the students on the double arrow sheet and then hang these in between the student's "I think you are great because…" poster.

Process and Reflection:
What?
- What did this activity convey as to how we should treat others?

So What?
- How did you go about thinking what you would write?
- Were there specific characteristics that you saw in the student from what he or she did?
- How would you summarize gratitude?
- Were there certain words or phrases you hoped that others would say about you? If so, were they on your poster? Why do you think that happened?

Now What?
- What do we mean when we say that caring is expressed by words and actions?
- What are the ways you think our class demonstrates caring?

- Do others care what we say about them? Why or why not?
- Share specific ways students in our class could show they are grateful for what they already have.

#70   Gratitude Ball Toss

Learning Objective: To understand the importance of gratitude
Materials: Tennis ball
Instructions:

- Before you begin, have students think about what they are grateful for.
- Have the students sit in a circle.
- The student who holds the ball says one thing in their life they are grateful for.
- They then toss the ball to someone else, who repeats what the previous just said, then states what they are grateful for, etc. Example: Ashley, "I am grateful for my dog." She tosses the ball to Xavier. He says, "Ashley is grateful for her dog, and I am grateful that it's sunny today."

Process and Reflection:
What?

- What does it mean to be grateful?

So What?

- What did you learn about your classmates?
- Why is it not only important but also necessary to be able to express gratitude?
- Why do you think some people never say they are grateful for anything?

Now What?

- In what ways can we show that we are grateful to others in our class?
- Identify one thing in your life you are grateful for and write about it in your journal. Try and add something each day.
- Find ten quotations or proverbs related to gratitude and then re-write them in your own words.

PERSEVERANCE

Touchstone Belief: When something doesn't work right, try again and again.

Supporting beliefs that will bring positive results and opportunity for student success:

- I am able to resist temptations and pressures to give up or quit, choosing instead to persist as long as I can.
- I will always finish what I start.
- I can learn to face and accept what happens in my life.
- I need to grow from my experiences, including the ones that hurt.

Explain it – Teach what students need to know

You've probably heard the quote, "If at first you don't succeed, try again," or seen the commercial that talks about falling down seven times and standing up eight. The lesson, of course, is that few people achieve anything great without first overcoming a few obstacles. After working with students for any length of time, we realize students aren't likely to get far in school or life without perseverance.

When you hear the life stories of famous scientists, inventors, artists, and visionaries, they always have one trait in common: amazing perseverance. Most of them failed repeatedly before they experienced success. However, an internal drive for success and a "never give up" attitude defined their life and their work. As a practical value, perseverance can be considered instrumental because it contributes to effectiveness, success, and the achievement of personal objectives irrespective of their moral content. Perseverance should be taught and nurtured not because steadfast and unrelenting students are necessarily good, but because possessing this value can be a contributor to success.

Students demonstrate perseverance by continuing to perform responsibilities and pursue goals with vigor and tenacity despite frustrations, mistakes, setbacks, and other obstacles that make their task difficult or seem impossible. Students are more likely to persevere when they can draw on specific strategies and tactics to deal with challenges and setbacks. They need actionable skills for taking responsibility and initiative, and for being productive under conditions of uncertainty: for example, defining tasks, planning, monitoring, changing course of action, and dealing with specific obstacles. Simply measuring how long someone works at a task does not adequately capture the essence of perseverance, because continuing to perform something that is fun or rewarding does not require one to endure and overcome setbacks.

It is important for students to consider the benefits of being able to bear difficulties and persist with a course of action calmly and without complaint. A few ways students show perseverance are:

- Giving up personal time to spend hours studying.
- Trying a new sport that is very difficult, but not giving up.
- Working hard to catch up after missing a week of school.
- Saving money and making sacrifices to buy something.
- Spending hours practicing a musical instrument.
- Studying and working hard to raise a grade.
- Trying out for something they weren't successful at the first time.
- Working a little harder or a few minutes longer on a task that they do not like.

Students must come to understand that perseverance and failure cannot coexist. Failure happens when one quits. To persevere means to stay with the challenge, or if it is one that can be modified, to change course, rather than simply give up. When all is said and done, perseverance can be referred to as 'stick–to–itiveness,' and is considered a necessary component of being an effective and successful student. Share with your students that perseverance is akin to the old adage of "getting up just one more time than you have been knocked down." Ultimately, students who persevere through the stumbling process will eventually be molded into individuals who can be counted on when things are not easily accomplished.

Explore it – What we can learn from others

1. Great works are performed, not by strength, but by perseverance. – Samuel Johnson
2. When the world says, 'Give up,' Hope whispers, 'Try one more time.' – Author unknown
3. Patience, persistence and perspiration make an unbeatable combination for success. – Napoleon Hill
4. It's not that I'm so smart, it's just that I stay with problems longer. – Albert Einstein
5. Failure is success if we learn from it. – Malcolm Forbes
6. When a door closes, try to re–open it. If it does not yield, look for another door. If you can't find one, look for a window. If there is no window, poke a hole in the wall and make one. There is always a way out. Nothing that confines you is stronger than your will to be free. – Michael Josephson
7. It's not whether you get knocked down, it's whether you get up. – Vince Lombardi
8. The difference between a try and a triumph is a little UMPH. – Author unknown
9. When you come to the end of your rope, tie a knot and hang on. – Franklin D. Roosevelt
10. The difference between perseverance and obstinacy is that one comes from a strong will, and the other from a strong won't. – Henry Ward Beecher
11. Nobody trips over mountains. It is the small pebble that causes you to stumble. Pass all the pebbles in your path and you will find you have crossed the mountain. – Author unknown
12. Consider the postage stamp: its usefulness consists in the ability to stick to one thing till it gets there. – Josh Billings
13. If one dream should fall and break into a thousand pieces, never be afraid to pick one of those pieces up and begin again. – Flavia Weedn
14. Perseverance is not a long race; it is many short races one after another. – Walter Elliott
15. People are always blaming their circumstances for what they are. I don't believe in circumstances. The people who get on in this world are the people who get up and look for the circumstances they want, and, if they can't find them, make them. – G.B. Shaw

Engage it – How beliefs and content can be taught at the same time

- Identify moral themes and dilemmas throughout history: prejudice versus civil rights, treatment of ethnic groups, greed versus giving, attitudes toward slavery, the family and its changing role.

- Have students write in their journals about difficult situations, and how they handled them without giving up.

- Discuss a poem about suffering, what can be learned from it, how to face it, how not to hurt others, and anything else about obstacles.

- Students can learn what it means to stick to a task through the retelling of the story "The Little Engine That Could." Personal application is made to their own experiences with the "I think I can..." statement.

- Have students write and illustrate something they can do now that required perseverance to accomplish (e.g., riding a bike or running a mile), and make a class art wall displaying these examples.

- Students can identify heroes in their local community, realizing that most heroes are ordinary people that just work hard and never give up.
- Read a children's book of heroes together and discover how the hero persevered.
- Make it a point to notice when your students are demonstrating perseverance and say things such as, "You stuck with that problem and tried it in a couple of different ways," or, "It can be frustrating to not get it the first time, but we stick with things and try again!"
- Have students research individuals from a historical perspective to document examples of perseverance.
- Have students create and illustrate the concept of perseverance through an acrostic poem.
- Have students discuss mistakes they have made and how they could have turned them into learning opportunities.
- Have students select a character from a favorite book or story. Tell them to list that character's traits and explain how these traits helped the character to overcome adversity. Then have them compare their own traits to those of their chosen character.
- Help your students think of a fun goal they can achieve within a short time, like finishing a book or completing a project. Completing a small goal will help give students an idea of the positive feelings they will have when they accomplish their long–term goals.
- Ask the students to make two lists: one list of things that are difficult for them, and another of things that are easy for them. Categorize these items under headings such as sports, school, home, friends, etc. Study how many are in each category and check if the students have listed more difficult things or easier things. Remind the students that if they keep persevering, the difficult items can be moved to the 'easy' list. You can also use this activity to teach about categorizing and percentages.
- Students could take part in a variety of writing exercises about the most important pastime or activity in which they participate, and the perseverance it takes to improve.

Enhance it – Learning from stories read, told or viewed
Stories Told

Story 1 – Moral Courage: The Engine of Integrity by Michael Josephson[18]

Mignon McLaughlin tells us, "People are made of flesh and blood and a miracle fiber called courage." Courage comes in two forms: physical courage and moral courage. Physical courage is demonstrated by acts of bravery where personal harm is risked to protect others or preserve cherished principles. It's the kind of courage that wins medals and monuments. Moral courage may seem less grand but it is more important because it's needed more often.

Moral courage is the engine of integrity. It is our inner voice that coaxes, prods, and inspires us to meet our responsibilities and live up to our principles when doing so may cost us dearly.

It takes moral courage to be honest at the risk of ridicule, rejection, or retaliation, or when doing so may jeopardize our income or career. It takes courage to own up to our mistakes when doing so may get us in trouble or thwart our ambitions. It even takes courage to stand tough with our kids when doing so may cost us their affection.

Like a personal coach, moral courage pushes and prods us to be our best selves. It urges us to get up when we'd rather stay in bed, go to work when we'd rather go fishing, tell the truth when a lie would make our life so much easier, keep a costly promise and put the interest of others above our own.

The voice of moral courage is also our critical companion during troubling times; it provides us with the strength to cope with and overcome adversity and persevere when we want to quit or just rest.

At unexpected and unwelcome times, we all will be forced to deal with the loss of loved ones, personal illnesses and injuries, betrayed friendships, and personal failures. These are the trials and tribulations of a normal life, but, without moral courage, they can rob us of the will and confidence to find new roads to happiness and fulfillment

Moral courage is essential not only for a virtuous life, but a happy one. Without courage, our fears and failures confine us like a barbed wire fence.

The voice of moral courage is always there, but sometimes it is drowned out by the drumbeat of our fears and doubts. We need to learn to listen for the voice. The more we call on it and listen to it and trust it, the stronger it becomes.

Story 2 – The Amazing 8–Watts[19]

In 1972, NASA launched the exploratory space probe Pioneer 10. The satellite's primary mission was to reach Jupiter, photograph the planet and its moons, and beam data to earth about Jupiter's magnetic field, radiation belts, and atmosphere. Scientists regarded this as a bold plan, for at that time no earth satellite had ever gone beyond Mars, and they feared the asteroid belt would destroy the satellite before it could reach its target.

But Pioneer 10 accomplished its mission and much, much more. Swinging past the giant planet, Jupiter's gravity hurled Pioneer 10 at a higher rate of speed toward the edge of the solar system. At one billion miles from the sun, Pioneer 10 passed Saturn. At some two billion miles, it hurtled past Uranus; Neptune at nearly three billion miles; Pluto at almost four billion miles. By 1997, twenty–five years after its launch, Pioneer 10 was more than six billion miles from the sun.

And despite that immense distance, Pioneer 10 continued to beam back radio signals to scientists on Earth. Perhaps most remarkable, those signals emanate from an 8–watt transmitter, which radiates about as much power as a bedroom night light, and takes more than nine hours to reach Earth.

"The Little Satellite That Could" was not qualified to do what it did. Engineers designed Pioneer 10 with a useful life of just three years. But it kept going and going. By simple longevity, its tiny 8–watt transmitter radio accomplished more than anyone thought possible.

Story 3 – The Concert

Ignace Jan Paderewski, the famous Polish composer–pianist, was once scheduled to perform at a great American concert hall for a high–society extravaganza. In the audience was a mother with her fidgety nine–year–old son. Weary of waiting, the boy slipped away from her side, strangely drawn to the Steinway on the stage. Without much notice from the audience, he sat down at the stool and began playing 'Chopsticks.'

The roar of the crowd turned to shouts as hundreds yelled, "Get that boy away from there!" When Paderewski heard the uproar backstage, he grabbed his coat and rushed over behind the boy. Reaching around him from behind, the master began to improvise a countermelody to 'Chopsticks.' As the two of them played together, Paderewski kept whispering in the boy's ear, "Keep going. Don't quit, son...don't stop...don't stop."
(This story has been re–created in a video clip on *The Foundations for a Better Life* web site at Foundations at www.values.com)

Stories Viewed

From Film Clips on Line

- Fellowship of the Ring – When the royal council argue about who should take the ring to the fires of Mordor, a unlikely outsider offers his services.

From Foundations for a Better Life

- Track Coach – The clip promotes the message that sometimes it takes someone else to see our potential and challenge us to do our best.

- The Wall – This clip promotes the theme that you should never says something cannot be done.
- Finish Line – Every goal begins with a dream. Challenges, obstacles, and distractions also seem to be part of what we must deal with on the way to achieving those goals.

From Wing Clips
- Arthur Christmas – Arthur and a feisty elf hurry to wrap and deliver the final Christmas present to Gwen before dawn.

From Motivational Media – Character in the Movies
- The Lone Ranger – John Reid, a young prosecutor, finds himself riding on a runaway train while shackled to an Indian named Tonto. As they make their way to the front of the train to stop the engine, they argue about the effort at hand. In this clip students will understand the importance of perseverance and determination in tough circumstances.

Cody McCasland – A clip about a 10–year–old boy who doesn't have any legs but has a wonderful attitude. Cody has had 20 surgeries and more. His dream is to compete in the 2016 Paralympic Games for swimming. https://www.youtube.com/watch?v=ladcCd9PRLc

Nic Vuvicic – No Limbs, No Limits https://www.youtube.com/watch?v=kD–fH5W_Ruk

Experience it – Using experiential activities leading to self–discovery
PERSEVERANCE

#71   Traffic Jam[20]

Learning Objective: To experience and reflect on the necessary skills to successfully complete with a small group a difficult problem–solving exercise

Preparation and Set Up:
- Divide students into small groups of 8–10.
- Each small group needs to have places marked on the floor. If outside, use chalk or inside you can use masking tape to mark the places for students to stand
- Number places 1–9 (shown below) to assist students in helping them find the solution.

Instructions:
1. Ask the students to stand on their markers facing the center marker that is empty.
2.

3. Explain to them that their 'side' members are the ones facing in the same direction.
4. The goal of the activity is for the two sides to exchange places–to get everyone from one side to the other side while remaining in the order and facing the direction their side is currently in.
5. This is not a competition between the two sides; they are working as one group together to complete the activity.
6. Tell them the rules allow for these kind of moves:
   - A player must move only to an unoccupied space in front of them.

- You may move past a player facing the opposite direction to get to the empty space behind him or her.
- You may not move past more than one player and remember they must be the ones facing the opposite direction
- You do not necessarily have to alternate turns with the people moving from the other side – you are working as one group to complete the activity.
7. Moves that are not allowed:
   - Players may not move backwards, nor turn around.
   - You may not move around anyone facing the same direction that you are facing.
8. If you attempt a solution and get stuck, your group must return to the starting position and begin again.

Here are two suggestions for assisting the students after they have grappled with finding the solution:
- Encourage them when they start over to mix up the order of the students standing there so the ones on the end do not disengage from the process.
- Provide them with paper and pencil so they can work together to diagram a solution.

If some groups are being successful and others are not, allow the groups that haven't gotten it yet to decide if they want assistance from the successful groups. Try not to allow any groups to quit without being successful. Consider having a successful group line up parallel and walk them through the solution.

Process and Reflection: Provide an opportunity for the groups to discuss some of these questions among themselves, and then ask for some shared comments with the entire group.

What?
- What were you asked to do?

So What?
- What strategies did your group use to figure out the solution? (include the option of watching others–did they consider that 'cheating' or using their resources? What is the difference? Is it different depending on the circumstances? Why or why not?
- How did your group handle themselves? Were they respectful and caring of people and their ideas?
- Did anyone want to give up? Did you? If not, why not? What kept you personally trying even when you were having problems finding the solution?

Now What?
- How does this activity reflect things that happen in your everyday life?
- What are some examples of times when it is important for you to persevere until you find the solution? Why is it sometimes hard?
- What do you do when you want to give up?
- Why do we hesitate sometimes to ask for help?

Solution to Traffic Jam Activity

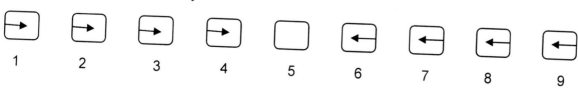

The solution involves using the numbers under the squares above. You may want to try this on paper with pennies or some other objects to represent the players. Keep in mind that the player on the square described, can only move in one direction. The arrows on the squares only show the direction of the player starting on that square. After the game starts, players can only move the direction they were facing at the beginning of the game.

square 4,
square 6, square 7,
square 5, square 3, square 2,
square 4, square 6, square 8, square 9,
square 7, square 5, square 3, square 1,
square 2, square 4, square 6, square 8,
square 7, square 5. square 3,
square 4, square 6,
square 5

Notice the pattern: L side – 1 move, R side – 2 moves, L side –3 moves, R side – 4 moves, L side – 4 moves, R side – 4 moves, L side – 3 moves, R side – 2 moves, L side – 1 move.

#72   Gone Fishing

Learning Objective: To help students realize that we all face challenges and fears but that we can possess the courage to overcome and persevere
Materials: A sheet of paper cut into fourths; two or three cans/pails; four dowel rods cut into two–foot lengths; string; four small magnets; paper clips
Instructions:

- Provide each student with a ¼ size sheet of paper. Have the students fold the paper in half. On the upper half, they can write down something they are, or were afraid of. On the bottom half, have them write what they did or could do to help get over this fear.
- Punch a hole through the top of both pieces of paper near the fold and attach a paper clip. Each student can then place the pieces of paper in a couple of pails or cans. Depending on the size of the class, figure on no more than eight students per can.
- Provide a couple of 'fishing poles' that have been created out of a two–foot piece of dowel rod that has a string and magnet attached to the end. Have the student take the pole and drop it into the can. The magnet will attach itself to a paper clip.
- The students can reel in the clip of paper and read whatever was written.

Process and Reflection:
What?

- What did you need to do in this activity?

So What?

- How hard was it to come up with a fear or challenge you have?
- Have you been successful in having the courage to overcome and persevere? If so, what strategy has worked for you?

Now What?

- Why is it hard for a student to face a fear or challenge?

146

- Failure is not an option. Do you agree or disagree? How does your response reflect what you would do to demonstrate perseverance?
- As you get older, what are other challenges you will most likely have to face?
- What are strategies you can use to overcome a specific situation you face?
- Why do you think some students lack the courage to overcome the fear they have?

#73   Stepping Up[21]

Learning Objective: To help students realize that if they face their problems by shaking off fear and stepping up, they will most likely have a better chance of being successful

Materials: *The Parable of the Wise Old Mule*

Instructions:

- Read *The Parable of the Wise Old Mule*
- Give students a copy of the worksheet or display the questions as part of a media presentation
- Group students to discuss responses to the questions.

The Parable of the Wise Old Mule – Author unknown

A parable is told of a farmer who owned an old mule. The mule fell into the farmer's well. The farmer heard the mule 'braying' – or whatever mules do when they fall into wells. After carefully assessing the situation, the farmer sympathized with the mule, but decided that neither the mule nor the well was worth the trouble of saving.

Instead, he called his neighbors together and told them what had happened and enlisted them to help haul dirt to bury the old mule in the well and put him out of his misery.

Initially, the old mule was hysterical! But as the farmer and his neighbors continued shoveling and the dirt hit his back...a thought struck him.

It suddenly dawned on him that every time a shovel load of dirt landed on his back...HE SHOULD SHAKE IT OFF AND STEP UP! This he did, blow after blow.

"Shake it off and step up...shake it off and step up...shake it off and step up!" he repeated to encourage himself.

No matter how painful the blows, or distressing the situation seemed the old mule fought panic and just kept right on SHAKING IT OFF AND STEPPING UP!

You're right! It wasn't long before the old mule, battered and exhausted, STEPPED TRIUMPHANTLY OVER THE WALL OF THAT WELL! What seemed like would bury him, actually blessed him – all because of the manner in which he handled his adversity.

Process and Reflection:
What?

- How does one handle adversity?

So What?

- What problem did the mule have to overcome?
- How did the mule handle the problem?
- Why is shaking it off and stepping up an admirable way to face adversity?

Now What?

- How does *The Parable of the Mule* relate to you as a student?

- What are examples you can share of people you know personally or people you have read or heard about who have shaken off adversity and stepped up?
- What happened to the people you cited as examples who shook off adversity and stepped up?
- Make a list of five ways that you can make shaking it off and stepping up to adversity a habit.

#74   The Frozen Penny

Learning Objective: To be persistent in even the most challenging of situations can allow us to be successful in meeting our goals

Materials: An ice cube for each student with a penny frozen inside

Instructions:
- Give each student an ice cube.
- Explain that the first person to get the penny out of their ice without putting it in their mouth or hitting it with another object is the winner.

Process and Reflection:
What?
- What did you have to do?

So What?
- How difficult was it to melt your ice cube?
- What strategies did you use to melt the ice cube?
- Did you observe what others in the class were doing?

Now What?
- How does melting the ice cube compare to reaching your goals?
- Did you ever feel like quitting? Why do some people quit before reaching their goals?
- Could you have gotten the penny quicker had you broken the rules? Would you feel as good about winning if you didn't follow the rules?
- How do hard work and perseverance help you achieve your goals?

#75   Sink or Swim[22]

Learning Objective: To understand how it is possible to work through challenges and achieve goals by reshaping one's attitude

Materials: Clear glass bowl with water; modeling clay (Not Play–Doh)

Instructions:
- Roll clay into four balls, three of them small and one a little larger (like small and big marbles).
- Drop each small one into the water and watch them sink. Tell the students that each ball represents a person that feels discouraged or frustrated by life's difficulties.
- Provide examples of situations that students face. Or you can ask the class to give examples.
- Next, take the larger clay ball and start reshaping it to form the shape of a simple canoe. Talk about how this person is not going to give up when faced with a problem. He is choosing to have a positive attitude and show perseverance.
- Discuss how it is possible to work through the challenges and achieve your goal by reshaping your attitude.
- Put the 'boat' in the water and watch it float.
- Now take each small ball and put them inside the boat.

148

Process and Reflection:
What?

- What did the balls of modeling clay represent?

So What?

- What were some of the challenges or problems that students face?
- Why is it a challenge to continue to try when it seems everything is going wrong?

Now What?

- What can happen when a student has a positive attitude and decides to persevere?
- Do you ever feel like quitting when things are hard? What do you do then?
- How can you demonstrate perseverance?
- What is one thing you can do this week to keep going and not give up?

#76   All Shook Up

Learning Objective: To realize that all it takes to triumph when facing a challenge is a little 'umph'
Materials: Three or four plastic jars with tight lids; a plastic bowl; three or four pints of whipping cream; honey; plastic knives; sliced bread
Instructions:

- Pour a pint of whipping cream into each container and place the lids on securely.
- Pass around the jars giving each student several moments to shake the jar before passing it on.
- While the students are shaking the jars you may want to read a story or watch a video clip on perseverance.
- After a few minutes of shaking, stop and ask them what would happen if they gave up now.
- Explain that quitting keeps great things from happening. If we lose patience and give up, nothing good will develop.
- It should take about 10 minutes for the cream to separate into a lump of butter in each jar.
- Carefully remove the butter and place it in a large plastic bowl.
- Drizzle honey over the butter. Invite the students to spread the treat on a piece of bread.

Process and Reflection:
What?

- What was this activity designed to represent?

So What?

- What did we have to do?
- Why couldn't we stop shaking the jar?
- Why did it have to take so long?

Now What?

- What are situations you face that seem too difficult to overcome?
- Why do students tend to give up?
- How do you show perseverance?
- What are the rewards in working hard to overcome a challenge you face?
- What conclusions can you draw from this activity?

RESILIENCE

Touchstone Belief: Even when life is tough, I know I can survive.

Supporting beliefs that will bring positive results and opportunity for student success:
- Negativity in life or in others does not change who I know I am.
- I identify myself as a survivor rather than a victim.
- I acknowledge that life comes with challenges and setbacks, which I can overcome.
- Challenging life experiences can be opportunities for growth and change.
- I can put negative experiences behind me and move forward with confidence and optimism.

Explain it – Teach what students need to know

Resilience is the ability to work with adversity in such a way that one comes through it unharmed or even better for the experience. For students, resilience means facing life's difficulties with courage and patience – refusing to give up. It is the quality of character that allows a person or group of people to rebound from misfortune, hardships, and traumas.

Resilience is a process, not a trait. It involves how we interact and negotiate with others and ourselves after facing adversity or misfortune. Everyone, regardless of age or circumstances, has the capacity for resilience. It just needs to be tapped.

Students can be taught that the way to demonstrate resiliency is by maintaining a positive outlook, and by drawing on their inner strength to muster the will and courage to bounce back from the pain and grief of personal traumas and tragedies, disappointments, failures, and misfortunes. Resilience is rooted in a tenacity of spirit – a determination to embrace all that makes life worth living even in the face of overwhelming odds. We are more resilient when we have a clear sense of identity and purpose, because we can hold fast to our vision of a better future.

A school is a natural environment for helping students cultivate their resilience, as conditions exist in the school setting that promote resilience. These include caring, encouraging relationships; role models and mentors; clear and fair expectations and structure; exploration of other worlds and possibilities; stories of overcoming adversity in literature, films, and history; and basic human respect and dignity.[23]

We have seen a growing number of parents who believe that it is important to help their children avoid difficulties and protect them from being hurt or treated unfairly. They do this out of love for their child, and they can't bear seeing them hurt or suffer from any pain. We have all heard of 'helicopter parents' who hover over everything that their child does. There are also 'bulldozer parents.' A bulldozer parent is one who is too involved in his or her child's life (especially at school), and is constantly complaining or intervening anytime there is a conflict or difficult situation. Often, it is this parent who makes excuses for their child's behavior. How can children develop resilience if they are not faced with adversity?

It certainly is not a bad thing to try to protect children from exposure to risk factors. I am not suggesting we should allow bad things to happen to our children. But when faced with a challenge, the way our children respond is key. A study on adversity and resilience found that "although preventing or minimizing risk factors should always be a goal, protective factors can foster resilience and mitigate some of the potentially negative influence of the risk factors when they are unavoidably present."[24]

How exactly does a student become more resilient? And how can schools most effectively capitalize on their power to promote resilience? The short answer is that a student's resilience is fostered when his or her internal and environmental protective factors are strengthened. These protective factors can buffer, ameliorate, and mitigate the effects of risk and stress, propelling the student to academic and life success.

Every caring adult within the school setting is a potential agent of protective factors. First, they can notice and reinforce students' internal protective factors – such as "easy temperament, good reasoning skills, self–esteem, and internal locus of control."[25] By engaging students in conversations and other interactions, they can help them recognize and grow these traits. Second, they can create classroom and school cultures that are infused with environmental protective factors like those already listed – regular structures, routines, civility, and caring.

According to Sagor, schools can provide support to students, particularly those at risk, through resilience–building experiences that focus on five themes:

1. Competency (feeling successful)
2. Belonging (feeling valued)
3. Usefulness (feeling needed)
4. Potency (feeling empowered)
5. Optimism (feeling encouraged and hopeful)[26]

Explore it – What we can learn from others

1. Success is not final, failure is not fatal: it is the courage to continue that counts.– Winston Churchill
2. When nothing in life seems to be going right.... Go Left! – Author unknown
3. I haven't failed. I've identified 10,000 ways this doesn't work. – Thomas Edison
4. People who soar are those who refuse to sit back, sigh and wish things would change. They neither complain of their lot nor passively dream of some distant ship coming in. Rather, they visualize in their minds that they are not quitters; they will not allow life's circumstances to push them down and hold them under. – Charles R. Swindoll
5. The strongest oak of the forest is not the one that is protected from the storm and hidden from the sun. It's the one that stands in the open where it is compelled to struggle for its existence against the winds and rains and the scorching sun. – Napoleon Hill
6. Be like the bird that, passing on her flight awhile on boughs too slight, feels them give way beneath her, and yet sings, knowing that she hath wings. – Victor Hugo
7. The bamboo that bends is stronger than the oak that resists. – Japanese proverb
8. I have missed more than 9,000 shots in my career. I have lost almost 300 games. On 26 occasions I have been entrusted to take the game winning shot... and I missed. I have failed over and over and over again in my life. And that's precisely why I succeed. – Michael Jordan
9. We are what we repeatedly do. Excellence then is not an act, but a habit. – Aristotle
10. Our greatest glory is not in never falling, but in rising every time we fall. – Confucius
11. He that can't endure the bad will not live to see the good. – Jewish proverb
12. Diamonds are nothing more than chunks of coal that stuck to their jobs. – Malcom Stevenson
13. What lies behind us and what lies before us are tiny matters compared to what lies within us. – Ralph Waldo Emerson
14. Do not let what you cannot do interfere with what you can do. – John Wooden
15. In the middle of difficulty lies opportunity. – Albert Einstein

Engage it – How beliefs and content can be taught at the same time

- Use examples from current events and literature to analyze how people face and bounce back from tragedy.

- Foster an interdependent learning environment where students learn from you and you learn from them.
- Implement "student–led family–school conferences" to encourage students to accept personal responsibility for their academic and school performance.
- Provide opportunities for peer tutoring, during which students can learn from each other.
- Allow students greater participation in and ownership of class and school activities and traditions.
- Assign rotating classroom chores/roles, set a tone of "we're all in this together," and provide frequent positive feedback.
- Discuss and implement reasonable student ideas for class and school rituals.
- Help your students develop a sense of purpose through participation in community service projects and events.
- Promote resilience in children and adolescents by increasing pro–social bonding.
- Encourage cooperative play rather than competitive play.
- Interact individually with students as frequently as possible and in ways that are mutually meaningful.
- Shared reading activities can center on stories in which the major characters exhibit resilience.
- Topics for journal writing can include factual narratives and personal reflections related to resilience.
- Scientific experiments can provide visible and tangible examples of resiliency.
- Interact with students in non–academic ways to get to know students' non–academic strengths and abilities.
- Create classroom and/or school rituals and traditions (i.e. bonding activities).
- Demonstrate pro–social behaviors in the classroom, cafeteria, during school events, etc.
- Discuss the concepts of friendship and qualities of a good friend within the learning environment.

Enhance it – Learning from stories read, told or viewed

Stories Told

Story 1 – Courage – You Can Stand Strong in the Face of Fear by Jon Johnston[27]

Ready for a baseball trivia question? Who is Clint Courtney? If you're unsure, don't bother requesting the answer from Cooperstown, N.Y. Clint never came close to making it into the Baseball Hall of Fame. In fact, it's very doubtful that his picture appeared on any bubble gum cards. This guy wasn't a legend in his own time — not even in his own mind. He was only a memory maker for his family, and a few die–hard fans who were inspired by his tremendous fortitude.

Clint played catcher for the Baltimore Orioles in the 1950s. During his career he earned the nickname of Scrap Iron, implying that he was hard, weathered, tough. Old Scrap broke no records — only bones. He had little power or speed on the base paths. As for grace and style, he made the easiest play look rather difficult. But armed with mitt and mask, Scrap Iron never flinched from any challenge.

Batters often missed the ball and caught his shin. Their foul tips nipped his elbow. Runners fiercely plowed into him, spikes first, as he defended home plate. Though often doubled over in agony, and flattened in a heap of dust, Clint Courtney never quit. Invariably, he'd slowly get up, shake off the dust, punch the pocket of his mitt once, twice, and nod to his pitcher to throw another one. The game would go on and Courtney with it — scarred, bruised, clutching his arm in pain, but determined to continue. He resembled a POW with tape, splints, braces, and other kinds of paraphernalia that wounded people wear. Some made fun of him — calling him a masochist. Insane. Others remember him as a true champion.

Story 2 – Andrew Jackson

The story is told that Andrew Jackson's boyhood friends just couldn't understand how he became a famous general and then the President of the United States. They knew of other men who had greater talent but who never succeeded. One of Jackson's friends said, "Why, Jim Brown, who lived right down the pike from Jackson, was not only smarter but he could throw Andy three times out of four in a wrestling match. But look where Andy is now." Another friend responded, "How did there happen to be a fourth time? Didn't they usually say three times and out?" "Sure, they were supposed to, but not Andy. He would never admit he was beat — he would never stay 'throwed.' Jim Brown would get tired, and on the fourth try Andrew Jackson would throw him and be the winner." Picking up on that idea, someone has said, "The thing that counts is not how many times you are 'throwed,' but whether you are willing to stay 'throwed'."

Story 3 – The Law of the Garbage Truck

One day I hopped in a taxi and we took off for the airport. We were driving in the right lane when suddenly a black car jumped out of a parking space right in front of us. My taxi driver slammed on his brakes, skidded, and missed the other car by just inches! The driver of the other car whipped his head around and started yelling at us!

My taxi driver just smiled and waved at the guy. And I mean, really friendly. So I asked, "Why did you just do that? This guy almost ruined your car and sent us to the hospital!" This is when my taxi driver taught me what I now call, "The Law of the Garbage Truck."

He explained that many people are like garbage trucks. They run around full of garbage (frustration, anger, and disappointment, etc.). As their garbage piles up, they need a place to dump it and sometimes they'll dump it on you. Don't take it personally. Just smile, wave, wish them well, and move on. Don't take their garbage and spread it to other people at work, at home, or on the streets.

The bottom line is that successful people do not let garbage trucks take over their day. Life's too short to wake up in the morning with regrets, so… love the people who treat you right and pray for the ones who don't. Life is ten percent what you make it and ninety percent how you take it!

Stories Viewed

From Film Clips on Line

- Bend it Like Beckham – In a girls' soccer match, a British player of Pakistani descent, reacts badly when she is insulted by her opponent.
- Chariots of Fire – A runner is tripped and falls, but gets up and wins the race.
- The Rookie – A coach encourages his players to take pride in themselves.

From Foundations for a Better Life

- Soccer – Perhaps one of the most important things we can do for someone is to give them a chance. When we allow someone the opportunity to fulfill their dreams, it gives us the pride of knowing we helped to make a difference in their lives.

From Wing Clips

- 12 Years a Slave – The true story of Solomon Northup, a free black man from upstate New York, who was abducted and sold into slavery. Solomon admonishes a fellow slave who is crying over being separated from her children, and tells her not to fall into despair.
- All About Color Freedom Writers – Erin challenges her students, who value the gang–life over education, about their sense of respect and purpose.

- The Karate Kid – After giving Dre a gift before the final tournament, Mr. Han tells Dre that he has taught him a valuable lesson.

Ordinary People Have Done Some Extraordinary Things www.youtube.com/watch?v=NLLMAcJJ3l0. (Produced by Farmers Insurance)

The Race – Heather Dorniden https://www.youtube.com/watch?v=xjejTQdK5OI

Experience it – Using experiential activities to promote learning by self–discovery
RESILIENCE

#77   Keypunch[28]

Learning Objective: To get students to demonstrate resilience by cooperatively working together to determine a solution

Materials: One boundary rope approximately 50' long; 30 rubber spots (or carpet squares or paper plates) numbered from 1–30; one cone

Preparation: Before class, form a rectangle with the boundary rope. Spread out the numbered spots within the boundary rope so that consecutive numbers are spread far apart from one another. This will form your keypad. Place the cone as a starting/ending point approximately 10 yards away from the keypad.

Instructions:
- Have students standing behind the starting point and explain that a terrible computer virus has infected the main computers at the State Department. Our class of computer experts has been hired to disinfect the system.
- In order to disinfect the system, the team must enter the 'restricted area' (anywhere beyond the starting cone, press the keys (spots) on the keyboard (anywhere within the rope boundary) in sequential order from one to 30, and get out of the 'restricted area' in less than 30 seconds, with the following stipulations:
  1. There may only be one person actually contacting the keyboard (i.e., the spots and/or the spaces between the spots, anywhere within the rope boundary) at any one time. Should two or more individuals be contacting the keyboard at one time, the board is fried and the group must begin again at number one. Time, of course, continues.
  2. Keys must be touched in order. If any keys are touched out of order, the board is 'fried' and the group must begin again at number one. Time, of course, continues.
- The class has a total of four attempts to disinfect the computer, time for each attempt beginning when the first person in the group moves past the starting cone on their way to the keypad and ending when the last person arrives back at the cone.
- At the end of 45 minutes, the computers will crash irrevocably with the terrible consequence that all of the money from everyone's paycheck will automatically be withdrawn.

Process and Reflection:
What?
- What was the assigned task in this activity?

So What?
- What was the initial reaction of the group?
- How well did the group cope with this challenge?
- What skills did it take to be successful as a group?

- What creative solutions were suggested and how were they received?
- Did everyone listen to each other's ideas?

Now What?
- What about this activity would be of help to you as a student?
- For your role in a class or school, why is it important to listen to others?
- What could be the benefits of getting others involved in arriving at a solution to a specific issue or problem?

#78 All Cracked Up

Learning Objective: To demonstrate how we manage stress in our lives
Materials: Egg; glass or dish
Instructions:
- Raise your arm so that it is visible to all the students.
- Conduct the first demonstration by picking up an egg. Squeeze the egg and explain that it did not crack because there was consistent pressure all around.
- Conduct the second demonstration. Show that the egg is raw by cracking it a clear glass or dish.

Process and Reflection:
What?
- What do you think the egg represented?

So What?
- Why did the egg not crack when it was squeezed on all sides, but cracked easily when it was hit against the side of the glass?
- What does stress mean?
- Provide an explanation as to how dealing with stress is related to resilience.

Now What?
- How can you relate this demonstration to real–world examples in the way we manage stress and deal with our emotions?
- What personally brings stress to you as a student?
- When does stress or dealing with emotions really become a challenge for you?
- What can we do to manage small stresses that are all around us?
- How do you compare the impact that a large stress can have with that of those small stress examples we face every day?
- What can we try to do to live a life that is balanced?

#79 Rejecting Rejection[29]

Learning Objective: To explore rejection and to emphasize that one can overcome challenges
Materials: A biographical sketch of famous people who have dealt with rejection and demonstrated resiliency. You can also have students develop their own biographical sketch of individuals who faced challenges and were successful in overcoming them. An excellent video clip to share as part of this lesson: *Ordinary People Have Done Some Extraordinary Things.* www.youtube.com/watch?v=NLLMAcJJ3l0. (Produced by Farmers Insurance)

Instructions:
- Divide the class into groups.
- Read the description of people who have been rejected.
- Have the groups identify the name of the person being described.

Process and Reflection:
What?
- What did the individuals have to do to overcome the challenges they faced in being rejected?

So What?
- What is it that all of these people have/had in common?
- What are specific qualities or traits that helped each of these individuals overcome the adversity of rejection?
- How does rejection hurt the ones who do the rejecting?

Now What?
- What are examples of rejection that students face at our school?
- What can you do to show resilience?
- React to this statement: "Rejection hurts only if we allow it to."
- Argue for or against the statement: "If you never quit, you'll never fail. You may lose, but you'll never fail."
- If you were able to create your own video of individuals who were successful in overcoming challenges, whom would you include?
- Would you be able to include stories of young people who demonstrated resilience? If so, provide examples and a brief description of their story.

Biographical Descriptions of Famous People
- He was born in Chicago by eventually moved to a Kansas farm.
- He wanted to study art but was only able to do it through correspondence school.
- He was a high school dropout.
- A newspaper editor fired him because "he lacked imagination and had no good ideas."
- He was forced to dissolve his company and at one point could not pay his rent and reportedly survived by eating dog food.
- He formed his first animation company in Kansas City, where he made a deal with a distribution company in New York, in which he would ship them his cartoons and get paid six months down the road.
- He tried to get a studio to distribute a cartoon he created but was told that the idea would never work because a giant mouse on the screen would terrify women.

Walt Disney

- She was a divorced single mother on welfare.
- Tried to attend school and write a novel at the same time.
- Her first novel was written on a manual typewriter.
- Twenty publishers rejected her novel.
- When she found someone to publish the book, she was encouraged to get a day job because there was no money in children's books.

156

- She once said, "You might never fail on the scale I did. But it is impossible to live without failing at something, unless you live so cautiously that you might as well not have lived at all – in which case, you fail by default."
- She went from depending on welfare to survive by becoming one of the richest women in the world in a span of only five years as the author of the Harry Potter series.

J.K. Rowling

- She endured a rough and often abusive childhood.
- At the age of 22, she was fired from her job as a television reporter because she was "unfit for TV."
- She was terminated from her post as co–anchor of the 6 o'clock weekday news on Baltimore's WJZ–TV after the show received low ratings.
- She was then demoted to morning TV.
- A comment she made once was that, "Challenges are gifts that force us to search for a new center of gravity. Don't fight them. Just find a new way to stand."
- She moved to Chicago and became one of the most iconic faces on TV as well as one of the richest and most successful women in the world.

Oprah Winfrey

- He was born in Milan, Ohio. His mother was a teacher.
- At age 12, he was selling fruit and candy on a railroad line.
- He was rejected as a student because of a severe learning disability.
- In his early years, teachers said he was "too stupid to learn anything."
- He was fired from his first two jobs for not being productive enough.
- Even as an inventor, he made 1,000 unsuccessful attempts at inventing the light bulb.
- He went on to invent not only the light bulb, but the phonograph, the movies and thousands of other inventions.

Thomas Edison

- He was born in Ulm, Germany and was rejected by many teachers who claimed they were unable to deal with such a poor student.
- He did not speak until he was four and did not read until he was seven, causing his teachers and parents to think he was mentally handicapped, slow and anti–social.
- Eventually, he was expelled from school.
- He was rejected admission to the Swiss Federal Institute of Technology because of poor test scores on the entrance exam.
- He persevered and went on to receive a Ph.D. from the University of Zurich.
- It might have taken him a bit longer, but most people would agree that he caught on pretty well in the end, winning the Nobel Prize and changing the face of modern physics.
- He gave the world the theory of relativity.

Albert Einstein

- In his first screen test, the testing director took note that this man, "Can't act. Can't sing. Slightly bald."
- He was told only that he was able to dance a little.

- A memo was written about him that said, "I am uncertain about the man, but I feel, in spite of his enormous ears and bad chin line, that his charm is so tremendous that it comes through even on this wretched test."
- He went on to become an Oscar–nominated actor, singer and dancer.
- He kept the negative note in his Beverly Hills home to remind him of where he came from.

Fred Astaire

- He was rejected from film school – three times.
- He eventually attended school at another location, only to drop out to become a director before finishing.
- Thirty–five years after starting his degree, he returned to school in 2002 to finally complete his work and earn his BA.
- He said, "I wanted to accomplish this for many years as a thank–you to my parents for giving me the opportunity for an education and a career."
- He added, as a personal note for his own family – and young people everywhere – about the importance of achieving their college education goals.

Steven Spielberg

- He started his dream at 65 years old.
- He got a social security check for only $105 and was mad. Instead of complaining he did something about it.
- He thought restaurant owners would love his fried chicken recipe, use it, sales would increase, and he'd get a percentage of it.
- He drove around the country knocking on doors, sleeping in his car, wearing his white suit.
- Unfortunately, 1009 times people said no before he got one yes.

Colonel Sanders

- He was given up for adoption at birth.
- In high school, he attended lectures at a small computer technology company called Hewlett–Packard.
- He dropped out of college because he thought it was expensive and didn't want to drain his parents' savings.
- He was a fired tech executive and an unsuccessful businessman.
- His own company was headquartered out of a garage in Los Altos, California.
- At 30–years old he was left devastated after being unceremoniously removed from the company he founded.
- He later said, "I didn't see it then, but it turned out that getting fired was the best thing that could have ever happened to me. The heaviness of being successful was replaced by the lightness of being a beginner again, less sure about everything. It freed me to enter one of the most creative periods of my life."
- After his return to Apple, he created several iconic products, including the iPod, iPhone and iPad.

Steve Jobs

- These brothers battled depression and family illness before starting a bicycle shop.
- They began to experiment with flight using the knowledge gained from the bicycle shop.

- On their first flight in their heavier–than–air machine only five people turned up.
- After numerous attempts at creating flying machines, several years of hard work, and tons of failed prototypes, the brothers finally created a plane that could get airborne and stay there.
- The brothers made their historic first powered flight on December 17, 1903, from Kill Devil Hill in Kitty Hawk, North Carolina. The longest of four flights that day lasted 59 seconds and covered a distance of 852 feet.

Wilbur and Orville Wright

- He was cut from his high school basketball team.
- After being cut from his high school basketball team, he went home and cried in the privacy of his bedroom.
- His father was shot and killed.
- He once said, "I have missed more than 9,000 shots in my career. I have lost almost 300 games. On 26 occasions I have been entrusted to take the game winning shot, and I missed. I have failed over and over and over again in my life. And that is why I succeed."

Michael Jordon

- In his youth he went to war a captain and returned a private.
- He was defeated for legislature in 1832.
- A year later he failed in business.
- He suffered a nervous breakdown.
- He was elected to Congress in1846 but two years later he lost renomination.
- He was rejected for Land Officer and defeated for Senate in 1854.
- Suffered defeat for nomination for Vice–President in 1856 and again defeated for Senate in 1858
- Elected President in 1860 and is remembered as one of the greatest leaders of our nation.

Abraham Lincoln

CHAPTER 6:
ACADEMIC BELIEFS
Action Steps to Instill the Key Beliefs

Touchstone Belief	
Growth Mindset	Intelligence and talent are not fixed; both can be improved with effort and practice.
Setting Goals	I will get better results if I set goals and plan out the steps to reach them.
Critical Thinking	It is important to understand and evaluate the information I am given.
Decision Making	I realize that my behavior and the choices I make affects others.

GROWTH MINDSET

Touchstone Belief: Intelligence and talent are not fixed; both can be improved with effort and practice.

Supporting beliefs that will bring positive results and opportunity for student success:
- The mind is a muscle that gets stronger with use.
- I can get better at anything if I put in the effort.
- I should seek challenges and learning, value effort, and persist effectively in the face of obstacles.
- People who limit themselves to doing what comes easy to them are much less successful than people who force themselves to be good at things that don't come easily.

Explain it – Teach what students need to know

Including growth mindset as one of the sixteen touchstones in this book reflects current studies on how we learn. Mindsets are beliefs – beliefs that one has about whom they are and their most basic qualities. These constitute how students frame themselves as learners, their learning environment, and their desire to exhibit continuous learning. Academically, they include beliefs, attitudes, dispositions, values, and ways of perceiving oneself. There is compelling evidence that mindsets can have a powerful impact on academic performance and are evident in how students behave and respond when faced with a challenge.

Have your students think about their intelligence, their talents, and the attributes or characteristics that best describe who they are. Are these qualities simply fixed traits that are carved in stone, with limited chance for improvement? Or are they attitudes and beliefs that students can cultivate throughout their lives?

Students with a fixed mindset believe their traits are just givens. They believe they have a certain amount of brains and talent, and nothing can change that. If they have a lot, they're all set, but if they don't, they are stuck on a track with the potential for limited success. Students possessing this mindset worry about their traits and how adequate they are. They will strive in class to prove to themselves and others that they can do something because of the level of intelligence or attributes that they have. Since they believe that they have only a certain amount of a valued talent or ability, their desire is to look good at all times. Students with a fixed mindset try to highlight their proficiencies while making sure they are able to hide their deficiencies.

Students with a growth mindset, on the other hand, see their qualities as things that can be developed through commitment and dedicated effort. They are happy if they're smart or talented, but to them that is just the starting point. They understand that no one has ever accomplished great things without passionate practice, dedication, and continuous learning. Students in the growth mindset understand that it takes effort to bring an ability to life and for it to reach its maximum potential. People with a growth mindset not only believe in the power of effort, but they also hold effort as a value.

Our work as teachers should be to have students approach learning and other aspects of their lives with a growth mindset, believing they can increase basic intellectual abilities and develop life skills, personal attributes, and moral virtues that enhance success in all areas of their lives. We need to challenge students to truly believe the idea that "My ability and competence grow with my effort."[1]

When the going gets rough, people in the growth framework not only take charge of improving their skills, they also take charge of their motivation. Despite setbacks – or even because of them – they find ways to keep themselves committed and interested.

It is important to encourage students to accept the belief that their basic qualities, whether talents or attributes, are things that can be cultivated through effort. Even though students may differ in their initial talents and aptitudes, interests, or temperaments, there needs to be an acceptance of the premise that everyone can change and grow through application and experience.

Explore it – What we can learn from others

1. It does not matter how slowly you go so long as you do not stop. – Confucius
2. Don't tell me how talented you are. Tell me how hard you work. – Arthur Rubenstein
3. There has to be this pioneer, the individual with the courage, the ambition to overcome the obstacles that always develop when one tries to do something worthwhile that is new and different. – Alfred P. Sloan
4. Whenever an individual or business decides that success has been attained, progress stops. – Thomas J. Watson
5. We find comfort among those who agree with us, and growth among those who don't. – Frank A. Clark
6. What you get by reaching your destination is not nearly as important as what you will become by reaching your destination. – Author unknown
7. There are three musts that hold us back: I must do well. You must treat me well. And the world must be easy. – Albert Ellis
8. It is never too late to be what you might have been. – George Elliot
9. There is no greater agony than bearing an untold story inside you. – Maya Angelou
10. Knowing what is and knowing what can be are not the same thing. – Ellen Langer
11. There isn't a person anywhere who isn't capable of doing more than he thinks he can. – Henry Ford
12. I don't divide the world into the weak and the strong, or the successes and the failures. I divide the world into the learners and the non–learners. – Benjamin Barber
13. Ask, 'How will they learn best?' not 'Can they learn?' – Jaime Escalante

14. Test scores and measures of achievement tell you where a student is, but they don't tell you where a student could end up. – Carol Dweck
15. You have to apply yourself each day to becoming a little better. By becoming a little better each and every day, over a period of time, you will become a lot better. – John Wooden

Engage it – How beliefs and content can be taught at the same time

- Give examples of people who decided early in life that they were not good at math, languages, or even school, and how those beliefs are self–limiting and false.
- Share an example with your students of something you now can do that you thought you couldn't.
- Praise effort and incremental improvement rather than grades, natural abilities, intelligence, or talent.
- Establish high expectations, as this increases motivation in vulnerable students. Let students know that you are challenging them because you know that all of them have the ability to meet those expectations.
- When introducing a new topic, you can tell your students, "This will be a challenging concept to learn, but all of us can reach the goal. I want you to stretch."
- Write comments to your students that contain specific feedback on ways to improve, along with an explanation that you are providing this feedback because you believe they have the capacity to develop a high level of skill in that area.
- Let your students know that you value challenge–seeking, learning, and effort above perfect performance, and that the amount of progress they make individually is more important than how they compare to others.
- Make it clear that mistakes are to be expected and that we can all learn from them.
- Ask students to share their 'best' mistake of the week with you, and what they learned from it (and do the same yourself).
- Give feedback that focuses on process – the things students can control, like their effort, persistence, and good strategies – not on their personal traits or abilities.
- Help your students understand the many ways to employ effort effectively, such as seeking out challenges, setting goals and making plans, using creative strategies, and sticking with it when they are having difficulty.
- Let students know that when they are practicing hard things, their brains are forming new connections and making them smarter. Instead of feeling dumb when they struggle, they will learn to 'feel' those connections growing.
- Teach students about how the brain physically changes while learning, and how they can strengthen their brains with effective learning strategies.
- Convince students that there is no such thing as 'smart' or 'dumb' people, but rather hard workers and not–so–hard workers.
- Reward effort and encourage students to achieve deep learning by allowing them to revise their work (e.g., rewriting a term paper using the teacher's feedback to improve their grade).

Enhance it – Learning from stories read, told or viewed
Stories Told

Story 1 – Will and Fern
Two frogs named Will and Fern fell into a deep pit together. At first, they thought it would be easy to jump out. But after lots of failed attempts they cried for help and a crowd of animals gathered around the pit.

Everyone agreed it was hopeless so they urged Will and Fern to accept their fate. The harder the trapped frogs jumped, the more the crowd yelled at them to give up. Finally, Will stopped trying. Fern refused to quit and with one mighty try she leaped out of the pit.

The crowd was amazed. Someone asked her why she kept trying when everyone told her she had no chance. Fern was baffled. "What are you saying?" she asked. "I'm a bit deaf. I was sure you were all cheering me on. I couldn't have done it without your encouragement."

Story 2 – Encouragement Found in an Unlikely Place

I learned of this story from a woman who was in a transitional housing program recovering from a long period of drug abuse, homelessness and hopelessness. She wanted everyone to understand how important positivism and encouragement can be to help people who seem down and out to get up and out. She said she got out of her own pit because caring people helped her believe in herself and gave her the confidence she needed to jump a little harder.

There will always be people in your life ready to tell you what you can't do. Real friends root for you, support you and help you discover your inner talents and strengths.

I hope you will find and treasure those kinds of friends and be one yourself.

Story 3 – How Your Attitudes Shape Your Life by Michael Josephson[2]

A long time ago a reporter visited a rock quarry where three men were cutting granite out of the walls. He asked the first what he was doing and the man grunted, "I'm making bricks." The second man grinned and said, "I'm making the foundation for a building." The third smiled, "I'm building a great cathedral."

All three were doing the same job, but their different attitudes about their work determined how they experienced their lives.

The first fellow saw his labor in a narrow way – making bricks to make a living. The second looked through a wider lens, realizing his bricks would be part of something lasting and important – the foundation to a building. The third man had the widest vision of all. He saw himself as part of a grand and uplifting enterprise – building a cathedral!

Could you guess which was the happiest? Which one would you hire?

Let's apply this story to teachers. The brick–maker type would say, "I teach math." The foundation–builder would say: "I teach math but I also teach my students how to learn so they can be more capable of anything." The cathedral–builder would say, "I teach math and lay a foundation for my students to learn other things, but I also help them see their full potential and build their character because each one is a cathedral!"

Which teacher would you rather have? Which do you think enjoys his or her life the most?

Could you apply this to your life? Are you just learning the least you have to so you get the grade you want, or are you taking the opportunity to build skills and habits that will help you achieve other goals? Imagine how much more you would get out of school if you saw yourself as a cathedral under construction, developing skills and character traits that will allow you to live a truly happy, rewarding and worthwhile life?

Remember, it's your attitudes not your circumstances that determine how far you will go and how much you will enjoy the journey.

Stories Viewed

From Foundations for a Better Life

- Power of the Dream – Falling off the beam was a real challenge to her! Yet she did very well. This spot also has an extra layer of meaning for those who know ESL (English Sign Language), which the hearing impaired gymnast and her coach are using to speak to each other.

- Rocket – The clip models the importance of mentoring and that it is worth hanging on to your dream.

From Film Clips on Line
- Akeelah and the Bee – A young girl from South Los Angeles tries to make it to the National Spelling Bee where she intentionally miss–spells a word only to have her opponent demand she do her best.

From Wing Clips
- Soul Surfer – Bethany encourages a young boy to venture into the water to surf, and she reflects on how helping people in need change your perspective. Upon arriving in Indonesia after the tragic tsunami swept through the region, Bethany is struck by the suffering of the people.

Growth or Fixed Mindset – A video clip that explains the difference between a person who has a growth mindset and person who has a fixed mindset.
https://www.youtube.com/watch?v=o8JycfeoVzg

Experience it – Using experiential activities to promote learning by self–discovery
GROWTH MINDSET

#80   Building a Better Me

Learning Objective: The importance of developing and maintaining a positive attitude
Instructions:
- Choose one student to come forward.
- Ask the student to hold out his or her arm straight to the side and resist as the teacher tries to push down on it. The challenge is for the student to not let the arm be pushed down.
- Now tell the student to look at the rest of the class and say 10 times in a row, "I am a loser." Have the others give a response as to what they think of the individual (i.e. uncaring words).
- When this is over, ask the student to again hold his or her arm out to the side and to resist as the teacher pushes down. You will find that the arm easily pushes down to the side.
- Now have the student say, "I am a good person" 10 times. The rest of the class says positive things.
- At the end of the 10 times ask the student to once again extend the arm and resist while the teacher pushes down on it.

As a class, complete questions either orally, in a journal or as a small group:
1. I am thankful for my alarm that goes off early each morning because…
2. I am thankful for adults who…
3. I am thankful for friends who…
4. I am thankful for the pile of homework I have each night because…
5. I am thankful for the responsibilities I have at home because…
6. I am thankful for the opportunities I have each day to…
7. I am thankful that I can…
8. I am thankful that my parents have…
9. I am thankful that I know when facing a difficult decision I am able to…
10. I am thankful for the other students in my school who…
11. I am thankful that I live in the community I do because…

Process and Reflection:
What?

- What did you have to do that made you reflect on gratitude?

So What?

- What did you do in this activity to understand the importance of overcoming everyday obstacles or failure?
- How does this approach help overcome what can be perceived as obstacles or failures?

Now What?

- Why does this not mean you are supposed to close your eyes to problems and obstacles in your life?
- How does one go about making good decisions?
- If you were to write the "I am thankful" statements, what would you add?
- Michael Levine says, "A pessimist is someone who complains about the noise when opportunity knocks." What's the difference between a pessimist and an optimist? Which one – a pessimist or an optimist – succeeds more often? Explain your answer.

#81   Affinity Diagrams

Learning Objective: To provide opportunity for students to organize large numbers of data into their natural relationships
Have students or work in small groups. The topic can be:

- Ethical dilemmas
- Strategies to teach students about how to make ethical decisions
- Integration of character education into subject matter curriculum through:
  1. Books
  2. Stories
  3. Media
- Immersion of character education in school with:
  1. Rituals, traditions and celebrations
  2. Classroom rules
  3. Codes and pledges
  4. Recognition
  5. Announcements

Instructions:

- On Post–it notes, have students write down a single thought or idea as a word or phrase that responds to the topic.
- Have the students sort the responses into categories and provide a heading for each category.
- Have them re–sort the responses into different categories.

Process and Reflection:
What?

- What were the various elements of this activity?

So What?

- What could you conclude from reviewing your finished product?

- Is there a process you used as a team to organize the information?
- What can you conclude about continuous learning or making sure we focus on the necessary effort to improve?

Now What?
- What did we just create for our class with this activity?
- How can we use the finished product?
- How did this activity allow for you as a group to reflect upon the opportunities to consciously, deliberately and consistently build character education into all aspects of a classroom and school?

#82   Strengths and Talents

Learning Objective: To understand that talents are like ingredients for baking a cake
Concept: If you saw the ingredients necessary to make a cake and randomly picked baking items, chances are your cake is not going to be very good. Maybe a 1 in 1000 chance that you will hit a near perfect cake your first time. Your talents are the ingredients in your pantry. Look at your ingredients (talents) and do what you can from there to make the best cake (strengths).

Instructions:
- Have students take a sheet of paper and draw a line vertically down the middle.
- Begin by asking students to write their strengths. Give them one minute to do this.
- After they have completed writing their five strengths in the left hand column, ask them to use their opposite hand to write the same strengths on each line in the right hand column. Give them one minute again to do this.

Process and Reflection:
What?
- What did this activity share about strengths and talents?

So What?
- How many of you finished the first list?
- How many of you finished the second list?
- Is one column easier to read than the other?
- What is the point of this exercise? Why did we do this?

Now What?
- Why are you better at writing with the dominant hand?
- What is the difference between strength and a talent?
- Science says that we will never be as good at writing with our non–dominant hand. We can attempt to make this weakness a strength, but the best it would ever be was mediocre. Do you think this statement is true or false? Why?
- What does this say about how we live our lives?

#83   Changing a Mindset[3]

Learning Objective: To help students understand what they can do to change their mindset from fixed to growth

Instructions:

- Divide the class into groups of five.
- Inform the groups that each will conduct a role-play of situations related to a 'Fixed vs. a Growth Mindset.'
- The setting for the role-play will be a School Improvement Committee meeting.
- The individual assignment for the role-play are as follows:
  o Administrator – responsible for stating the problem
  o Alex – as a student who responds as one with a fixed mindset
  o Sophia – as a student who responds with a growth mindset
  o Community member – representing what an employer is looking for in an employee
  o Mr. Dungan – the teacher representative on the committee
- The role-play will involve all five representatives on the School Improvement Committee and utilize the following steps from Carol Dweck:

1. The administrator identifies the issues to be discussed. With the rigor of Common Core and ever-increasing mandates, the administrator wonders what mindset the students have related to what they are able to accomplish in school. Are they focused on being smart or are they willingly putting forth the hard work, engaged in the learning process and being recognized for effort?

   Have students learn to hear their fixed mindset 'voice.' When students approach a challenge, there may be a voice saying, "Are you sure you can do it? Maybe you don't have the talent." "What if you fail – you'll be a failure" "People will laugh at you for thinking you had talent." "If you don't try, you can protect yourself and keep your dignity." Then, when they are confronted with a setback, the voice might say, "This would have been a snap if you really had talent." "It's not too late to back out, make excuses, and try to regain your dignity."

   When facing criticism, they might hear themselves say, "It's not my fault. It was something or someone else's fault." They might feel yourself getting angry at the person who is giving you feedback. "Who do they think they are? I'll put them in their place."

2. The second issue is how to make student understand and recognize that they have a choice. How they interpret challenges, setbacks, and criticism is their choice.

   They can interpret them in a fixed mindset as signs that fixed talents or abilities are lacking. Or, they can interpret them in a growth mindset as signs that what is needed is to ramp up their strategies and effort, stretch themselves, and expand their abilities.

3. Students should talk back to their shortcomings with a growth mindset voice. In approaching a challenge:

   THE FIXED–MINDSET says, "Are you sure you can do it? Maybe you don't have the talent."

   THE GROWTH–MINDSET answers, "I'm not sure I can do it now, but I think I can learn to with time and effort."

   FIXED MINDSET: "What if you fail–you'll be a failure."

   GROWTH MINDSET: "Most successful people had failures along the way."

   FIXED MINDSET: "If you don't try, you can protect yourself and keep your dignity."

   GROWTH MINDSET: "If I don't try, I automatically fail. Where's the dignity in that?"

   When bumping up against a setback:

   FIXED MINDSET: "This would have been a snap if you really had talent."

   GROWTH MINDSET: "That is so wrong. Basketball wasn't easy for Michael Jordan and science

wasn't easy for Thomas Edison. They had a passion and put in tons of effort."
Whenever they face criticism:
FIXED MINDSET: "It's not my fault. It was something or someone else's fault."
GROWTH MINDSET: "If I don't take responsibility, I can't fix it. Let me listen–however painful it is– and learn whatever I can."

4. The community member will interject and identify what role the growth mindset will play in the individuals he hires for his business.
5. The teacher will lead a discussion as to what specific strategies teachers at the school could consider when working with students to instill a growth mindset.

Process and Reflection:

- The role-play concludes by summarizing action that students can take related to the growth mindset.
- Over time, which voice students heed becomes pretty much their choice. This will be evident when students:
  - Take on the challenge wholeheartedly
  - Learn from setbacks and try again
  - Hear the criticism and act on it is now in their hands.

- Discuss specific ways teachers can work with students to instill a growth mindset.

SETTING GOALS

<u>**Touchstone Belief: I will get better results if I set goals and plan out the steps to reach them.**</u>

Supporting beliefs that will bring positive results and opportunity for student success:

- I will be more in control of my life if I set goals that will improve my way of facing problems.
- I will possess effective strategies to establish plans that will meet my goals.
- I need to formulate and follow specific plans to meet my goals.
- I understand that my goals are the road maps that will guide me and show me what is possible for my life.

<u>Explain it – Teach what students need to know</u>

Basil S. Walsh said, "If you don't know where you are going, how can you expect to get there?" An ancient Chinese proverb notes that no wind is favorable if one does not know to which port one is sailing. Goals provide a standard against which students can gauge their progress, and setting goals can have a substantial impact on student self–efficacy and achievement. Setting and measuring goals are probably the most effective classroom modifications teachers can make to increase student confidence. When students achieve short–term goals, they gain an initial sense of self–efficacy for performing well, which is later substantiated as they observe their progress toward long–term goals.

Goals are effective in two ways. First, they provide a student with direction for their effort. Second, they provide a way to measure, and thus draw attention to, previous achievement. Past performance can be a strong indicator of self–efficacy, and helping students set, measure, and record achieved goals draws their attention to their past performance.[4]

It is important for educators to understand that student goal setting should not only be used to set performance targets, but more importantly should be used as a part of the learning process to set learning targets. Student goal setting for learning and self–assessment of that learning are both important steps in the overall classroom assessment process.

Students demonstrate self–management by formulating and prioritizing short–term and long–term goals related to school, career, and personal life. They identify intermediate objectives to help them reach their goals. Students setting their own goals in regards to learning allows them to set learning targets and then develop strategies to reach those goals. The self–assessment process allows students to monitor and evaluate their performance during a lesson or unit of instruction. Research has shown that using goal setting and self–assessment not only increases student performance but also increases a student's responsibility for their own learning and critical thinking skills.

<u>Explore it – What we can learn from others</u>

1. A goal is a dream with a deadline. – Napoleon Hill
2. Goals are the fuel in the furnace of achievement. – Brian Tracy
3. The significance of a man is not in what he attains but in what he longs to attain. – Kahlil Gibran
4. If you don't know where you are going, you'll end up someplace else. – Yogi Berra
5. Aim at the sun, and you may not reach it; but your arrow will fly far higher than if aimed at an object on a level with yourself. – J. Howes
6. A good archer is known not by his arrows but by his aim. – Thomas Fuller
7. The future belongs to those who believe in the beauty of their dreams. – Eleanor Roosevelt

8. The people who get on in this world are the people who get up and look for the circumstances they want and if they can't find them, make them. – George Bernard Shaw
9. I have learned, that if one advances confidently in the direction of his dreams, and endeavors to live the life he has imagined, he will meet with a success unexpected in common hours. – Henry Thoreau
10. Your goals are the road maps that guide you and show you what is possible for your life. – Les Brown
11. If you're bored with life – you don't get up every morning with a burning desire to do things – you don't have enough goals. – Lou Holtz
12. Living without an aim is like sailing without a compass. – Dumas
13. When it is obvious that the goals cannot be reached, don't adjust the goals, adjust the action steps. – Confucius
14. You can achieve anything you want in life if you have the courage to dream it, the intelligence to make a realistic plan, and the will to see that plan through to the end. – Sidney A. Friedman
15. There is always a step small enough from where we are to get us to where we want to be. If we take that small step, there's always another we can take, and eventually a goal thought to be too far to reach becomes achievable. – Ellen Langer

Engage it – How beliefs and content can be taught at the same time

- Illustrate how students can set goals for large assignments and tasks by breaking them into small steps, and also show them how to make a plan.
- Point out the organizational and time–management strategies you utilize in the classroom.
- Incorporate organizational skills into research–based or multi–part assignments, such as lab experiments and history projects.
- Consider conducting student–led conferences in which students present their learning to their teacher and parents, as an opportunity for students to reflect on the learning that has taken place over a period of time and the goals they have for the rest of the term.
- Have students create a portfolio that will be used to help them reflect on what they have learned and help them to state clear goals for future learning, based on the areas where they need to make more progress.
- Create a graphic organizer for students, as it organizes facts, concepts, ideas, or terms in a visual or diagrammatic way, making the relationship between the individual items clearer.
- Have students assume responsibility for the setting of their learning targets and also for the monitoring or tracking of those targets.
- Use the S.M.A.R.T. acronym as a way of guiding students in the design of a learning target. In this acronym: S = Specific, M = Measurable, A = Achievable or Attainable, R = Relevant, and T = Time–bound. The S.M.A.R.T. method of setting learning targets:
  o *Specific* – The learning target must be specific rather than general.
  o *Measurable* – There must be some way of measuring whether the learning target has been accomplished.
  o *Achievable* – The achievement of the learning target must be something the student is capable of attaining.
  o *Relevant* – The learning target needs to be significant and relevant to the student's present learning. If students are left to set learning targets without any guidance, there is the danger that their targets will be less relevant than if they are set in the context of understanding.
  o *Time–bound* – Students should specify by when they aim to achieve the target.

- Delineate what is called for in student homework assignments, and also in the resources (time, study materials, research databases, etc.) that will be needed to complete them.
- Teach note organization by suggesting ways to summarize lecture content and fill in gaps in notes.
- Work with your students to set three goals each week.
- Help students set improvement (rather than benchmark) goals. For example, a student may decide to increase the number of homework assignments they complete, as opposed to completing twelve (or any other set number of) homework assignments. The first goal promotes achievement while improving performance.

Enhance it – Learning from stories read, told or viewed
Stories Told

Story 1 – Pursuit of Excellence by Michael Jordan[5]

I approach everything step by step. I had always set short–term goals. As I look back, each one of the steps or successes led to the next one. When I got cut from the varsity team as a sophomore in high school, I learned something. I knew I never wanted to feel that bad again. So I set a goal of becoming a starter on the varsity. That's what I focused on all summer. When I worked on my game, that's what I thought about. When it happened, I set another goal, a reasonable, manageable goal that I could realistically achieve if I worked hard enough. I guess I approached it with the end in mind. I knew exactly where I wanted to go, and I focused on getting there. As I reached those goals, they built on one another. I gained a little confidence every time I came through. If your goal is to become a doctor and you're getting Cs in biology then the first thing you have to do is get Bs in biology and then As. You have to perfect the first step and then move on to chemistry or physics.

Take those small steps. Otherwise you're opening yourself up to all kinds of frustration. Where would your confidence come from if the only measure of success was becoming a doctor? If you tried as hard as you could and didn't become a doctor, would that mean your whole life was a failure? Of course not.

All those steps are like pieces of a puzzle. They all come together to form a picture. Not everyone is going to be the greatest. But you can still be considered a success. Step by step, I can't see any other way of accomplishing anything.

Story 2 – Tell Me the Secret of Success

A young man asked Socrates the secret to success. Socrates told the young man to meet him near the river the next morning. They met. Socrates asked the young man to walk with him toward the river. When the water got up to their neck, Socrates took the young man by surprise and ducked him into the water. The boy struggled to get out but Socrates was strong and kept him there until the boy started turning blue.

Socrates pulled his head out of the water and the first thing the young man did was to gasp and take a deep breath of air. Socrates asked: "What did you want the most when you were there?" The boy replied: 'Air.' Socrates said: "That is the secret to success. When you want success as badly as you wanted the air, then you will get it. There is no other secret."

The motivation to succeed comes from the burning desire to achieve a purpose. Napoleon Hill wrote: "Whenever the mind of man can conceive and believe, the mind can achieve." A burning desire is the starting point of all accomplishment. Just like a small fire cannot give much heat, a weak desire cannot produce great results.

Story 3 – Take Control of My Life

High on a hilltop overlooking the beautiful city of Venice, Italy, there lived an old man who was a genius. Legend had it he could answer any question anyone might ask of him. Two of the local boys figured they could fool the old man, so they caught a small bird and headed for his residence.

One of the boys held the little bird in his hands and asked the old man if the bird was dead or alive. Without hesitation the old man said, " Son, if I say to you that the bird is alive, you will close your hands and crush him to death. If I say the bird is dead, you will open your hands and he will fly away. You see, son, in your hands you hold the power of life and death."

In your hands you hold the seeds of failure or the potential for greatness. Your hands are capable but they must be used – and for the right things – to reap the rewards you are capable of attaining.

Stories Viewed
From Foundations for a Better Life
- Imagine – Every good thing that has ever been achieved began with an idea – a dream that something better is actually possible. Our society depends upon ordinary people to think the extraordinary – someone to simply ask, even in the face of criticism, why not?

From Film Clips on Line
- Coach Carter – A controversial high school basketball coach benches his undefeated team because of their poor academics.

From Wing Clips
- Unlimited – What Are Your Goals? When Simon finds himself stranded on Harold's orphanage, Harold asks him what his main three goals are in life.
- The Mighty Macs – Before the championship game, Cathy gives an inspired speech to her team about believing in themselves that they will win.

Experience it – Using experiential activities to promote learning by self–discovery
SETTING GOALS

#84   Take What You Need

Learning Objective: To help students see the importance in setting goals
Materials: Roll of toilet paper
Instructions:
- Gather students into a circle either on the floor, in chairs or by arranging their desks.
- Don't say anything, just take out a roll of toilet paper, tear off a length with about 10 squares, hand the roll of toilet paper to the student sitting next to you, and just say, "Take what you need."
- Let each student take as much or as little as they want, then pass it to the next student.
- When everyone has had a turn, tell them that for each square of toilet paper they have taken, they will now share specific goals that they have for the class this school year or future plans.
- Demonstrate the type of information you'd like them to share by modeling – you go first.

Process and Reflection:
What?
- What was the purpose of this activity?

So What?
- What did you think this activity would be about?
- What did you learn about your classmates?
- Was it hard for anyone to come up with enough information particularly if you took a bunch of squares? What made this activity a challenge for you?

Now What?

- What does this activity have to do with what you hope to accomplish this school year?
- Why is it important for the students in our class to set goals?
- What would be the benefits associated with having goals?
- Explain the process you will use to help meet the goals you have set. What do you think makes this process effective?

#85   Goal Setting

Learning Objective: To encourage students to reflect upon character traits and to focus on striving for improvement

Materials: Sentence strips; worksheet

Instructions:

- In groups of three, have students define a specific character trait.
- Have each group write their definition on a sentence strip.
- Display the sentence strips on the classroom wall or bulletin board.
- Refer to the definitions periodically as part of an academic lesson. Students can also be asked for examples of the behavior they have noticed in their own lives (personal, in classes, in their studies) or in the world: TV, politics, social media, movies).
- Have students complete the worksheet and keep it as an assessment of progress on the goal.

Process and Reflection:

What?

- What were you asked to do related to goals?

So What?

- What is the benefit of setting goals?
- How can we establish goals related to values, non–cognitive skills or character traits?
- Did you find this activity a challenge? If so, what made it challenging for you as a student?
- Can you identify all of the ways you can measure results?

Now What?

- By completing this activity, what can be direct benefits for you as a student?
- If you have done this on a regular basis in our class, what have you noticed over time?
- The cynic may say that it makes no sense to try and work on changing one's behavior because all that counts in our school is academics. Agree or disagree? Explain your position.
- How could this activity be helpful for all students in our school?

Worksheet:

The character trait I would like to work on developing is: _____

The specific actions I will take are:

_____

_____

_____

_____

The results of my actions will be:

_____

_____

_____

➤ In what specific ways will this result in a change in my attitude and/or behavior?

➤ Think about a specific time when the value or character trait was important and write a few sentences about it.

➤ When was that time? Why was it important to you then?

➤ Read the three phrases:
  This value has influenced my life.
  In general, I try to live up to this value.
  This value is an important part of who I am.

  Write one of five ratings next to each one –Very Strongly Agree, Strongly Agree, Agree, Strongly Disagree, or Very Strongly Disagree

➤ How can I measure the results?

#86   Life Highlights Game

Learning Objective: To understand what is important in one's life and what it takes to make dreams a reality

Instructions:

- Begin by asking students to close their eyes for one minute and consider the best moments of their lives. This can include moments they've had alone or those they've shared with family or friends. These moments can pertain to success in the classroom or an extra-curricular activity, community involvement, personal revelations, or exciting life adventures.
- After the students have had a moment to run through highlights of their lives, inform them that their search for highlights is about to be narrowed.
- Keeping their eyes closed, ask students to take a moment to decide what 60 seconds of their life they would want to relive if they were given the opportunity.
- Pair students and have them share what it they chose as highlights and explain why they chose what they did.
- Have pairs identify what they can do now to create additional life changing experiences.
- To conclude the activity, have each pair identify the key elements of what it was that they believe has been significant in their life.

Process and Reflection:
What?

- What has been determined to be significant in the lives of students?

So What?

- How hard was it to decide on the significant moments in your life?
- Should we do this kind of activity when we are still young? Explain.
- What is the benefit of thinking about the best moments in one's life?

Now What?

- Why do you think this activity can be a challenge for students?
- What can you learn from what you shared as to your defining moments in your life?
- Identify specific things you learned about the experiences of others in your class.
- What can you do to create additional life changing experiences?
- What does this activity have to do with setting goals?
- How did character or being a good person and making wise choices play a role in what you decided to be important and potentially life changing?
- What would you like to be remembered for after you leave our school?

CRITICAL THINKING

Touchstone Belief: It is important to understand and evaluate the information I am given.

Supporting beliefs that will bring positive results and opportunity for student success:

- I can use what I know to figure out problems and explain situations.
- My experiences and my assumptions can affect how I understand information and see the world.
- I can use what I've learned to think of new ideas and ways of looking at things.
- My understanding and interpretation of information should be based on reliable facts and solid information.

Explain it – Teach what students need to know

Critical thinking skills are skills that students need to learn to be able to solve problems. This includes analyzing and evaluating information that is provided, whether that information is through observation, experience, or communication. The core of critical thinking is being responsive to information, and not just accepting it. The most important part of critical thinking is questioning information. It is a part of scientific, mathematical, historical, economic, and philosophical thinking, all of which are necessary for any future success in the 21st century workplace.

Being able to master the necessary critical thinking and problem–solving skills is vital for student success in the classroom, higher education, and workplace. Learning how to be a critical thinker leads students to develop other skills, such as a higher level of concentration, deeper analytical abilities, and improved thought processing.

Students demonstrate progressively complex cognitive abilities to become knowledgeable, logical, critical, and creative thinkers, especially in the areas of reading, writing, speaking, and listening. We want students to demonstrate the ability to acquire, recall, and retain basic and complex forms of information. This can be accomplished if we see evidence of students demonstrating the ability to understand the meaning and significance of facts, assertions, ideas, concepts, and theories acquired by listening, through experiential learning, or by reading expository or literary writings.

We as teachers can strive for our students to be able to apply their knowledge in new situations and in useful ways. Regarding academic content, it is important to provide opportunities for students to demonstrate creative thinking, innovativeness, and an openness to challenge assumptions and preconceptions. This can be achieved by reclassifying, recategorizing, reorganizing, or rearranging information. Students can then develop the necessary skill sets to combine, integrate, and reconcile divergent theories and approaches, or they can consider supplementing existing theories and explanations with new perspectives or approaches. Within the context of the academic curriculum, strive to get students to demonstrate perceptiveness, keen observation skills, and discernment while reading, listening, and watching resources.

Explore it – What we can learn from others

1. It is the mark of an educated mind to be able to entertain a thought without accepting it. – Aristotle
2. It is the supreme art of the teacher to awaken joy in creative expression and knowledge. – Albert Einstein
3. An education isn't how much you have committed to memory, or even how much you know. It's being able to differentiate between what you do know and what you don't. – Anatole France

4. Too often we give children answers to remember rather than problems to solve. – Roger Lewin
5. The eye sees only what the mind is prepared to comprehend. – Henri Bergson
6. The direction in which education starts a man will determine his future life. – Plato
7. Out of the questions of students come most of the creative ideas and discoveries. – Ellen Langer
8. Invest a few moments in thinking. It will pay good interest. – Author unknown
9. He who asks a question is a fool for five minutes; he who does not ask a question remains a fool forever. – Chinese proverb
10. Knowing a great deal is not the same as being smart; intelligence is not information alone but also judgment, the manner in which information is collected and used. – Carl Sagan
11. Time given to thought is the greatest time saver of all. – Norman Cousins
12. No way of thinking or doing, however ancient, can be trusted without proof. – Henry David Thoreau
13. A great many people think they are thinking when they are merely rearranging their prejudices. – William James
14. Did you ever stop to think, and forget to start again? – Winnie the Pooh
15. It is well for people who think, to change their minds occasionally in order to keep them clean. – Luther Burbank

Engage it – How beliefs and content can be taught at the same time

- Assign articles for students to read on a selected topic from different points of view.
- When a student asks the question "Why?" respond with "Why do you think?" to encourage the student to draw his or her own conclusions.
- Compare and contrast items and topics, which allows for students to tell the ways things are similar and different and helps them analyze and categorize information.
- Comparing and contrasting stories is another way to encourage critical thinking.
- Students can analyze characters, settings, plot and other story elements when they list the way stories are the same and different.
- Provide opportunity for students to restate, paraphrase, explain, and summarize facts, definitions, methods, rules, theories, and concepts.
- Understand the literal meaning and the implications of information conveyed in all forms of nonfiction writings (e.g., textbooks, diagrams, graphs, instruction manuals).
- Illustrate or simplify information with pictures, diagrams, charts, and graphs.
- Provide exercises and projects that let students interpret and apply information.
- Compare various resources on the same topic: online encyclopedia vs. news article vs. blog.
- Analyze claims in advertisements targeted at the students' age group and compare with researched information and statistics.
- Challenge, question, and test the accuracy and validity of recommendations, claims, and assertions by identifying a) internal inconsistencies, b) logical flaws, c) unproven or unstated assumptions, d) the existence of contradictory evidence and opinions, e) factors that bear on the objectivity and reliability of the sources of information (e.g., credentials, prejudice, bias, attitudes, motivations, and conflicts of interest).
- Evaluate the relevance and weight assigned to specific evidence or arguments by: a) distinguishing between facts, opinions, speculations, and feelings and b) considering the expertise, personal knowledge, character, and credibility of the source.
- Use case studies and projects that require proposing ideas and formulating plans.

- Explain and illustrate how our beliefs and ideas about things can change as we are exposed to new ideas and experiences, starting with minor things (favorite foods or music) to major things (political values).
- Read and discuss biographies of accomplished individuals. Encourage students to be discerning, seeing that an individual may have flaws but still be capable of much admirable action.
- Have students relate the story to their own lives or outside events. This is the beginning important critical thinking skill called synthesizing, where children begin to use the information in new ways and apply it to different ideas.
- Telling a story without an ending and asking students to finish the story is another way by taking the information they know and creatively compile it, draw conclusions and come up with their own ending.

Enhance it – Learning from stories read, told or viewed
Stories Told

Story 1 – The Boulder That Couldn't Be Moved
When St. Petersburg, one of the most splendid and harmonious cities in Europe, was being laid out early in the eighteenth century, many large boulders brought by a glacier from Finland had to be removed. One particularly large rock was in the path of one of the principal avenues that had been planned, and bids were solicited for its removal. The bids submitted were very high. This was understandable, because at that time modern equipment did not exist and there were no high–powered explosives. As officials pondered what to do, a peasant presented himself and offered to get rid of the boulder for a much lower price than those submitted by other bidders. Since they had nothing to lose, officials gave the job to the peasant.

The next morning he showed up with a crowd of other peasants carrying shovels. They began digging a huge hole next to the rock. The rock was propped up with timbers to prevent it from rolling into the hole. When the hole was deep enough, the timber props were removed and the rock dropped into the hole below the street level. It was then covered with dirt, and the excess dirt was carted away.

It's an early example of what creative thinking can do to solve a problem. The unsuccessful bidders only thought about moving the rock from one place to another on the city's surface. The peasant looked at the problem from another angle. He considered another dimension – up and down. He couldn't lift it up, so he put it underground.

Story 2 – The Woodcutter's Story
Once upon a time, a very strong woodcutter asked for a job in a timber merchant and he got it. The pay was really good and so was the work condition. For those reasons, the woodcutter was determined to do his best. His boss gave him an axe and showed him the area where he supposed to work.

The first day, the woodcutter brought 18 trees. "Congratulations," the boss said. "Go on your way!"

Very motivated by the words of his boss, the woodcutter tried harder the next day, but he could only bring 15 trees. The third day he tried even harder, but he could only bring 10 trees. Day after day he was bringing less and less trees.

"I must be losing my strength." the woodcutter thought. He went to the boss and apologized, saying that he could not understand what was going on.

"When was the last time you sharpened your axe?" the boss asked. "Sharpen? I had no time to sharpen my axe. I have been very busy trying to cut trees."

Story 3 – Test Of Three

In ancient Greece (469–399 BC), Socrates was widely lauded for his wisdom. One day the great philosopher came upon an acquaintance who ran up to him excitedly and said, "Socrates, do you know what I just heard about one of your students?"

"Wait a moment," Socrates replied. "Before you tell me I'd like you to pass a little test. It's called the Test of Three."

"Test of Three?"

"That's right," Socrates continued. "Before you talk to me about my student let's take a moment to test what you're going to say. The first test is Truth. Have you made absolutely sure that what you are about to tell me is true?"

No," the man said, "actually I just heard about It."

"All right," said Socrates. "So you don't really know if it's true or not. Now let's try the second test, the test of Goodness. Is what you are about to tell me about my student something good?"

"No, on the contrary…"

"So," Socrates continued, "you want to tell me something bad about him even though you're not certain it's true?"

The man shrugged, a little embarrassed.

Socrates continued. "You may still pass though, because there is a third test – the filter of Usefulness. Is what you want to tell me about my student going to be useful to me?"

"No, not really."

"Well," concluded Socrates, "if what you want to tell me is neither True nor Good nor even Useful, why tell it to me at all?"

Stories Viewed

From Film Clips on Line

- Dead Poets Society – A teacher challenges his pupils to celebrate their unique qualities and think for themselves.

From Motivational Media – Character in the Movies

- The Hobbit 2 – The dwarves have learned that Bard the Bowman is a direct descendant of Dale's ruler, Girion. Thorin now stands before them and the townspeople and makes the argument that everyone can get back their stolen riches. The clip shows the importance of people being careful and making good decisions before it's too late.

How to Think Critically https://www.youtube.com/watch?v=LmgmgrwpIP4
Above and Beyond https://www.youtube.com/watch?v=7KMM387HNQk

Experience it – Using experiential activities to promote learning by self–discovery
CRITICAL THINKING

#87   Significant Insight

Learning Objective: To reflect on a discussion of character or specific values that requires students to identify a most significant insight

Materials: One sentence strip (or index card); marker for each student

Instructions:

- Distribute to each student a sentence strip (or index card).
- Instruct students to reflect on what they learned yesterday, and to write down on the strip or card one of their 'a–ha!' moment – when they had an epiphany or realization what was new and significant to them.

- Go around the room and have students share their significant insights. An alternative is to have the first group of eight read their sentence strip; a second group will sing their insight; the third group will sing and dance what they wrote.
- Once everyone has read their insight, collect them and hang them somewhere in the room.
- If you opt for using the index card, have students share their insights with a partner.

Process and Reflection:
What?
- What did each of us have to do?

So What?
- What were common themes you heard?
- How would you categorize the various insights that were shared?
- Which of the insights seem to be based on knowledge gained while other may be associated with an emotional response?

Now What?
- What do you think we should do with the insights you wrote?
- Take out a sheet of paper and respond, "I learned that…"
- How could these insights be used by each of us in reflecting upon character and its impact on our class?

#88   Group Drawing

Learning Objective: To debrief content for teamwork, individual differences, diversity, problem solving or planning
Materials: Drawings of shapes; a large chalkboard or flip chart
Instructions:
- Divide the class into small groups of three and assign a role to each person in the group.
  - **Drawers.** The drawers attempt to recreate one of the predrawn designs, which they cannot see. They can only draw and listen. They may not talk and they stand with their backs to the group so they cannot receive nonverbal messages.
  - **Talkers.** The talkers attempt to describe the design to the drawers. The talkers also do not see the design.
  - **Viewers.** The viewers are the only ones to see the design. They may not talk and must communicate nonverbally. The talkers may question the viewers who must respond nonverbally. The viewers may not draw the design in the air or use any other nonverbal communication, which actually shows the design.
- The initiative is complete when the viewers are satisfied with what the drawers have created.

Process and Reflection:
What?
- What did you do?

So What?
- Why were there different roles?
- What role had the most responsibility for the success of this project?
- What were the challenges you faced as a group?
- What steps did you use to complete the assignment?

Now What?

- Do we have different roles and levels of responsibility within our class? Our school?
- Which role is the most important?
- When confronted with a challenge, what process do we use to complete the project?
- How do we measure success?

#89   The Marshmallow and Toothpick Tower[6]

Learning Objective: To build a tower using only marshmallows and toothpicks that helps to teach communication and critical thinking skills

Materials: Half a bag of mini marshmallows per group; 25 wooden toothpicks

Instructions:

- Each team will be given the marshmallows and toothpicks to build the tallest tower.
- The tower must be able to stand on its own without any helping hands or another object (freestanding). This means no holding the tower or leaning it against another object.
- Recommended time limit of 10 minutes
- Here's a helpful hint. Print out some pictures of famous buildings or towers from around the world to help get students thinking about different structural designs.
- After the towers are built, measure all the towers to determine the tallest.

Extension:

Test how much weight the structure can hold by placing a few pennies in a margarine tub lid and setting it on top of the tower. Add pennies one by one and see how many it takes to bust the tower.

Alternatives:

- Draw a 5" x 5" square on a piece of paper and hand out to the students or teams. They should build the tower in this square and the base cannot go outside this square.
- Students have 10 minutes to construct the tower. When only two minutes are left for construction, have the students use two large marshmallows. They must use them both somewhere in their tower.
- Assign a dollar value to the toothpicks and marshmallows. Make the activity more like a project with a budget and the students can 'buy' more materials if needed, they get an 'incentive' (extra money) if they finish ahead of schedule.

Process and Reflection:
What?

- What were you required to do with the marshmallows and toothpicks?

So What?

- What did your group do before beginning to build the tower?
- What were some of the ideas your group considered on how to build the tallest tower?
- How did your group decide what you were going to do?
- What shapes did your group use that made for a good design for a tower.
- How would you compare the use of triangles and squares to see which is the strongest?

Now What?

- How did communication play a role in this activity?
- What do you think this activity had to do with enhancing critical thinking skills?

- As a student, how do you analyze and evaluate information that is provided, whether that information is through observation, experience or communication?

#90   Using Both Fact and Opinion

Learning Objective: To distinguish a fact (something that is true or can be proven) from an opinion (feelings or how someone else feels about a topic)

Instructions:
Write one fact and one opinion for each topic.

> Example: Elephants
> Fact: African elephants have bigger ears than Asian elephants.
> Opinion: Elephants are fun to watch at the zoo.

Sample topics to consider:
1. Friendship
   Fact: _____
   Opinion: _____
2. Having a job
   Fact: _____
   Opinion: _____
3. Money
   Fact: _____
   Opinion: _____
4. Healthy lifestyle
   Fact: _____
   Opinion: _____
5. Bullying
   Fact: _____
   Opinion: _____

Process and Reflection:
What?
- What is the difference between a fact and an opinion?

So What?
- Share what process you used to determine fact from opinion.
- If you were a newspaper reporter what would you need to use in a story: opinion or fact? Explain.
- What is going to be more credible when communicating with others? Why?

Now What?
- How can a student distinguish fact from opinion when discussing academic content, reading a story or a non–fiction account?
- What are specific examples of comments that students make that you would consider opinions?
- What should be your response when others only share what they think by using opinions vs. facts?

#91   Penny Pondering

Learning Objective: To know how to figure out problems and explain situations
Materials: Prepared question sheet; a penny for each student

Instructions:

- Hand each student the prepared question sheet and a penny
- Pair students to complete the questions

Question Sheet: On a Lincoln head penny:

Locate the following:		
1. A serving of corn	8. Part of a stream as it enters a river	15. One's boyfriend (or wooden part of railroad tracks)
2. A fruit	9. A messenger is…	16. The side of a road
3. A type of flower	10. A sacred place	17 An odor
4. A cold or hot beverage	11. A policeman	18. A visitor
5. A large body of salt water	12. A grain	19. A country
6. An animal	13. Freedom	20. An implement of war
7. Part of a needle (or myself)	14. Married	21. One who is worshiped

Answers:

1. Ear
5. 'C' or sea
9. One cent/one sent
13. Liberty
17. Scent (Cent)
21. God

2. Date
6. Hair (hare)
10. Temple
14. United
18. Caller (Collar)

3. Two lips
7. Eye
11. Copper
15. Bow (or Tie)
19. America

4. 'T' or tea
8. Mouth
12. Wheat
16. Shoulder
20. Arms

Process and Reflection:

What?

- What was the purpose of this activity?

So What?

- What did you learn about what can be found on a penny?
- How did you analyze information to make a decision?

Now What?

- Review the life of Abraham Lincoln and see where character played a significant role. A few resources that can be used by students include:
  - Lincoln's Legacy of Character – *Washington Times* http://communities.washingtontimes.com/neighborhood/truth–be–told/2010/feb/12/abe–lincolns–legacy–character/
  - The Lincoln Institute – http://www.abrahamlincolnsclassroom.org
  - The Abraham Lincoln Presidential Library and Museum – https://www.illinois.gov/alplm/Pages/default.aspx

DECISION–MAKING

Touchstone Belief: I realize that my behavior and the choices I make affects others.

Supporting beliefs that will bring positive results and opportunity for student success:

- I can make the best decisions if I consider all the options carefully and thoughtfully.
- Learning how to make a variety of choices will enhance the outcomes of my actions.
- When confronted with an ethical dilemma, I am able to make a decision that ensures my actions are rational, ethical, and effective.
- Decisions that have the potential of monumental consequences are determined on what will produce the best possible result.

Explain it – Teach what students need to know

The ability to make good decisions is crucial in order for a student to be successful. Fortunately, decision–making skills can be taught. The goal for teachers is to have students demonstrate the ability to make effective decisions that efficiently use the least amount of time and resources to accomplish the desired result, without causing unintended and undesirable consequences.

There are key concepts and definitive truths related to choices:

1. Every person affected by a decision is a stakeholder, because he/she has a 'stake' in that decision and a moral claim on the decision–maker to make the decision wisely and ethically.
2. Students have the power to choose what they say, do, and think. As a result, all of their words, actions, and attitudes reflect choices.
3. Even when students don't like the alternatives, they still have a choice.
4. Choosing not to choose is a choice. If one chooses not to act, this is still a choice.
5. Although students don't always have the power to do what they want to do, they always have the power to do what they can.
6. Students need to accept that they are morally responsible for the consequences of their choices – even those made subconsciously.
7. Good choices lead to personal success and greater happiness. Bad choices lead to rocky student opportunities, poor career experiences, and unhappy lives.

As teachers, we need to be direct in teaching students that there are two main components of a good decision. 'Right' or 'good' decisions are:

- Effective – The practical aspect of a decision focuses on its ability to efficiently accomplish intended and desirable objectives. An effective decision can be described as correct, successful, or wise. We say a decision is effective if it accomplishes an intended goal without causing unintended negative consequences.
- Ethical – The moral aspect of a decision focuses on issues of legality and ethical propriety. An ethical decision complies with the law and honors ethical values. Decisions that accomplish goals at the cost of ethical principles are not acceptable.

Students must grasp the concept that most problems can be solved and nearly all situations can be addressed in a variety of ways that are effective and ethical. In teaching students how to make effective and ethical decisions, we must focus on the fact that every decision has consequences; the greater the potential consequences, the higher the stakes. When the stakes are high, there is a need for more careful decision–making. The decision–maker takes responsibility for evaluating these options and choosing the one most likely to produce the best possible result, an outcome that honors ethical principles, preserves trust, produces the most good, and minimizes harm. The choice needs to be evaluated in terms of core ethical principles and the elimination of any option that is illegal or unethical.

Finally, students must demonstrate the ability to discern the ethical implications of their choices by systematically considering core ethical principles and the discipline to do what they think is right even when it is difficult, risky, or personally costly. In so doing, students need to be cognizant and aware of the principle that they are morally and legally accountable for the consequences of their decisions. Students must understand that in dilemmas where ethical principles compete (e.g., honesty versus kindness, loyalty versus fairness), they should choose the option most likely to produce the greatest good for the greatest number (i.e., the best possible result).

Explore it – What we can learn from others

1. Once you make a decision, the universe conspires to make it happen. – Ralph Waldo Emerson
2. Nothing is more difficult, and therefore more precious, than to be able to decide. – Napoleon Bonaparte
3. When you have to make a choice and don't make it, that is in itself a choice. – William James
4. It's not hard to make decisions when you know what your values are. – Roy Disney
5. Choices are the hinges of destiny. – Attributed to both Edwin Markham and Pythagoras
6. Some persons are very decisive when it comes to avoiding decisions. – Brendan Francis
7. When one bases his life on principle, 99 percent of his decisions are already made. – Author unknown
8. Life is the sum of all your choices. – Albert Camus
9. Indecision becomes decision with time. – Author unknown
10. The doors we open and close each day decide the lives we live. – Flora Whittemore
11. To decide is to walk facing forward with nary a crick in your neck from looking back at the crossroads. – Betsy Cañas Garmon
12. Where there is no decision there is no life. – JJ Dewey
13. Greatness is not a function of circumstance. Greatness, it turns out, is largely a matter of conscious choice, and discipline. – Jim Collins
14. Decision is a sharp knife that cuts clean and straight; indecision, a dull one that hacks and tears and leaves ragged edges behind it. – Gordon Graham
15. One's philosophy is not the best expressed in words; it is expressed in the choices one makes. In the long run, we shape our lives and we shape ourselves. The process never ends until we die. And, the choices we make are ultimately our own responsibility. – Eleanor Roosevelt

Engage it – How we can teach beliefs and content at the same time

- Provide examples so students can understand the difference between a rationalization and a rational decision.
- Provide scenarios that allow students to determine a course of action that is based on rational decision–making.
- While discussing a fictional story, nonfiction writing, or historical document, ask if an effective decision was made. Ensure that students can grasp alternative choices along with potential consequences.
- Provide opportunities to discuss the fact that one's behavior or action taken is a result of a choice that was made.
- Use literary works or historical documents to discuss if the choices made were rational or rationalizations.

- Explain and illustrate how different decisions can lead to alternative outcomes.
- Review the actions of celebrities who are notorious in the press for behaving badly, and have students create best possible result mind maps for how things could have turned out.
- Demonstrate to students how to gather and analyze information.
- Provide students with a variety of media presentations of the same story and analyze how the reporting is different depending on the media outlet.
- Ensure that students understand that responsible decision–making affects interpersonal and group relationships.
- Have students use the newspaper to write their own moral dilemmas.
- Use case studies in media and literature to illustrate how our choices impact others.
- Share stories of ethical conflict from literature or current subjects in the news or movies/TV shows.
- Provide student–based scenarios in which the decisions that are made will produce the best possible result.
- Have students interview someone they think displays ethical actions.

Enhance it – Learning from stories read, told or viewed
Stories Told

Story 1 – A Moment of Indecision

Former president Ronald Reagan once had an aunt who took him to a cobbler for a pair of new shoes. The cobbler asked young Reagan, "Do you want square toes or round toes?" Unable to decide, Reagan didn't answer, so the cobbler gave him a few days. Several days later the cobbler saw Reagan on the street and asked him again what kind of toes he wanted on his shoes. Reagan still couldn't decide, so the shoemaker replied, "Well, come by in a couple of days. Your shoes will be ready." When the future president did so, he found one square–toed and one round–toed shoe! "This will teach you to never let people make decisions for you," the cobbler said to his indecisive customer. "I learned right then and there," Reagan said later, "if you don't make your own decisions, someone else will."

Story 2 – Making Good Decisions

"Sir, What is the secret of your success?" a reporter asked a bank president.

"Two words."

"And, sir, what are they?"

"Good decisions."

"And how do you make good decisions?"

"One word."

"And sir, what is that?"

"Experience."

"And how do you get Experience?"

"Two words."

"And, sir, what are they?"

"Bad decisions."

Story 3 – The Summer Job Conundrum by Michael Josephson[7]

Julia, an 11th grader was thrilled when she got an A+ on an assignment to design an advertising brochure in an art class. And when her teacher, Mr. Roberts, told her she should consider a career in advertising Julia realized that was exactly what she'd like to do.

186

A few days later, Mr. Roberts told Julia he talked with Max, a former student, who was now the chief creative director for a prestigious advertising firm. "The firm doesn't hire high school students," he said, "but I persuaded Max to give you a summer job. It only pays minimum wage, but you'll get great experience. Do you want it?"

Julia was excited: "Absolutely, I'm honored you recommended me." Julia's parents were so proud they told all their friends.

When Julia reported to work, Max was very nice but didn't seem to know what to do with her. He had her run errands most of the time, but she occasionally was allowed to sit in creative meetings. Julia thought she was going to get some hands–on mentoring and she was very disappointed.

After two weeks on the job, a friend told Julia the summer camp she was working at needed a new counselor immediately since one of the girls quit without notice. Her friend said, "It's really fun. There are tons of cute guy counselors. And it pays twice what you're getting at the advertising agency." Julia really wanted to take the job.

What do you think? Should she take it? What are the possible consequences if she decides to stay or leave?

The fact is, it would be a terrible mistake with long–term consequences if Julia quit. Mr. Roberts went out on a limb for her and he's not likely to do so again if she lets him down. She would also create a very bad impression with Max, a person who could be enormously helpful to her later in life.

It's easy to come up with rationalizations to justify breaking a commitment, but people of character keep their word even when it turns out to be costly or inconvenient.

Julia should understand that doing this job exceptionally well, proving her integrity as well as her gratitude for the opportunity, would make Mr. Roberts proud that he recommended her and Max glad that he hired her – and this is worth much more than a fun summer and a little more money.

Treat every job as if it's an audition for the next job. Do more than you have to do. Approach even routine tasks as an opportunity to shine. And, above all, keep your word.

Stories Viewed
From Foundations for a Better Life

- Truck Stop – "With so much riding on the choice at hand, the spirit of a boy, or the wisdom of a man."
- Umpire – Because every choice that you made is born somewhere in between who you are today and who you'd like to be. And no matter that decision there will be one more coming through – the easy way out or the right thing to do.

From Wing Clips

- King's Faith – Brendan asks his foster parent, Mike, if he should bring his friends back to the neighborhood where all his troubles started.
- Admission – The Princeton board of admission starts the stringent process of choosing their next class of students.
- Groundhog Day – Phil decides to take advantage of his conundrum by living recklessly and disobeying the law.

Experience it – Using experiential activities to promote learning by self–discovery
DECISION MAKING

#92   Ethical Decision–Making

Learning Objective: To provide understanding of priorities, questioning, ranking and what constitutes a good decision

Instructions:

- Choose a decision–making scenario to analyze and have students apply a decision–making model to the scenario. Ask students to:
  - State the nature of the problem or dilemma
  - List possible alternatives
  - Discuss the positive and negative consequences of each alternative and rank the alternatives.
- Have each student write a scenario in which a student is faced with a situation requiring a decision. Ask each student to:
  - Use the decision–making model to determine alternatives and the consequences or outcomes of each.
  - Choose the alternative that he or she thinks best and give reasons for selecting it.
- Have students present their scenario, alternatives, and decision (with reasons) to the class or a small group. Then have the class or group discuss whether the decision–making model has been applied appropriately and whether the decision is one that produces the best possible result.

Examples of Ethical Decision–Making Scenarios

Misty and Sonja – No Sale

Misty and Sonja are best friends. They were neighbors from the time they were little until they were in eighth grade, when Sonja's parents got divorced and Sonja and her mom moved to an apartment across town.

One Saturday while they were shopping at a mall, Sonja took a bunch of clothes into the dressing room to try on. Misty waited for her, and they left the store together. Just outside the store, Misty asked, "Why didn't you get any of the outfits you tried on?" "I got all of them!" Sonja replied. "I got the five–finger discount. I had a big shopping bag from this store folded up in my purse. No one even noticed. And I took the sweater you liked for you. Here, take it."

Standing outside the story, Misty is nervous and upset. She knows it is wrong to shoplift, and she's afraid that Sonja will get caught. Misty is also afraid she will be accused of stealing because she was with Sonja, especially if she takes the sweater she was offered. She is disturbed and disappointed that her friend was willing to steal but she doesn't want to make a big deal about it. She doesn't want to ruin the friendship or make Sonja feel bad because she knows Sonja's family doesn't have much money.

But she also worries that if she doesn't try to help Sonja see what she did was wrong, it could ruin her character and reputation. Finally, she worries that if her friend continues on this path, she will continually make bad choices that could mess up the rest of her life.

Questions:

- Should Misty let Sonja think stealing is okay or, just as she would try to stop a friend from hurting herself or driving while drunk, should Misty try to stop Sonja?
- Would a good friend just turn the other way or try and intervene and counsel?
- If Sonja's parents had good values, what do you think they would do if they found out what Sonja was doing? Is that parental perspective appropriate or inappropriate for a caring friend?
- If Misty was your daughter, and she came to you with this problem, what would you do?

Melanie the Store Clerk

Melanie is a store clerk at a local store. One night she catches a 17–year–old stealing school supplies and a pair of sneakers for his little brother. Melanie knows the store policy about shoplifting. In fact she had to sign a code of conduct saying that she would turn in anyone she caught.

After confronting the 17–year–old, ready to turn the kid in, he pleads with Melanie saying it is the first time he has stolen anything. Then he tells her that his little brother is being teased at school for not having the stuff that other kids have. Their mother, a single parent, works all day and doesn't have time or money for her children. Melanie does not know what to do. How should she handle the situation?

Questions:

- Should Melanie turn the 17–year–old into the store manager? Or, does she rationalize that he had a good reason to steal?
- What should Melanie think about in making her decision?
- How can the decision she makes have an impact on her own goals?
- What are the options?
- If Melanie was your daughter, and she faced this dilemma, what do you hope she would do? Why?

Kenny and the Bully

Les is known as a troublemaker and bully in school. He never does his homework and constantly interrupts class with his unruly behavior and smart–mouth comments. He hangs around with a group of guys who share his lack of interest in school and his knack for getting into trouble. Les and his buddies don't like the 'jocks' or the 'study nerds' in the school, and they aren't shy about letting everyone know how they feel about those students.

Kenny is one of the study nerds that Les doesn't like. Les often threatens and picks on Kenny in class and in the halls, but Kenny just lets it slide. He knows some kids who talked back to Les, and they got beat up by Les and his friends.

One night after school, Kenny walks out to the parking lot and finds Les 'keying' the principal's car. Kenny tries to act like he hasn't seen it, but Les walks up to him and grabs him by the shirt collar.

"If you breathe a word about what you saw, you will die!" Les whispers. "No problem, man, I didn't see a thing," says Kenny.

A few minutes later, while Kenny is waiting at the bus stop, the principal leaves and notices that his car has been damaged. He walks over to the bus stop and says, "Kenny, I trust you. Did you see who did this to my car?"

Questions:

- What should Kenny do?
- What should Kenny do if the principal mistakenly blames another student for the vandalism?
- What should Kenny be thinking about here in terms of his immediate and long–term goals? What are the most important goals that could be affected by the choice he is about to make?
- What should Kenny know to make a different decision?
- If Kenny's immediate objection is to avoid being beaten up, what options does he have other than lying to the principal? List everything Kenny could do.
- What values are involved in the choices Kenny faces? Who are the 'stakeholders?'

#93   Finish the Story[8]

Learning Objective: To understand that we have the power to decide what we think, what we say and what we do

Instructions:

- Read each fictitious story, and creatively finish them in two different ways by having the characters respond in the most irresponsible way and then in a responsible way.

Story #1: "Cheating"

After graduation, Jamie found herself at a big university. Her parents were so proud. She was looking forward to four years of undergrad in the pre–med program, followed by med school, and then a career as a doctor. The first classes were brutally tough. Then came her first mid–term exam! She read the first question of the exam, and her mind went blank. She looked at the second question. She didn't know the answer. As she wiped the tears from her eyes, she tried to concentrate. She looked up, and there it was: an answer sheet in plain view, right on the desk in front of her... (You finish the story from here)

When you're done writing the endings to the story, answer these questions:
1. What were the consequences for those who made irresponsible decisions?
2. What were the benefits to the characters that made the responsible decisions?
3. Why is it that we often know what it takes to be responsible, and yet we don't always make a good decision?
4. Does someone always have to experience the negatives of a situation in order to learn responsibility?
5. What five things need to happen for you to be more responsible in your own life?
6. Why would cheating never prosper someone (list at least five reasons)?

Story #2: "Who Is To Blame?"

Joshua doesn't come from a family that anyone would call 'ideal.' His mom is an alcoholic, his father beats his mother, and the family never has any money. Joshua's never done very well in school; he feels there's nothing to motivate him to do a good job. No one at home cares what grades he gets, except when they are embarrassed by getting more than one call from the same teacher. So it wasn't a big deal when Joshua started partying, forging absence notes, and ditching school. His GPA dropped below a 1.0. For a while, no one seemed to notice that things were going downhill. Then Joshua's counselor called him in to say that he wasn't going to graduate. "What's the problem, Joshua?" asked the counselor. "I can't believe it," said Joshua... (You finish the story from here)

When you're done writing the endings to the story and answer these questions:
1. At what point in your life are you willing to take the blame for your actions?
2. Who would be considered the 'stakeholders' in the story?
3. How is personal responsibility related to integrity?
4. When are you old enough to take control and determine your own direction?
5. At what point in life are you able to overcome the influences around you?

Process and Reflection:
What?
- What does this activity say about making decisions?

So What?
- What are the differences that exist related to decisions that students make?
- What needs to be taken into consideration when making a decision?
- What were key elements of the story you wrote?
- What were potential consequences of actions taken in each story?

Now What?
- Why should one be concerned about the decisions one makes?
- What is the process you use when making a decision?

- Why is it sometimes hard for students to make a good choice?
- Have you ever helped someone make a good choice?

#94   Magic Carpet Ride[9]

Learning Objective: To develop decision–making skills from a team perspective
Materials: A tarp, blanket or large piece of paper measuring 5 feet x 5 feet (one for every six to eight students)
Instructions:

- Have a group of six to eight students stand close together on the tarp. The students must work together to turn the tarp over without stepping off.
- The activity can be initiated with the following narrative. "Everyone on board…keep your arms and legs in at all times. The school year is ready to start, the students are moving in and we don't have a plan. We just realized that all the instructions for having a successful year are on the bottom part of this magic carpet. The only problem is that we are at a cruising altitude of 20,000 feet. We need everyone aboard to get through the year. If anyone touches the ground (which is thin air) we have lost him or her. The group will have to start again."

Process and Reflection:
What?

- What were you asked to do as a group?

So What?

- Were you successful? Why? Why not?
- Was this too close for comfort?
- What process did you use to make decisions?
- How do you think your group could have done this activity quicker?

Now What?

- What roles did everyone play?
- Did someone take a more active leadership role? Did anyone in your group want out?
- In what way is this activity a good metaphor for conflict you may experience in groups?
- What do groups need to do in order to work through conflict?
- How do we as students want to handle conflict when it arises?

#95   Identify Defined By Choices Made

Learning Objective: To understand that our character is reflected in the outcomes of the choices we make
Materials: Story words; decision-making worksheet
Instructions:
Part 1

- Divide the class into groups of either 4 or 5 students
- When groups have formed, determine which students will be the first to begin the activity. Each group needs to determine who will be #1 by selecting the student who had the most recent birthday. Then moving clockwise from #1, have the students count off up to 10.

- Introduce the activity by saying, "We have no control over some things that happen; other times we do have control and that is exercised by what it is we say and do. Then, there are some situations by the choice we make, we can influence the outcome."
- The activity will include 10 words put up individually on a screen or board with which students will tell a story.
- The rules to be followed are:
  1. Once the word is put on the screen and told to your group, the #1 student will have 15 seconds to tell a story with the word.
  2. The story can be fictional or true.
  3. After 15 seconds, the next word will be shown and shared with each group, and the student clockwise from #1 will tell a story with that word. The student does not have to repeat what was said before – he or she is in total control of what is said.
  4. Again, after 15 seconds, another words is shared and the next student tells a story with the assigned word.
  5. The pattern continues until all 10 words have been used and stories told.

Words that could be used: (note that any 10 words will work)

Las Vegas	My Best Friend	Bill Clinton	Common Core
Thunderstorm	Taxi	Lady Gaga	Integrity
NASCAR	Airplane		

Process and Reflection:
What?
- What did this activity have to do with decision-making?

So What?
- What did you not have control over?
- What did you have control over?
- What could you influence with the choice of words that you shared when it was your turn to tell the story?
- Why is it important to make good decisions that are effective and ethical?

Now What?
- What are examples of some things that students face over which they have no control?
- Even when we have no control over what exists, a decision or choice will need to be made. Provide an example of what that choice will look like.
- "Every student has the power to decide what he or she will say and do." Do you agree or disagree? Explain your answer.
- Complete this sentence: Decision-making is not easy but…

Part 2
Instructions:
- Using the same groups, students in a role-play will discuss a decision-making scenario.
- The student with the next birthday will be Brent (or Brenda).

Scenario:
Brent is a High School Junior. As part of his science class, he is one member of a cooperative learning group that has to complete a project by the following Monday.

Each member of the group has a specific responsibility to complete for the project. The group has decided to work on Friday after school and on Saturday morning to put together the project so it can be completed by the Monday deadline. On Thursday, Brent's good friend invited him to a concert on Friday evening. Brent quickly responds that he would love to go. Before he leaves on Friday, he meets with the other members of his group to share his decision to go to the concert and that he will not be in any condition to get up early on Saturday to work on the project. Sunday is out as two other members of the group have a family commitment.

In the role-play, Brent (Brenda) needs to:
- Present arguments that explain the choice made.
- Convey the process used to make the decision to go to the concert.

The other three – four students are members of a cooperative learning group. Each will need to:
- Respond to Brent about the choice made.
- Identify who the stakeholders are in his decision.
- Discuss what is important in order to accomplish the assigned project.
- Share what are the unintended consequences of the choice Brent has made.

Brent (Brenda) will try to rationalize the choice as he (she) refutes the key points being made by the members of the cooperative learning group.
Finally, as a group, discuss what could be a decision that Brent (Brenda) may make to produce the best possible result.

#96   Pass a Problem

Learning Objective: To identify and solve a problem related to character.
Materials: Worksheet of possible problems; recorder sheet
Instructions:
- Divide students into small groups.
- Have each group spend up to five minutes solving a problem related to character and choices.
- Students are to brainstorm possible solutions and then reach consensus as to one that they believe will produce the best possible result. A recorder for the groups writes down the solution to the problem.
- Have the groups pass their problem with solution to another group for review and then the second group can add to the original solutions.
- Continue until all groups have had a chance to see/solve each problem. When each group gets back its original problem, they are to review all solutions and either pick the best one or create a new one that synthesizes two or more of the solutions.

Process and Reflection:
What?
- What did you have to do?

So What?
- How easy was it to come up with a solution to the problem?
- Why did you have differing points of view?
- What was the strategy that your group used to determine a possible solution?
- How significant were the difference in the solutions other groups gave to the problem?

Now What?

- What process do you use when you have to make a decision?
- What makes choosing a solution with the best possible result hard for a student to actually do?
- Were the solutions you chose as the best, ones that the majority of students at our school would also do? Why or why not?

Possible problems to discuss:

1. You're grounded and your parents are away for the evening. Friends drop by and ask you to join them for a hamburger. It will be two hours before your parents come home. Your friends say the punishment given by your parents was unfair.

2. Your best friend drives you to a party. After three hours, it's time to go. You smell alcohol on his breath, and he seems rowdier and louder than normal. You tell him you'd rather drive. Offended that you think his driving would be impaired, he refuses. This is the third weekend in a row this has happened. What do you do for yourself? For your friend?

3. It's the first week of a new school year. Your best friends tease a new student who's moved into the neighborhood. They joke about how she looks and talks. While walking home after school, one of them picks a fight with her. Before you know it, others join in.

4. When you see your best friend take cash from the secretary's desk at school, she asks you to promise not to tell anyone. The incident could lead to suspension and possible expulsion. She says if you tell, she'll never speak to you again. And, she'll tell your parents about how you lied to them about staying overnight at her house when you were really with your boyfriend.

5. A clerk at a record store forgets to charge you for one of the DVDs you purchased. You realize this as you leave the store. You turn to go back but see a long line at the register. You rationalize: Not my mistake. Maybe it'll teach the clerk a lesson about being more careful. And I'm really hungry. The money I just saved could feed me nicely.

6. You find a wallet containing $500. No one sees you pick it up. There's identification inside, but the address isn't close to your house. No one will know you found the wallet. You could really use the cash. ?

7. At lunch time you realize you forgot to do your math homework. The assignment has 45 problems to complete. Instead of eating, you hurriedly try to get through it. A friend sees what you're doing and offers his completed assignment to copy.

8. Carlos is your best friend. Your class is taking a math test. You notice him peeking at your paper and writing down your answers. Earlier, Carlos told you he went to the mall's game arcade last night instead of studying (while you were at home cramming).

9. Now that you're a high school senior, your dad's on your case whenever you go out on Saturday night. It all started when you told him your friends drink at parties and always pressure you to do so. You've been honest with your dad and said you have no interest in drinking because if you're caught, you'll be off the basketball team and lose your scholarship. Your dad concocts a strategy: Next time you're asked to drink, lie and say your dad gives you a breathalyzer test after every party. This bothers you because it's not the truth.

10. The principal announces over the intercom that a teacher's laptop has been stolen. If it's not turned in by noon, all lockers will be searched. You remember seeing your friend, whose locker is next to yours, stuffing what looked like a laptop in his backpack that morning.

Recorder sheet

Problem	Solutions

EPILOGUE

Having spent time working in schools as a teacher, principal, and superintendent, I have come to the conclusion that, more than ever before, education is undergoing significant changes. From the Common Core, 21st century skills, high–stakes testing, and the increasing emphasis on non–traditional forms of education, we can see evidence of what society deems as valuable for students to learn in addition to the standard curricula.

From my perspective, schools can concentrate on not only academic learning but also character development as the standard for what our students should acquire during their years in school. With an emphasis on skills that can be tested, the concept of promoting character as a function of schooling may seem to some to be of little value. It is my hope that this book can serve as a resource for parents, teachers and administrators to guide the direction of a school with specific ideas, strategies, and tools to assist in promoting the integration of values, character traits and non–cognitive skills. If implemented, I would like to think these strategies will help any school to become a venue in which not only academic learning is valued, but a place where life skills are acquired, leaders are made, and the talents of students are unleashed. This is what the American public considers to be necessary and important in preparing students for higher education and the workforce. Unfortunately, the American public believes that schools are lacking in preparing students for life after high school. A recent Gallup poll cited, "just 17 percent of Americans think high school graduates are ready for work, and just 29 percent think they're ready for college."[1]

What can be done to change the perception of the American public? I am sure you will agree with me that students are important not only to their schools and families, but also to their communities, to their future workplaces, and to the world around them. Each student has potential. Opportunities need to be provided and promoted by schools to assist students in reaching their potential not only in terms of academics but in their ability to make good choices. Integrating academics with character development is the most promising way to accomplish this goal.

No one ever said this would be easy. Schools today are inundated with standards, mandates, and demands, even as their resources shrink. Teachers claim that supplemental programs can be considered a burden as they impact a valued commodity of instructional time. Moreover, teachers are obligated to face the challenge regarding integration of ancillary programs with basic school curricula. As social and emotional standards and character development become mandated, teachers find themselves juggling and often times attempting to sustain multiple supplementary programs that tend to detract from a unified focus.

In spite of these difficulties facing teachers, consideration needs to be given to the importance of the role character development plays in the life of school. Just like the bundle of assessments that now have to be administered to students, our schools need teachers to lead the way toward preparing students for the tests they will face in life, for the responsibilities of citizenship, and for adopting a lifestyle that is built on a foundation of honesty, responsibility, respect and caring. This can be accomplished in the school environment where academics social/emotional, and character lessons are taught within the context of the school curriculum and not separately.

What a school looks like that promotes the "touchstones of character"

I began this book by writing that what was to be shared would not be a theoretical treatise on character, its history or even the merits of developing a character program. Rather, it was my desire to move beyond the rhetoric and provide practical tools for implementing and instilling key beliefs identified throughout the book as "touchstones of character." But, now that I reached the end, allow me to focus attention on creating a school that intentionally and explicitly addresses the need to develop the character of its students.

To be effective as a school in promoting a culture that advocates the development of the "touchstones of character" included in this book, one must consider an initiative that is meaningful, measurable, and sustainable. These are the defining elements that are desired when schools implement a successful CHARACTER COUNTS! framework. To have a meaningful initiative, strategies need to be in place to effectively deal with issues that are relevant and significantly impact students, staff, the school, and community. With implementation, a school should be expected to demonstrate effectiveness in terms of measurable changes in attitudes and conduct. Finally, there should be a commitment to create and promote a sustainable program that becomes part of the DNA of a school so that the values promoted will endure changes in leadership. Simply, it needs to become the "way we do school."

I am convinced that effective schools strive to develop students socially, ethically, and academically by infusing character development into every part of their curriculum and culture. Specifically, schools committed to character development explicitly identify and publicly stand for specific core values, and disseminate them to all members of the school community. A survey, reported in *Primary Sources: America's Teachers on Teaching in an Era of Change*, found that, "Nearly all teachers (99%) see their roles extending beyond academics to include things like reinforcing good citizenship, building resilience and developing social skills. Eight in 10 (84%) agree that it is teachers who have the greatest impact on student achievement in school. As one teacher said, "I believe teaching is more than just teaching subjects. It changes lives and should be about teaching social skills and respect as well."[2]

Think about this. What I have proposed can be characterized as putting into action the mission and values espoused by a school. The established values should be defined as specific behaviors that can be observed in the life of the school. What is captured as key beliefs, written in terms of positive expectations are taught, enforced, discussed and modeled, forming the basis for all relationships and interactions that occur in the school. Furthermore, the staff and students strive to uphold the values while accepting accountability of consistently applied standards of conduct. When there is visible and tangible evidence of the key beliefs being put into action, there is recognition and celebration of their manifestation with those in the school and community. The sixteen "touchstones of character" can truly form the basis for this schoolwide effort.

When training teachers, I have found that the effort to promote academic, social and emotional, and character beliefs will work in nearly every school environment, from small schools to large schools and from urban to suburban to rural. I have seen character education work in both public and private schools, and with unique school populations and structures, such as charter, magnet, faith–based, and at–risk. And, character education is not just restricted to schools in the United States. Many foreign countries have adopted, promoted or in some cases mandated character development.

Just as there is a need for intentionally and explicitly teaching character and key beliefs, a school must effectively plan and develop a strategy for implementation of a character initiative. This should not be left up to chance or simply mandated for teachers to include character development into the curriculum. The success of CHARACTER COUNTS! has been evident as thousands of schools, communities, public agencies and nonprofit organizations that have embraced, implemented and support an initiative focusing on key beliefs.

Randy Doerksen, an elementary school principal and colleague of mine, has created a model that addresses implementation of a CHARACTER COUNTS! initiative that will promote the implementation of key beliefs. For a successful character initiative to be created and supported, a change in how a school's staff thinks and behaves must be seriously considered. The staff must be convinced that a change is needed not only in the way we teach but also in the way we incorporate key beliefs into the curriculum. There should be a conviction that such a change is worth it because more will be gained than what one would have to give up.

According to Doerksen, the successful character initiative needs six key elements to produce lasting results:

- Vision
- Commitment on the part of staff
- Professional development or training
- Assessment
- Resources for teachers to integrate character into the curriculum
- Action plan

Vision	Commitment	Professional Development	Assessment	Resources	Action Plan	→	Lasting Results
What staff wants the school to be	Staff buy–in to integrate the beliefs in classrooms	In–service opportunities are provided	Measures in place to assess change	Availability of time, materials, strategies	Clearly identifiable goals to accomplish		Meaningful, measurable & sustainable change
⊘	Commitment	Professional Development	Assessment	Resources	Action Plan	→	Confusion
Vision	⊘	Professional Development	Assessment	Resources	Action Plan	→	Sabotage
Vision	Commitment	⊘	Assessment	Resources	Action Plan	→	Anxiety
Vision	Commitment	Professional Development	⊘	Resources	Action Plan	→	Uncertainty
Vision	Commitment	Professional Development	Assessment	⊘	Action Plan	→	Frustration
Vision	Commitment	Professional Development	Assessment	Resources	⊘	→	False Starts

If any factor is missing, a meaningful, measurable, sustainable change will not happen.[3]

Implementing the above framework would focus attention on having a school intentionally develop and initiate the following key concepts associated with promoting an environment that is truly conducive to learning. This can be accomplished by any school that clearly strives to promote:

1. An established framework for instilling key beliefs associated with character, social and emotional learning, and academics that is aligned with and integrated into a school's curricular requirements, Common Core, and 21st century skills.
2. Active and direct involvement, by a school administrator who enthusiastically accepts the responsibility for supporting and advocating the implementation and sustainability of a high quality program. The administrator needs to promote academic growth, the instilling of social and emotional skills and the development of specific character traits that will be of direct benefit to students now and for the future.

3. A schoolwide team, created and charged with the responsibility of initiating, coordinating, and assessing the efforts to promote character development.
4. Direct instruction on the part of all who work with students as well as the implementation of strategies that encourage, advance and maintain caring, supportive classrooms and a positive school culture.
5. Creating a culture that pervasively and repetitively ensures the key beliefs are espoused, recognized and supported throughout all aspects of school life.
6. The existence of a regular and consistent form of assessment that measures changes in student behavior and attitudes related to the key beliefs.
7. Implementation of ongoing professional staff training for all teachers as a vital an essential element for growth as character educators.
8. The collaborative involvement of parents and the greater schoolwide community as an essential and critical component in promoting these key beliefs.

From my role as a school district administrator and in my work as a character education trainer, I have come to the conclusion that CHARACTER COUNTS! provides the model to support the development of a school that promotes the integration of academics, social and emotional learning, and character. I have found that CHARACTER COUNTS! is a comprehensive, integrated, values–based school improvement and student development system. When implemented, a school will be explicitly and deliberately developing the character of each student by instilling core ethical values and attributes. The school will also be developing positive social and emotional life skills to help children and adolescents achieve their goals and live happy and constructive lives. Finally, an initiative instills educational values and develops essential academic skills to help students reach their intellectual potential and meet or exceed state standards.

It is my hope that you, your students, and your school will benefit from the strategies included in this book, and that you will recognize that effective character education is neither a program nor a prescription for 'fixing' students who need behavioral changes. Rather, by instilling the "touchstones of character," you will create a continuous, creative and deliberate practice of expecting students to "know the good, love the good, and do the good."[4] If you are part of the noblest of professions that educates the minds of a communities most precious resource, I hope you have seen in these pages a little of what you know, plenty worth thinking about and much about which you deeply feel truly matters.

May you go forth to face the challenges and joys of teaching with the desire, enthusiasm, and commitment as reflected on by Emerson: "People of character are the conscience of society."

NOTES

INTRODUCTION

1. C.S. Lewis, *Of Other Worlds: Essays and Stories* (New York: Mariner Books, 2002).
2. Hal Urban, *Positive Words, Powerful Results: Simple Ways to Honor, Affirm, and Celebrate Life* (New York: Touchstone, 2004).
3. The quotation from Maya Angelou can be found in numerous sources. Throughout the book, quotes will be shared with only the identification of the individual who spoke or wrote it. Sources for quotes used throughout the book include: http://josephsoninstitute.org/quotes/; http://www.quotationspage.com/subjects/character/; http://www.brainyquote.com/quotes/keywords/character.html; http://www.goodreads.com/quotes/tag/character
4. Josephson Institute of Ethics, *Model Standards for Academic, Social, Emotional and Character Development.* These Model Standards, integrating critical outcomes from each of these domains, draw heavily upon the hands–on experience of thousands of educators involved in the Josephson Institute's CHARACTER COUNTS! school and student development improvement efforts, the most current research and theories regarding the whole child, school climate; connectedness, behavior modification; the growth mindset, research–based instructional strategies, as well the research, reports, recommendations and standards presented by the National Governor's Association's COMMON CORE *Standards Initiative*, the *Partnership for 21st Century Skills' Framework for 21st Century Learning: Student Outcomes and Support Systems*, the *Illinois State Standards for Social and Emotional Learning*, the *Kansas State Standards for Social, Emotional, and Character Development*; *ASCD Whole Child Initiative* and the work of the *Collaborative for Academic, Social, and Emotional Learning* (CASEL); *Character Education Partnership*, the *Institute for Excellence & Ethics*, the *Center for the 4th and 5th Rs*, and the *National Center for Mental Health Promotion and Youth Violence Prevention* (2013), http://charactercounts.org/
5. Christine Brouillard, a School Counselor at Mill Pond School, a 2010 National School of Character, wrote a lesson in collaboration with the Mill Pond School Character Education Committee, http://www.character.org/
6. Thomas Lickona, *Character Matters* (New York: Simon & Schuster, 2004).
7. Ignite Nation, "Culture First, Achievement Follows," *Schoolwide Touchstones*, http://www.igniteforschools.com/
8. Josephson Institute of Ethics.
9. Josephson Institute of Ethics.

CHAPTER 1

1. Michael Josephson, Josephson Institute of Ethics, CHARACTER COUNTS! *Character Development Seminar, 1997/2014.* Over the past 25 years, Josephson has built on all available sources of research and writing to summarize, formulate and often, create, strategies and definitions. As one of the foremost experts in character development and applied ethics, he has been instrumental in writing and developing the CHARACTER COUNTS! framework, the most widely implemented approach to character education, reaching millions of youth. http://charactercounts.org
2. Hilary Wilce, *Backbone: How To Build The Character Your Child Needs To Succeed* (London, UK: Endeavour Press Ltd, 2013).
3. Josephson Institute of Ethics, *Aspen Declaration.* In July 1992, the Josephson Institute of Ethics hosted a summit conference in Aspen, Colorado. A diverse group of ethicists, educators and

youth–service professionals convened to find ways to work together and boost their character–education efforts. The declaration that concluded this meeting would form the intellectual foundation for the CHARACTER COUNTS! movement, started by the Institute the following year. http://charactercounts.org/

4. Barbara A. Lewis, *What Do You Stand For? For Teens: A Guide to Building Character* (Minneapolis: Free Spirit Publishing, 2005).

5. Kerry Patterson, Joseph Grenny, David Maxfield, Ron McMillan, Al Switzler, *Influencer: The Power to Change Anything* (New York: McGraw Hill, 2011).

6. Thomas Lickona, *Educating for Character: How Our Schools Can Teach Respect and Responsibility* (New York: Bantam Books, 1992).

7. John Easton, Director of the Department of Education Institute of Educational Sciences. Quoted in: *Promoting Grit, Tenacity, and Perseverance: Critical Factors for Success in the 21st Century* (U.S. Department of Education Office of Educational Technology, 2013).

8. Kristin Fink, and Karen Geller, *Integrating Common Core and Character Education: Why It Is Essential and How It Can Be Done* (Character Education Partnership, 2013), http://www.character.org/

9. Fink and Geller.

10. Howard Gardner, *Five Minds for the Future* (Boston: Harvard Business Review Press, 2009).

11. Justin Minkel, "True Grit," *Education Week* (October 7, 2013).

12. Richard Roberts, *What Measuring the Harder Stuff Tells Us About Students* (Educational Testing Service National Conference: Can You Relate? Critical Relationships for Teacher Leaders (July, 2013).

13. *The MetLife Survey of the American Teacher: Preparing Students for College and Careers* (2010).

14. Richard Rothstein, "Accountability for Non–cognitive Skills – Society values traits not covered on academic tests, so why aren't they measured in school?" *The School Administrator* (December 2004).

CHAPTER 2

1. Thomas Lickona, 2004.

2. Lickona.

3. Video clips will be a strategy for teachers to use when teaching the beliefs. Specific web sites for the clips mentioned in this chapter and under specific practices to initiate the use of vicarious experiences are: Foundations for a Better Life, (http://www.values.com), Wing Clips (http://www.wingclips.com), Film Clips Online (www.filmclipsonline.com), Teach With Movies (http://www.teachwithmovies.org/), Motivational Media – Character in the Movies (http://themarketingteacher.myshopify.com/products/character–in–the–movies).

4. Michele Borba, "Raising a Moral Child," Article is found at: http://www.beliefnet.com

5. Lickona.

CHAPTER 3

1. Barbara Taylor, Debra Peterson, P. David Pearson, Michael Rodriguez, "Reading Growth in High–Poverty Classrooms: The Influence of Teacher Practices That Encourage Cognitive Engagement in Literacy Learning," *Elementary School Journal*, 104 (2003).

2. P. K Cross, "Teaching for Learning," *American Association of Higher Education*, Bulletin 39 (1987).

3. Michael Strauss and Toby Fulwiler, "Writing To Learn In Large Lecture Classes," *Journal of College Science Teaching*, 19(3) (1989/1990).

4. "State of America's Schools – The Path to Winning Again in Education," *Gallup Inc.* (2014).

5. Tom Jackson, *More Activities That Teach* (Boulder, CO: Red Rock Publishing, 2003).

6. John Dewey, *Experience and Education* (New York: Macmillan Co., 1938/1997).

7. David Royse, *Teaching Tips for College and University Instructors, A Practical Guide* (Upper Saddle River, NJ: Pearson Publishing, 2001).

8. Dewey.

9. Edgar Dale, *Audio–Visual Methods in Teaching*, 3rd ed. (Austin, TX: Holt, Rinehart & Winston, 1969).
10. Except as otherwise noted, the skills definitions are derived from the "Partnership for 21st Century Skills Framework," (2012), www.21stcenturyskills.org.
11. Rothstein 2004.
12. Jim Eison, *Using Active Learning Instructional Strategies to Create Excitement and Enhance Learning*, http://www.cte.cornell.edu
13. Adapted from David Kolb, Experiential Learning Cycle Chart, *Experiential Learning: Experience as the Source of Learning and Development* (Englewood Cliffs, NJ: Prentice Hall, 1984).
14. Robert Fisher, *Teaching Thinking: Philosophical Enquiry in the Classroom* (London, UK: Continuum, 1998/2003).
15. Illinois State Board of Education, *Illinois 5Essentials Survey*. The Illinois 5Essentials Survey is a diagnostic tool based on 20 years of research, measuring schools' level of strength – or implementation – on leading indicators of school improvement. Survey results help schools organize, prioritize, evaluate and achieve sustainable improvement (2013), http://www.isbe.net
16. "Cooperative Learning: Great Grouping Strategies for Your Classroom," *Daily Teaching Tools*, http://www.dailyteachingtools.com/cooperative–learning–grouping.htm.

CHAPTER 4

1. Michael Josephson, *Commentary: The Seven C's of Character*, 756.2 (January 2, 2012), http://charactercounts.org/
2. Tom Jackson, 1995.
3. Adapted from *Foundations for Life Teacher's Resource Guide*, Josephson Institute of Ethics, www.FFL–essays.org
4. Adapted from "Play for Performance," *Words and Pictures*, Seriously fun activities for trainers and facilitators by workshops by Thiagi, Inc. (June, 2003). A number of activities in the book have been adapted from Thiagi, Inc., are included and reprinted with permission. http://www.thiagi.com
5. Thiagi, "Thiagi Gameletter," *Dodgeball Review* (July, 2012).
6. James Neill, "Mirror Image," Wilderdom – a project in natural living and transformation (2005), http://www.wilderdom.com/games/descriptions/MirrorImage.html
7. Josephson, *Something To Think About For Teens #8: Trust, Promises, and Good Friends* (May 10, 2012), http://charactercounts.org/
8. Peggy Atkins, *Exercising Character: A Workout Guide For Teenagers Who Make Character Count!* (Los Angeles: The Josephson Institute, 1995).
9. Thiagi, "Thiagi Gameletter," *Who and Why* (August, 2013), www.thiagi.com
10. Josephson. *Commentary: RESPECT. 690.5.* http://charactercounts.org/
11. Josephson, *Something to Think About For Teens #10: Jesse Owens and Luz Long* (May 17, 2012), http://charactercounts.org/
12. Silvasaliam Thiagi, *I'm a...* , (1997). www.thiagi.com
13. Bernard Brown, Adapted from the original story. http://www.sermonillustrations.com/a–z/r/responsibility.htm
14. Josephson, *Commentary 775.3 and Something to Think About For Teens #9: Lessons From the Monkey Pot* (May 15, 2012), http://charactercounts.org/
15. Thiagi, "Play for Performance," *Leadership Advice from Your Role Model*, (November, 2004). www.thiagi.com
16. Stuart Wolpert, "Fairness Is More Rewarding Than Money," *UCLA Newsroom*, http://newsroom.ucla.edu/portal/ucla/brain–reacts–to–fairness–as–it–49042.aspx
17. A yoga story adapted from www.wordpress.com.

18. Josephson, *Something To Think About For Teens #15: A Teacher's Dilemma About Grades* (June 6, 2012), http://charactercounts.org/

19. Charlotte–Mecklenburg Schools, Beverly Woods Elementary School, *Justice and Fairness*. This is an activity from the school's resource guide for character. http://schools.cms.k12.nc.us/beverlywoodsES/Documents/Janjustice.pdf

20. Josephson, *Commentary: Too Poor to Give, 842.3* (August 27, 2013), http://charactercounts.org/

21. Josephson, *Something To Think About For Teens #16: Teenagers Lead The Way* (June 13, 2012), http://charactercounts.org/

22. Activity was conducted by Cathy Fisher in Lombard School District 44 and is credited to Louisiana State Agricultural Center https://www.lsuagcenter.com/

23. Kamaron Institute, "K through 5th Grade Classroom Guidance," *Apple Activity*, www.kamarn.org.

24. Josephson, *Commentary: Shopping Carts and Rationalizations, 787.2* (August 6, 2012), http://charactercounts.org/

25. Adapted from a story at: http://www.ushistory.org/more/hoover.htm

26. Josephson, *Something To Think About #3: Leadership On A Bus* (April 23, 2012), http://charactercounts.org/

27. Alanna Jones *Team–Building Activities for Every Group* (Lusby, MD: Rec Room Publishing, 2000). Adapted from an activity at Team Building: http://www.teambuildingportal.com/games/sneek–peek

CHAPTER 5

1. James Surowiecki, *The Wisdom of Crowds: Why the Many Are Smarter Than the Few and How Collective Wisdom Shapes Business, Economies, Societies and Nations* (New York: Knopf Doubleday Publishing Group, 2005).

2. Partnership for 21st Century Skills, 2012.

3. Michael Josephson, *Something To Think About #4: I Just Have To Outrun You* (April 26, 2012), http://charactercounts.org/

4. Jackson, 2004.

5. Alanna Jones, *104 Activities That Build: Self–Esteem, Teamwork, Communication, Anger Management, Self–Discovery, Coping Skills* (Lusby, MD: Rec Room Publishing, 1998). Adapted from an activity at Games for Groups: http://gamesforgroups.com/teambuildingactivities.html

6. "Are They Really Ready To Work?" *Employers' Perspectives on the Basic Knowledge and Applied Skills of New Entrants to the 21st Century U.S. Workforce*, The Conference Board (2006).

7. Michael Firmin, "Using Debate to Maximize Learning Potential: A Case Study," *Journal of College Teaching & Learning*, Volume 4, Number 1 19 (January 2007).

8. Adapted from: Roger M. Boisjoly, "Telecon Meeting Ethical Decisions – Morton Thiokol and the Challenger Disaster," *Online Ethics Center for Engineering* (2006).

9. Tom Jackson, *Activities That Teach* (Boulder, CO: Red Rock Publishing, 1993).

10. Thiagi, "The Games Newsletter," *Miss–Understanding* (July 2011), www.thiagi.com

11. Attributed to Delta Gamma Fraternity, *Changing of the Tides* (Rev. October, 2001). http://csi.ucdavis.edu/wp–content/uploads/2012/04/L13teamwork_games.pdf

12. Sivasailam Thiagarajan and Barbara Steinwachs, *The Instructional Design Library* (Boston: Intercultural Press, 1990).

13. The Greater Good Science Center, *Expanding the Science and Practice of Gratitude*, http://greatergood.berkeley.edu/expandinggratitude/

14. Robert Emmons, *Thanks!: How the New Science of Gratitude Can Make You Happier* (New York: Houghton Mifflin, 2007).

15. Michael Josephson, *Commentary: Gifts From the Heart Are Gifts of the Heart, 866.2* (February 10, 2014), http://charactercounts.org/

16. *The Global Village: A Summary of the World*, http://www.nationsonline.org/oneworld/global–village.htm

17. Josephson, *Something To Think About For Teens #2: Is This Generous Or Just Dumb?* (April 18, 2012), http://charactercounts.org/
18. Josephson. *Commentary: Moral Courage: The Engine of Integrity, 751.3* (November 29, 2011), http://charactercounts.org/
19. Craig Brian Larson, *Pastoral Grit: The Strength to Stand and to Stay* (Grand Rapids, MI: Bethany House Publishers, 1998).
20. Karl Rohnke, *Silver Bullets: A Revised Guide to Initiative Problems, Adventure Games and Trust Activities,* Project Adventure Inc. (Dubuque, IA: Kendall Hunt Publishing, 2013).
21. Michael Koehler and Karen Royer, *First Class Character Education Activities Program* (New York: Prentice Hall, 2001).
22. Charlotte–Mecklenburg Schools, Sterling Elementary School, *Perseverance.* This is an activity from the school's resource guide for character. http://schools.cms.k12.nc.us/sterlingES/Documents/AprilPerseverance.pdf
23. Nan Henderson, "Havens of Resilience," *Educational Leadership,* Vol. 71.1 (September, 2013).
24. Amity Noltemeyer, Kevin Bush, "Adversity And Resilience: A Synthesis Of International Research," *School Psychology International,* 34(5) (October, 2013).
25. Bonnie Benard, *Resiliency: What We Have learned* (San Francisco: WestEd, 2004).
26. Richard Sagor, "Building Resiliency in Students," *Educational Leadership,* 54(l) (September, 1996).
27. Jon Johntson, *Courage – You Can Stand Strong in the Face of Fear,* SP Publications (1990).
28. Directed Action Professional Associates, *First Steps Training: Keypunch,* http://www.firststepstraining.com/resources/activities/archive/activity_keypunch.htm
29. Koehler and Royer.

CHAPTER 6

1. Carol Dweck, *The Mindset of a Champion.* Attributed to a quote at: https://champions.stanford.edu/perspectives/the–mindset–of–a–champion/
2. Michael Josephson, *Something To Think About For Teens #7: Building Cathedrals – How Your Attitudes Shape Your Life* (May 7, 2012), http://charactercounts.org/
3. The role-play presented in the activity is adapted from the strategies of Carol Dweck, *Mindset: The New Psychology of Success* (New York: Random House, 2006).
4. Del Siegle, *Help Students Set Goals,* http://www.gifted.uconn.edu/
5. Michael Jordon, *I Can't Accept Not Trying: Michael Jordan on the Pursuit of Excellence* (New York: Harper, 1994).
6. SC ETV's K–12 Educational Web Portal, *Marshmallow and Toothpick Tower,* www.knowitall,org.
7. Josephson, *Something To Think About For Teens #17: The Summer Job Conundrum* (June 14, 2012), http://charactercounts.org/
8. Media International, *Finish the Story* (2002), http://www.mediainternational.com/support/PDF/POWER%20SURGE/Resp.pdf
9. Adapted from "Teamwork and Team Play," *Magic Carpet Ride,* http://www.teamworkandteamplay.com/resources.html

EPILOGUE

1. "State of America's Schools – The Path to Winning Again in Education," *Gallup, Inc.* (2014).
2. *Primary Sources: America's Teachers On Teaching In An Era Of Change 3rd Edition* (New York: Scholastic Press, 2013). Source is at: http://www.scholastic.com/primarysources/
3. Adapted by Randy Doerkson from Tim Knoster, Richard Villa and Jacqueline Thousand, *A Framework For Thinking About Systems Change, Restructuring for Caring and Effective Education: Piecing the Puzzle Together* (Baltimore: Paul H. Brooks Publishing Co., 2000).
4. Kevin Ryan and Karen Bohlin, *Building Character in Schools* (San Francisco: Jossey–Bass Publishers, 1999).

INDEX OF GAMES AND ACTIVITIES

About the Author

Gary Smit holds bachelor's and master's degrees and a doctorate in educational administration from Northern Illinois University. Committing 34 years to public education, he has been a teacher, principal and served 25 years as a school superintendent. His most recent superintendency was Lombard School District 44 in suburban Chicago where he was instrumental in the adoption and implementation of CHARACTER COUNTS!

Now, as one of the Josephson Institute's most popular, experienced, and versatile speakers, Gary has trained educators and community leaders in character development, ethics in sports and school administrator ethics. His trainings have been held throughout the United States, and in Puerto Rico, Colombia, Ecuador, United Arab Emirates, Singapore, Bermuda and Nigeria.

An attention-grabbing and practical presenter, Gary speaks not only to the head but the heart. No one leaves without grasping the passion and desire to live a life in which character truly matters. Gary is the author of numerous journal articles and has co-authored the resource guide, *Living the Four-Way Test – The Rotary Ethical Leadership Framework for Youth.*

CPSIA information can be obtained
at www.ICGtesting.com
Printed in the USA
FFOW04n0338131115
18427FF

3 1531 00444 1702

9 781621 374